The Band CRIME
Punk77 Revisited

Photographs and Text Documenting the Band Crime 1976 - 1978
by James Stark
Edited by Pilar Covamebias

I0793499

For James
who takes holy photographs
Nico.

The Band CRIME • Punk77 Revisited

Photographs and Text Documenting the Band Crime 1976 - 1978
by James Stark
Edited by Pilar Covamebias

Published by
Last Gasp of San Francisco
Ronald E. Turner, Publisher

777 Florida Street
San Francisco, CA 94110

www.lastgasp.com

All rights reserved. No part of this book may be reproduced or transmitted in any form or by any means, electronic or mechanical, including photocopying, recording, xerography or any information storage or retrieval system, without permission in writing from the author and publisher.

This edition ©2009 James Stark
Published by Last Gasp
ISBN: 978-0-86719-715-0
Printed in China
6 5 4 3 2 1

Table of Contents

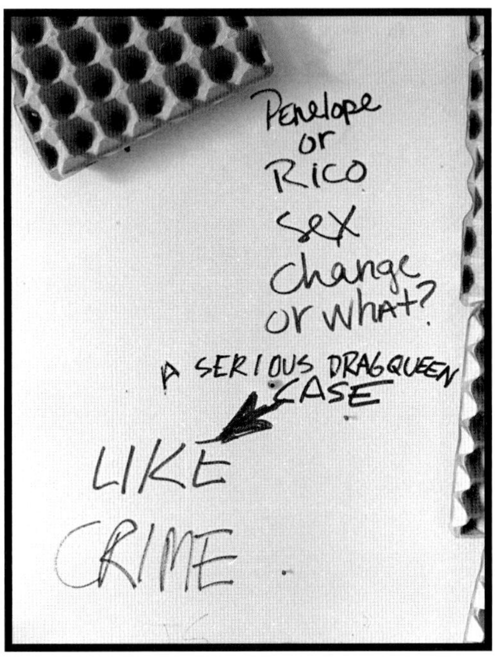

Comment about sexual identity on the wall of a South of the Slot Rehearsal studio, San Francisco, circa 1977.

Introduction by James Stark

Rock and roll had lost its essence. Its rebellious streak had become merely a facade, a false front meant to conceal the corporate control that determined which bands would be concocted, which records would be released, which songs would be played on the radio. And that was determined by what those corporations thought would make money while keeping the populace placated—nothing too dangerous.

Punk set out to change all that. In the days before the Internet, punk was the ultimate do-it-yourself movement. Loud, out of tune and in your face, punk came screaming out of the garages and gutters of America, announcing itself with hand-made posters or simply by word of mouth. Taking place entirely outside the normal commercial framework of rock and roll, punk would be the last real alternative underground the U.S. would produce. It was the end of bohemia.

Crime was there from the beginning, blasting away at the establishment. When I first heard Crime it reminded me of the first time I heard the Velvet Underground at Andy Walhol's Exploding Plastic Inevitable at the Dom. Crime put on its own shows, pasted its own posters on walls, made and distributed its own records. Although Crime seemed headed for something big, in the end they became just another casualty on the road to rock and roll fame.

Introduction by Jack H.

I met James Stark at Nine in the heyday of the Brit bike revival. He had a 1971 Norton Commando and I had a Triumph TT Special. James always seemed to be on the cutting edge of what was happening. He was part of the original group of people who created the Punk scene in San Francisco. His work with Crime is legendary. James created the Crime logo, designed posters and shot the photographs that help create the Crime look.

James' genius is seen in his book "Punk77, an inside look at the San Francisco rock n' roll scene." Now he has put the best of his Crime photographs into a new book, The Band CRIME, Punk77 Revisited, along with some of his inside observations. Crime didn't record much, and James' work has done much to add to the Crime mystique. Each image is fresh and shows the hard edge of life in the underground.

Before meeting James, I had enjoyed his photographs, and they influenced how I approached making images. Punk77 was a guide for young people learning how to shoot, and now Part Two is here. Check it out.

Preface

I went to the first Crime show in early 1977 and walked out thinking, "God, they looked cool. I couldn't hear a thing they were singing, but, boy, did they look cool..."
Joey Swails

What does a person do with a box full of negatives that chronicle the life of a rock 'n' roll band that started off creating a lot of excitement but ended up in the dust bin of history? I hooked up with Crime at the beginning, before they'd even played a show. That in itself offered both opportunities and challenges: how to fit in and help out while also taking photographs that meant something. To me, good photography is about access to the subject, and being with Crime offered that access, not just to the band but to the whole punk scene that was happening at that time. This book is about sharing that access and inspiring other photographers in similar circumstances.

The early photographs seen here were taken using an Nikon S2 range finder camera, everything manual. I later got a state-of-the-art Canon AE1, one of the earliest aperture-priority automatic cameras. The Canon also had a flash that could automatically set the exposure according to the distance from the subject. This was especially helpful during live shows. When the lighting was right I could turn it off, or I could use flash when the lighting was poor.

For Frankie, Brittley, and Ricky

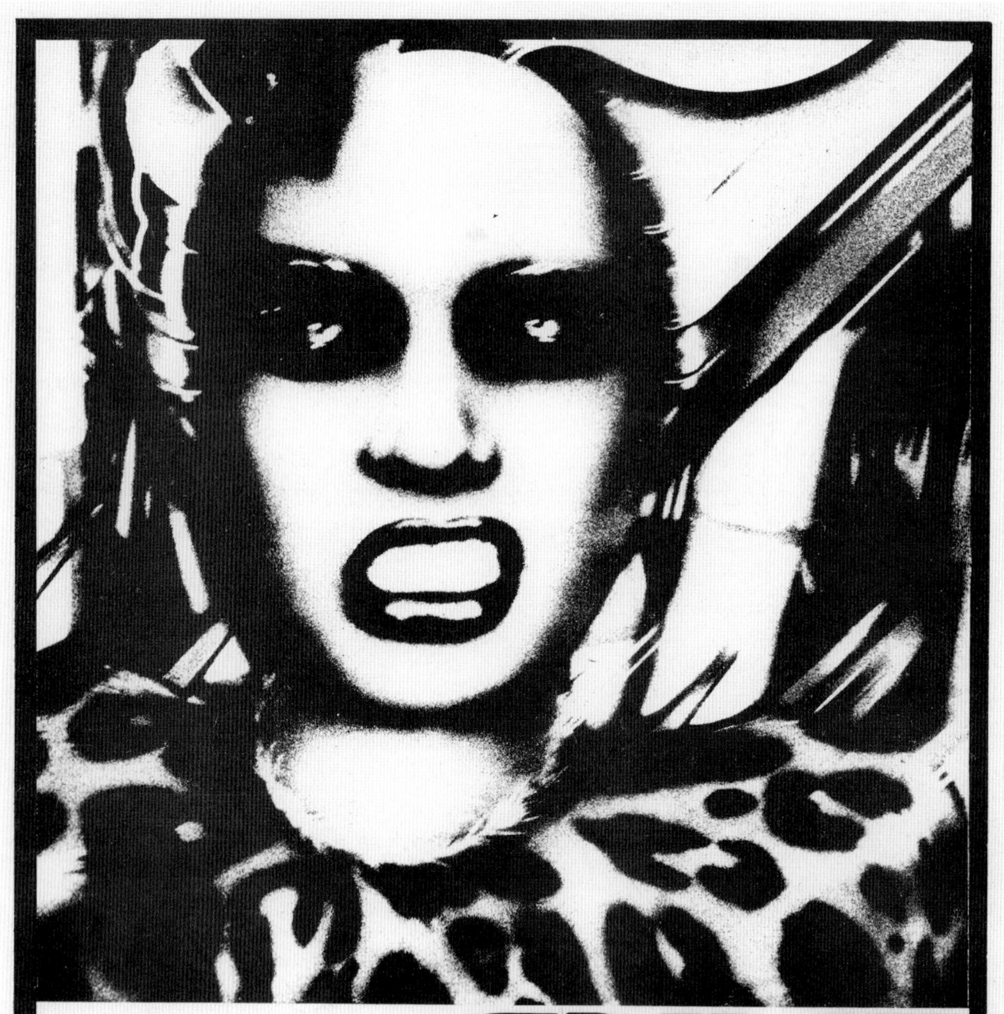

First Crime show, January, 1977

The Beginning

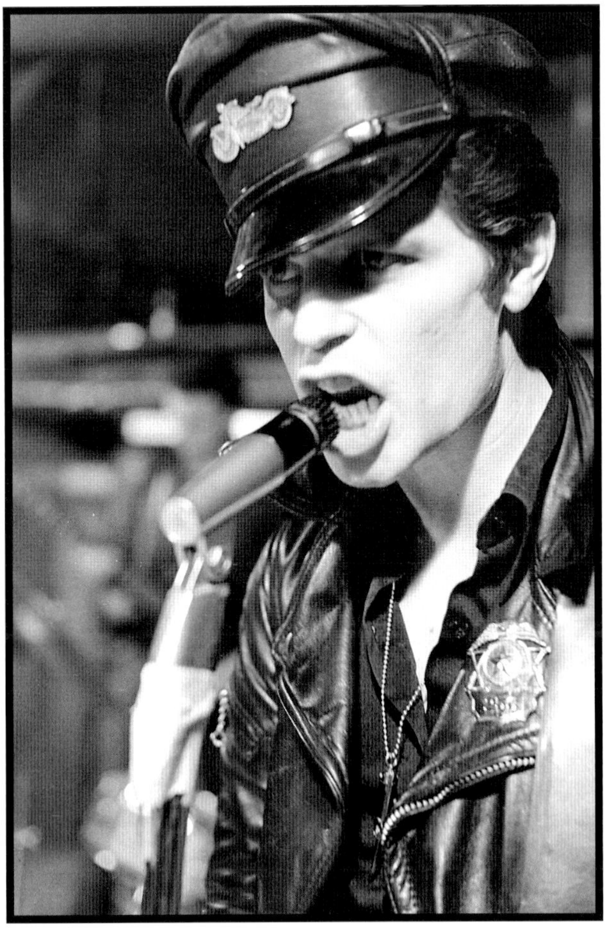

Frankie at the rehearsal studio, circa 1976

Before Crime, Frankie Fix and Johnny Strike were known as the Space Invaders. It was their take on glam, influenced by David Bowie in his Spiders From Mars period. Though they never played any shows, Frankie and Johnny created quite a stir being seen around San Francisco in full space drag. In mid-1976, Ron Greco was approached by Johnny at the Mount Olympus Disco where Johnny was a waiter. He asked Ron if he played bass and if he was interested being part of new band that he and Frankie were putting together. Ron was actually a guitarist and didn't play bass, but he was intrigued and said he did. When he met with them later, he liked where they were coming from. They knew very little about music, but their lyrics and melodies were interesting. With Ron's musical background, he figured they might be able to do something together. The name Crime was provided by Tony Steel, a friend of Frankie and Johnny's.

Soon thereafter, Ron asked me if I'd be interested in taking photos of his new band. I'd met Ron a few years earlier when I'd taken photos of the band he'd had then, Hell and High Water. The new band was called Crime, and none of the photographers they'd already used, Nori Ezio among others, had been able to get the "street" look that would get across what they were about.

I showed up at the South of Market warehouse on Howard Street in San Francisco where the band rehearsed. Two guys—Frankie and Johnny—were standing in front of Marshall stacks in gay leather drag. Ron and the band's drummer, Chris, were in street clothes. The scene reminded me of the Velvet Underground shows I'd gone to at the Dom when I was living in New York City. The music was loud and dissonant, a wall of noise with a solid beat behind it, and it appealed to me right away. We arranged to do a photo shoot at their rehearsal space within the next few days.

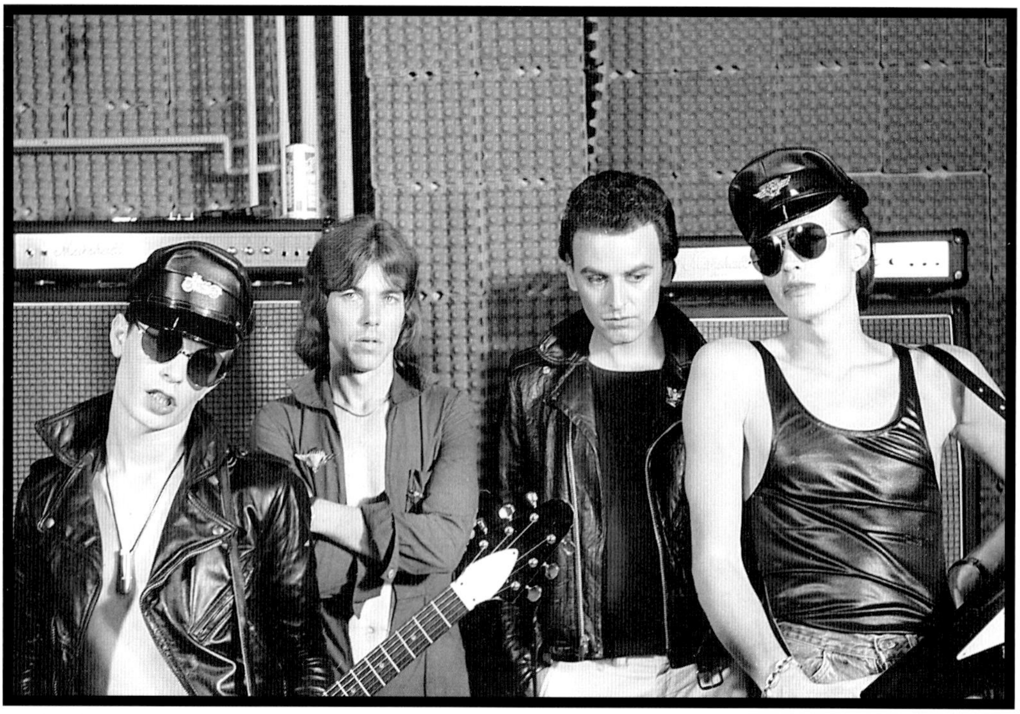

The first version of Crime: Frankie Fix (guitar and vocal), Chris Kat (drums), Ron "The Ripper" Greco (bass), Johnny Strike (guitar and vocal). Frankie and Johnny in leather bar drag.

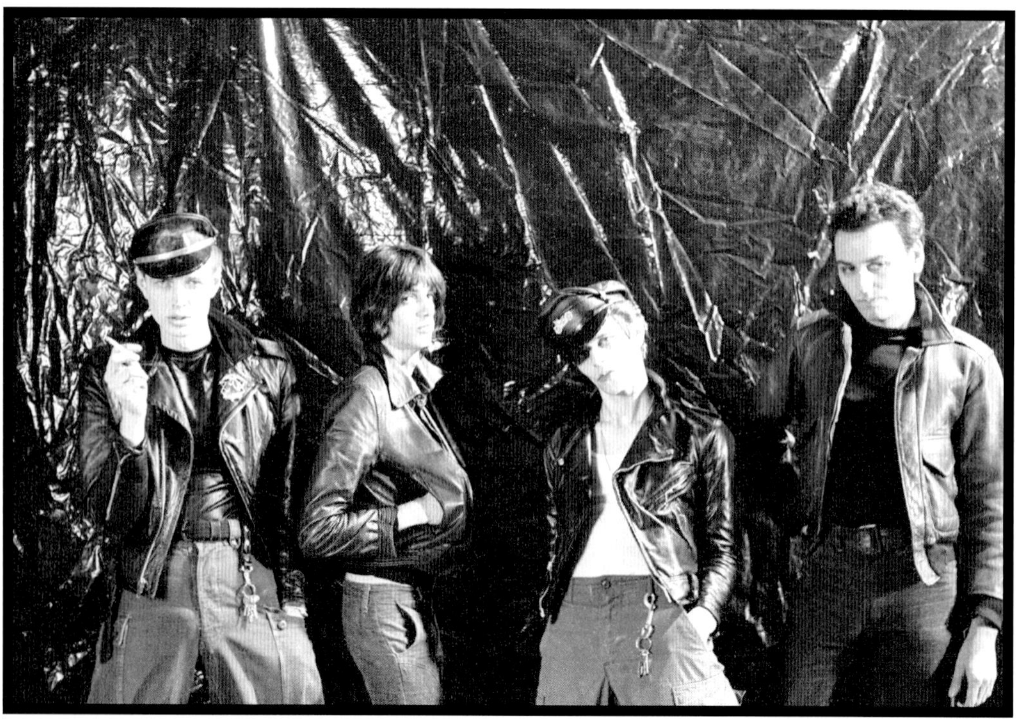

Photo used for the first Crime single: Johnny Strike, Ricky Williams, Frankie Fix, and Ron "The Ripper." The photo also appeared in Rock Scene's *new band section. Chris Kat was replaced by Ricky Williams.*

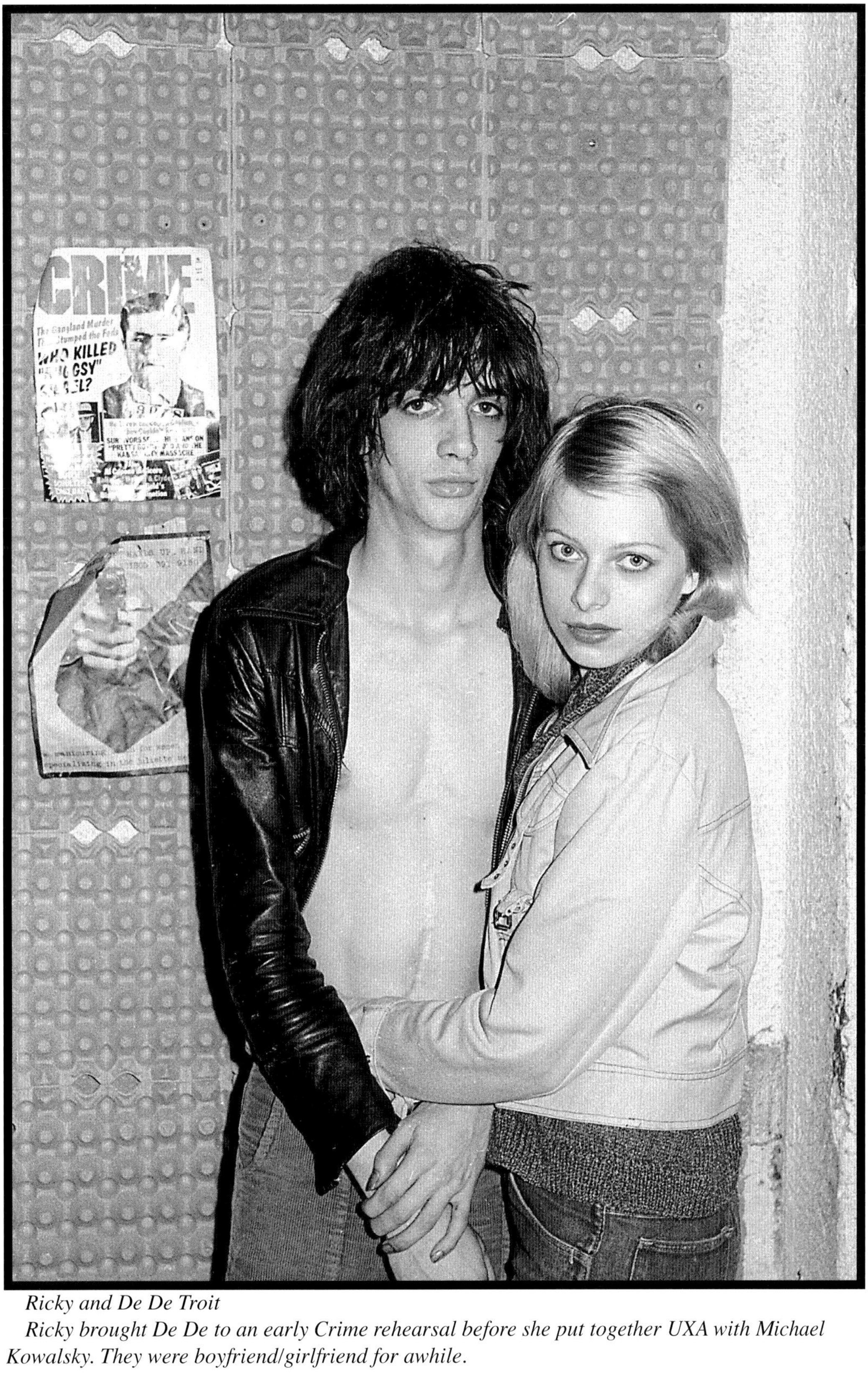

Ricky and De De Troit

Ricky brought De De to an early Crime rehearsal before she put together UXA with Michael Kowalsky. They were boyfriend/girlfriend for awhile.

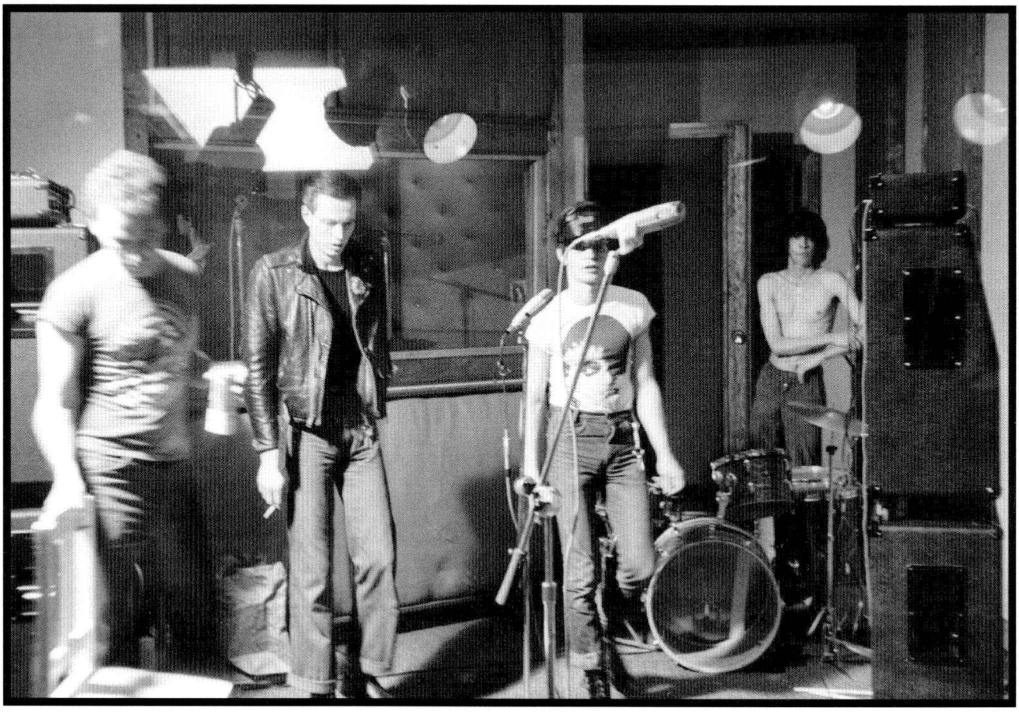

Crime at Blue Bear Studios

In November, 1976, Crime recorded its first 45 ("Hot Wire My Heart" and "Baby You're So Repulsive") in San Francisco at Blue Bear Studios, just down from the rehearsal space on Howard Street. We pushed or carried all of the equipment down the sidewalk to the studio and set it up in a room that was approximately fifteen by ten feet. The engineer said, "You guys can't use all of that equipment! The sound will be distorted!" At that time, the goal was getting a "clean sound," and bands generally let the engineer decide what equipment would be used.

The Blue Bear engineer didn't know to deal with a band like Crime, who recorded with all the equipment plugged in and with the knobs turned up. They were after an authentic sound, something like an old Charlie Patton blues record. I always thought that "Hot Wire my Heart" and "Frustration" were the 1970s equiv-alent of old blues recordings.

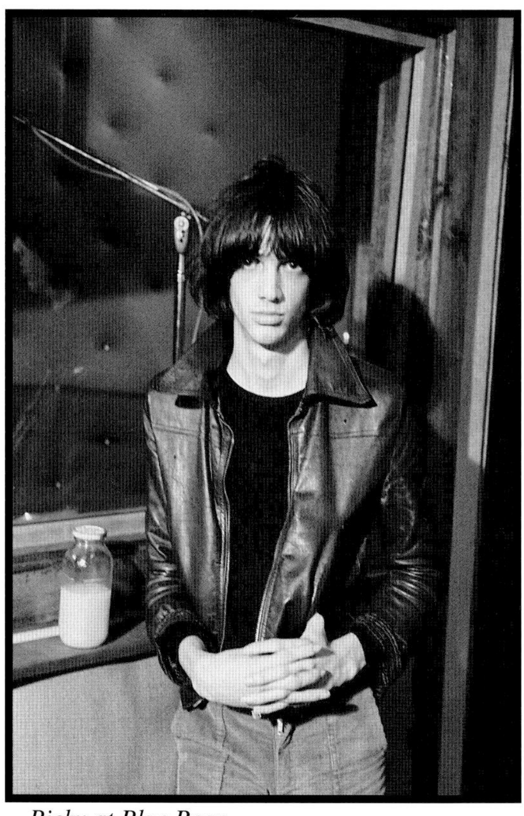

Ricky at Blue Bear

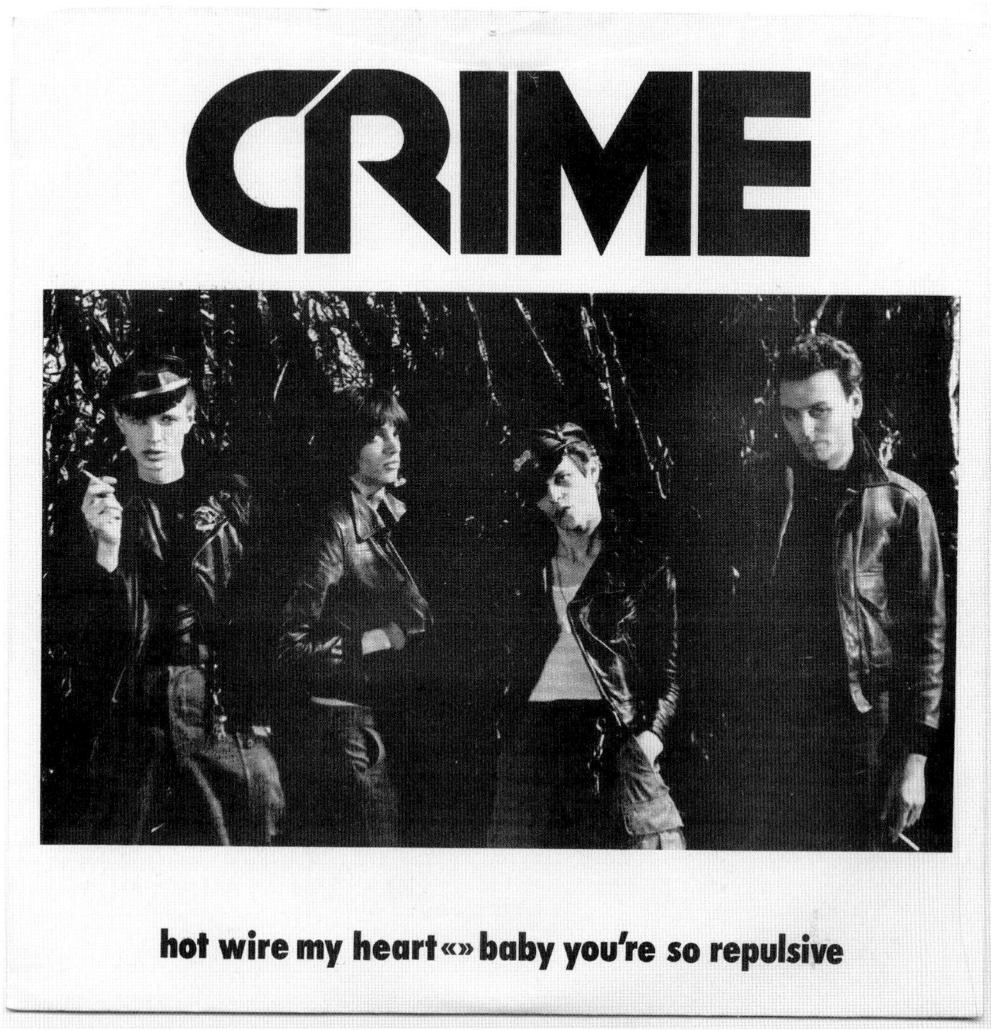

The first single made the chart in Sounds, an English music magazine. Sonic Youth would later cover Hot Wire My Heart.

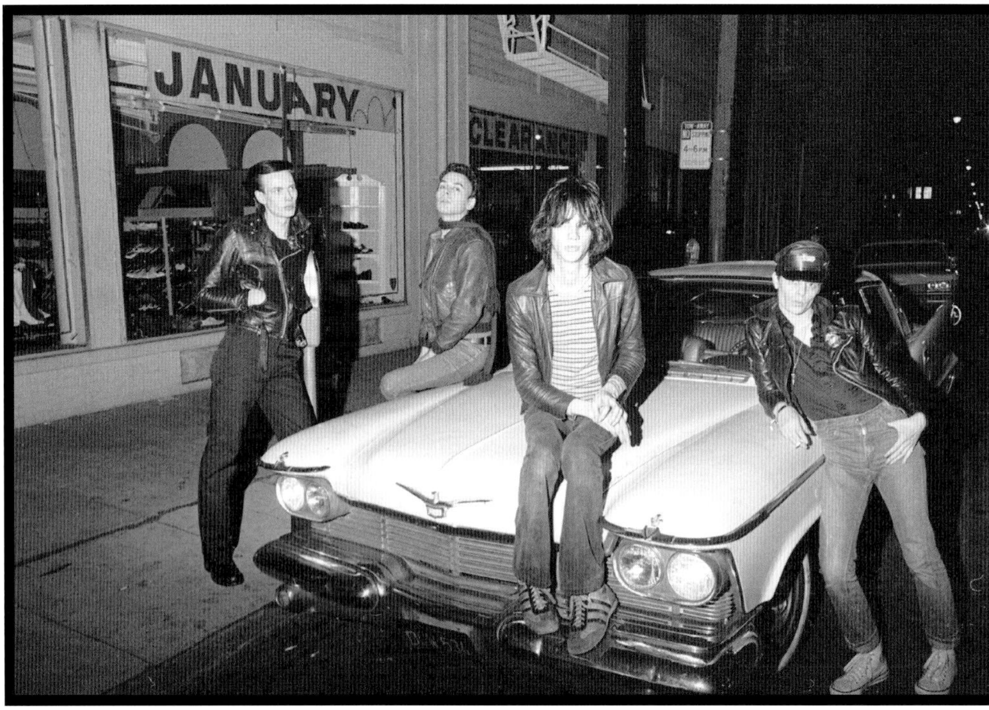

Frankie pictured himself as a gangster. Legend was that Frankie's father was a small time gangster on the East Coast, around Philadelphia. Frankie and Johnny came to California from Hershey, Pennsylvania. The band is posing around Frankie's 1956 Chrysler Imperial.

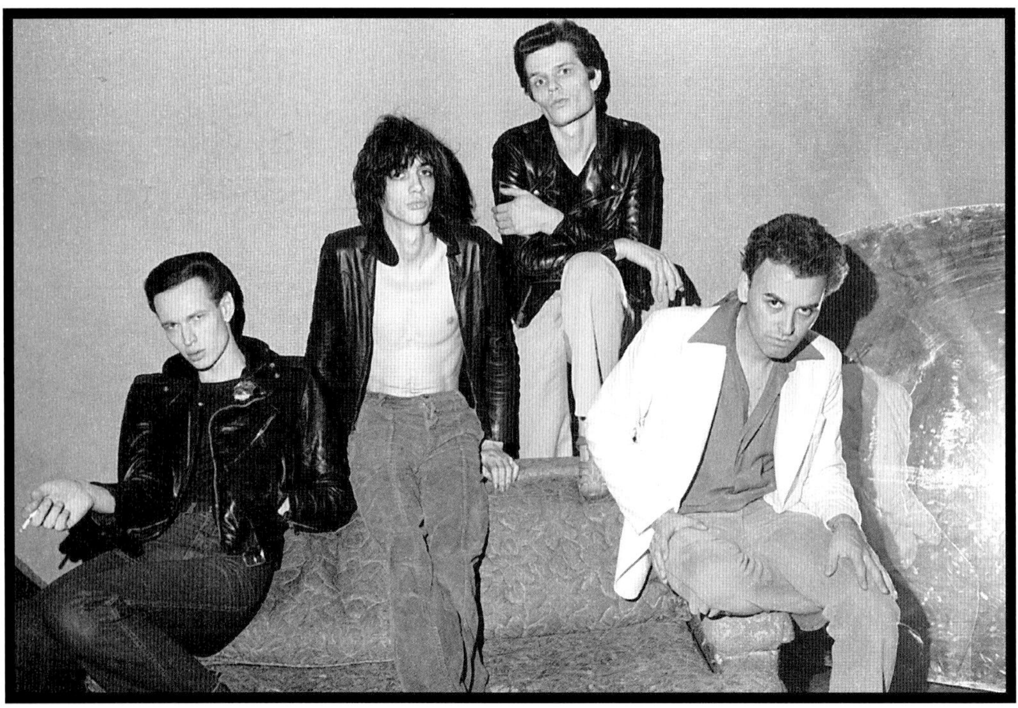

One of my favorites, shot at the studio during rehearsal.

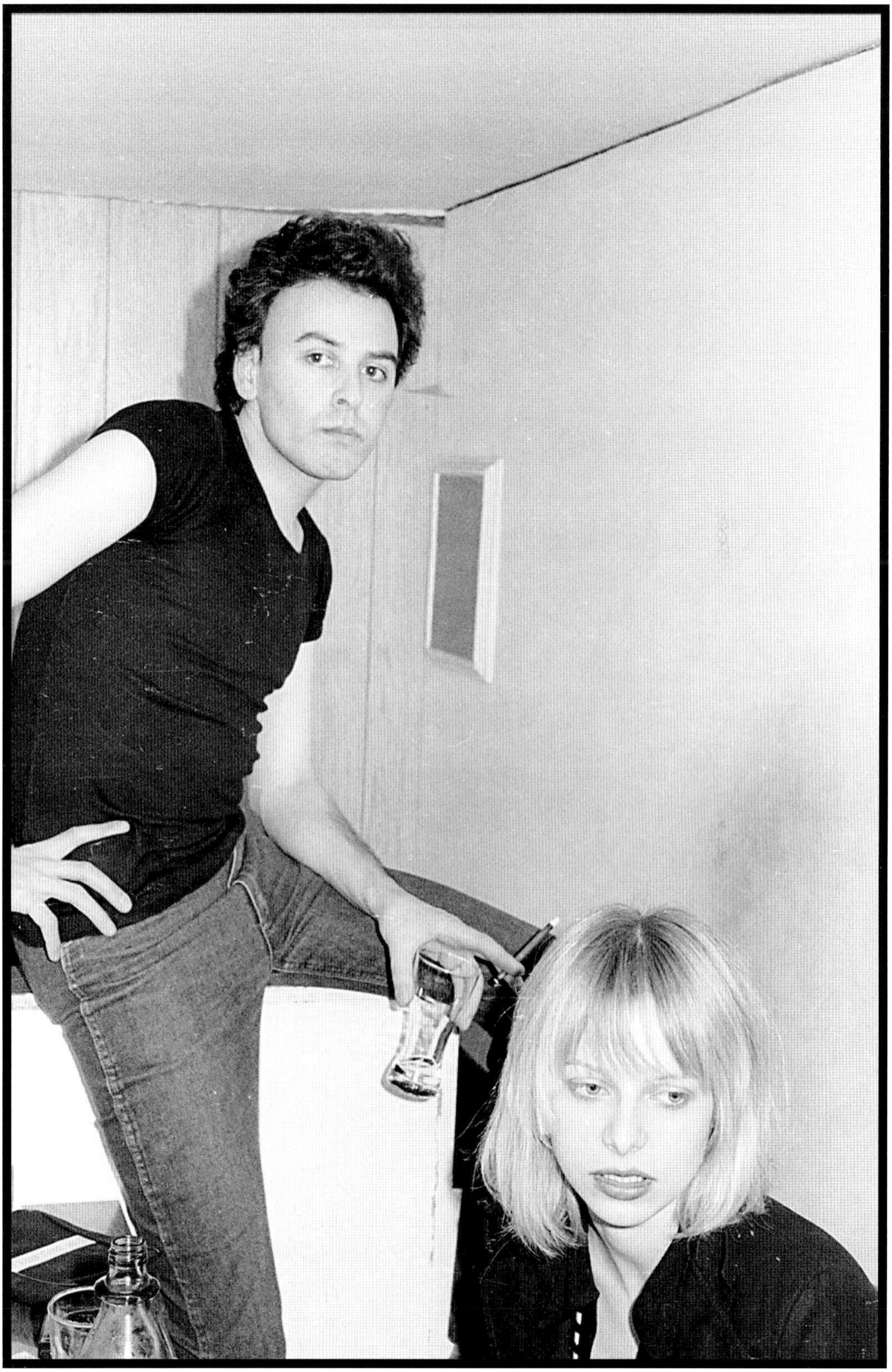

Ron "The Ripper" Greco and De De Troit.

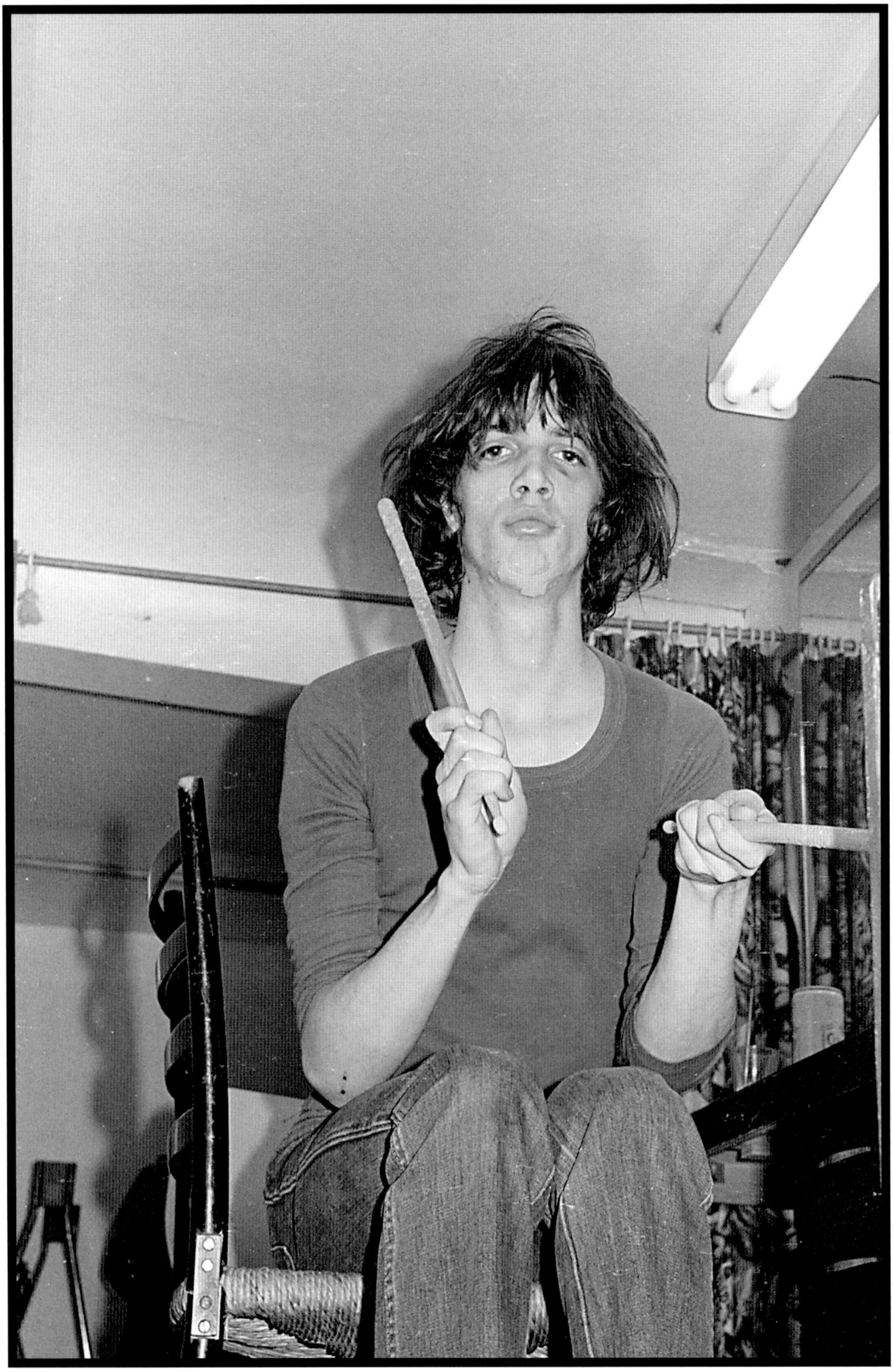

Ricky Williams waiting to play.

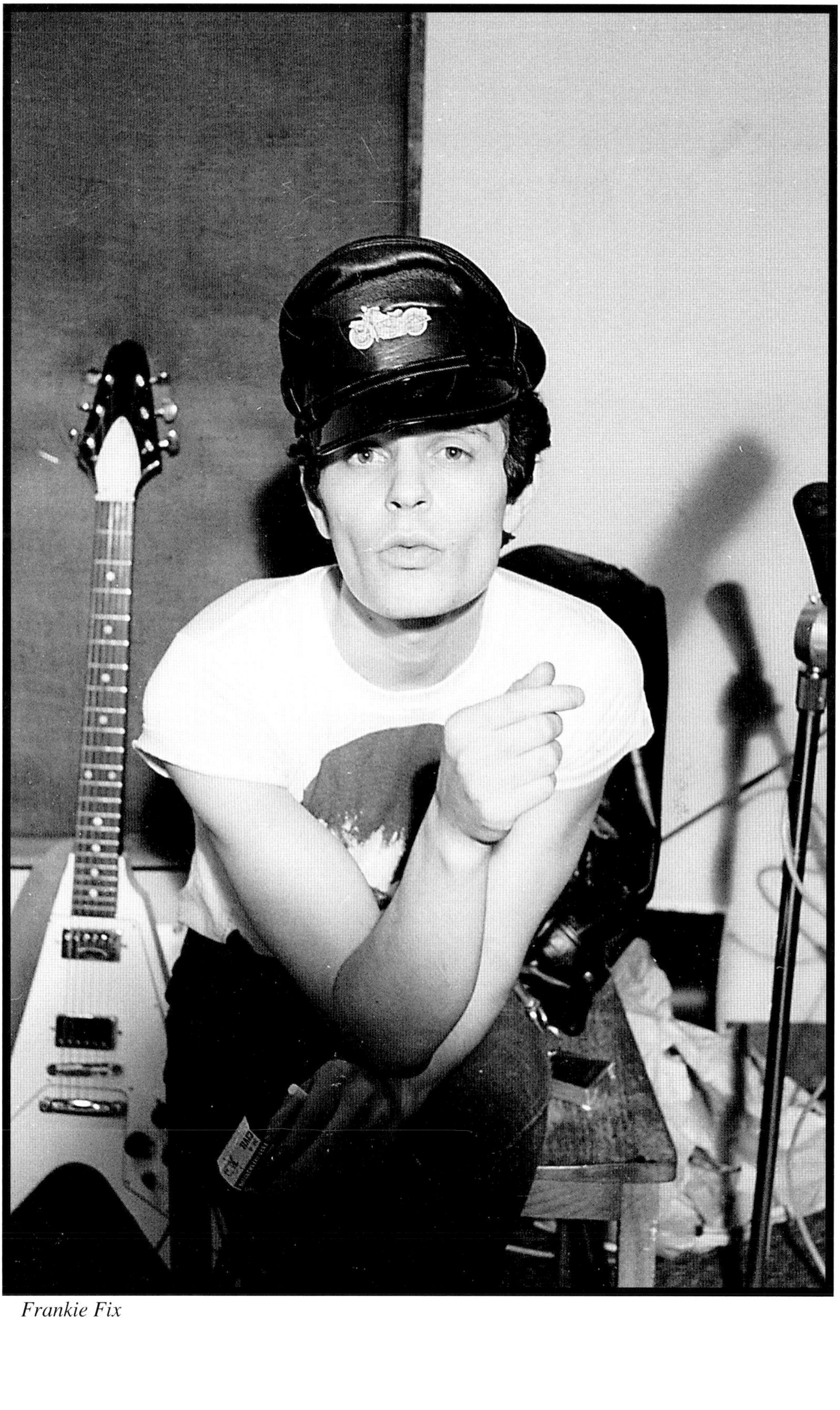

Frankie Fix

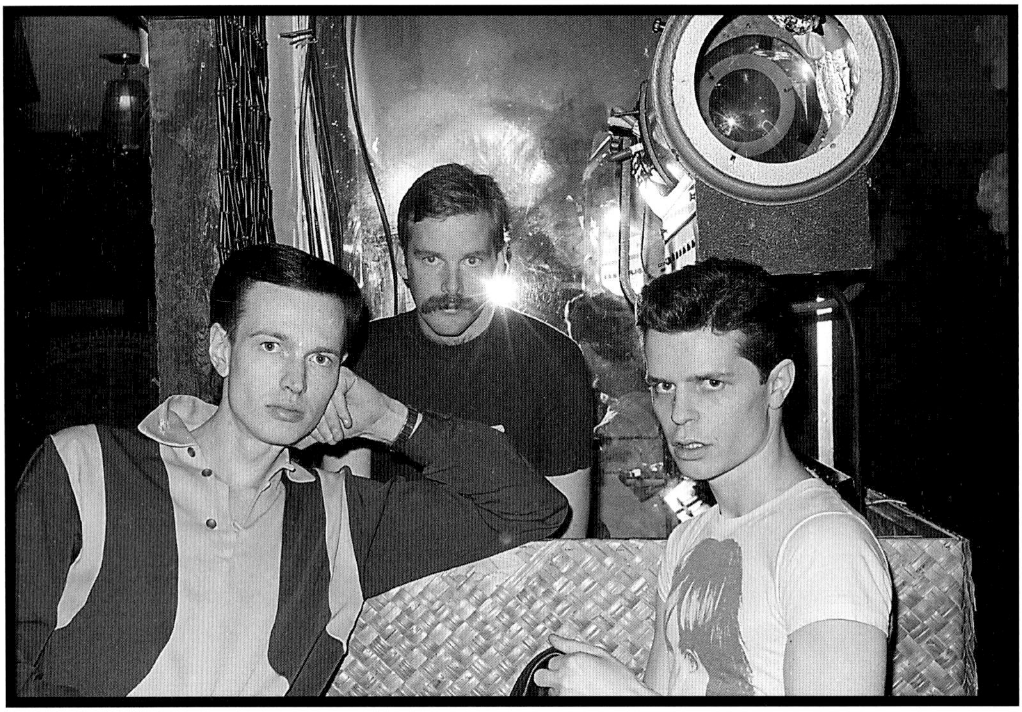

Johnny Strike, Tony Steel, and Frankie Fix
Tony helped with lighting and publicity. He came up with the name Crime and along with his friend Melissa published the fanzine No Exit.

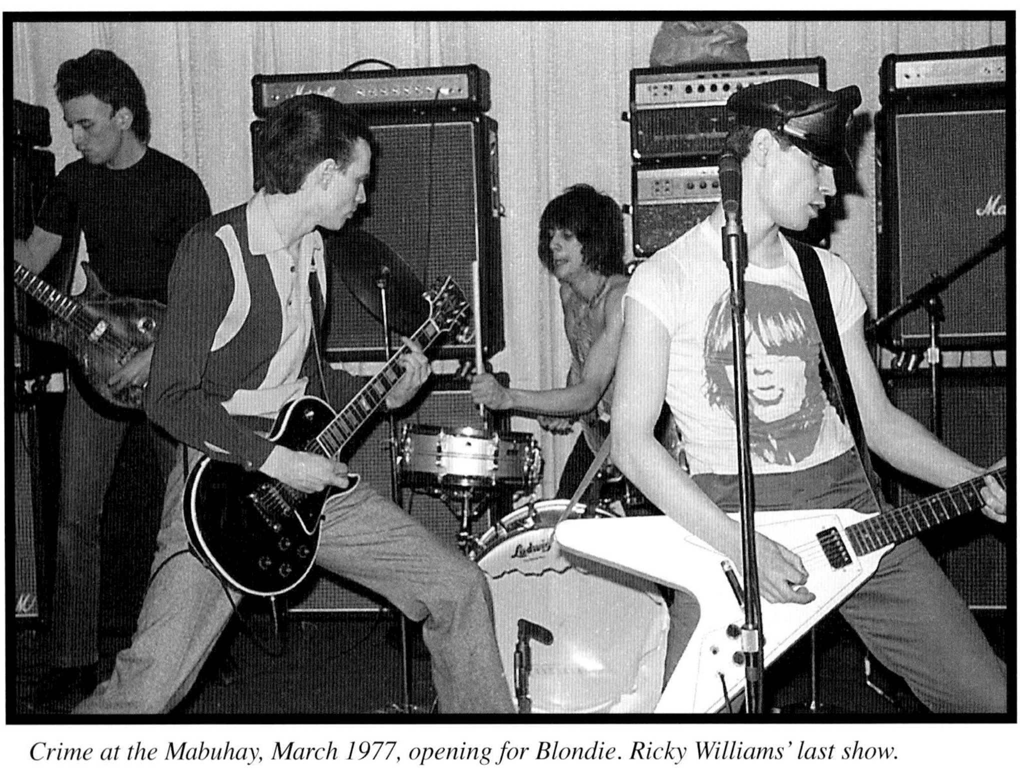

Crime at the Mabuhay, March 1977, opening for Blondie. Ricky Williams' last show.

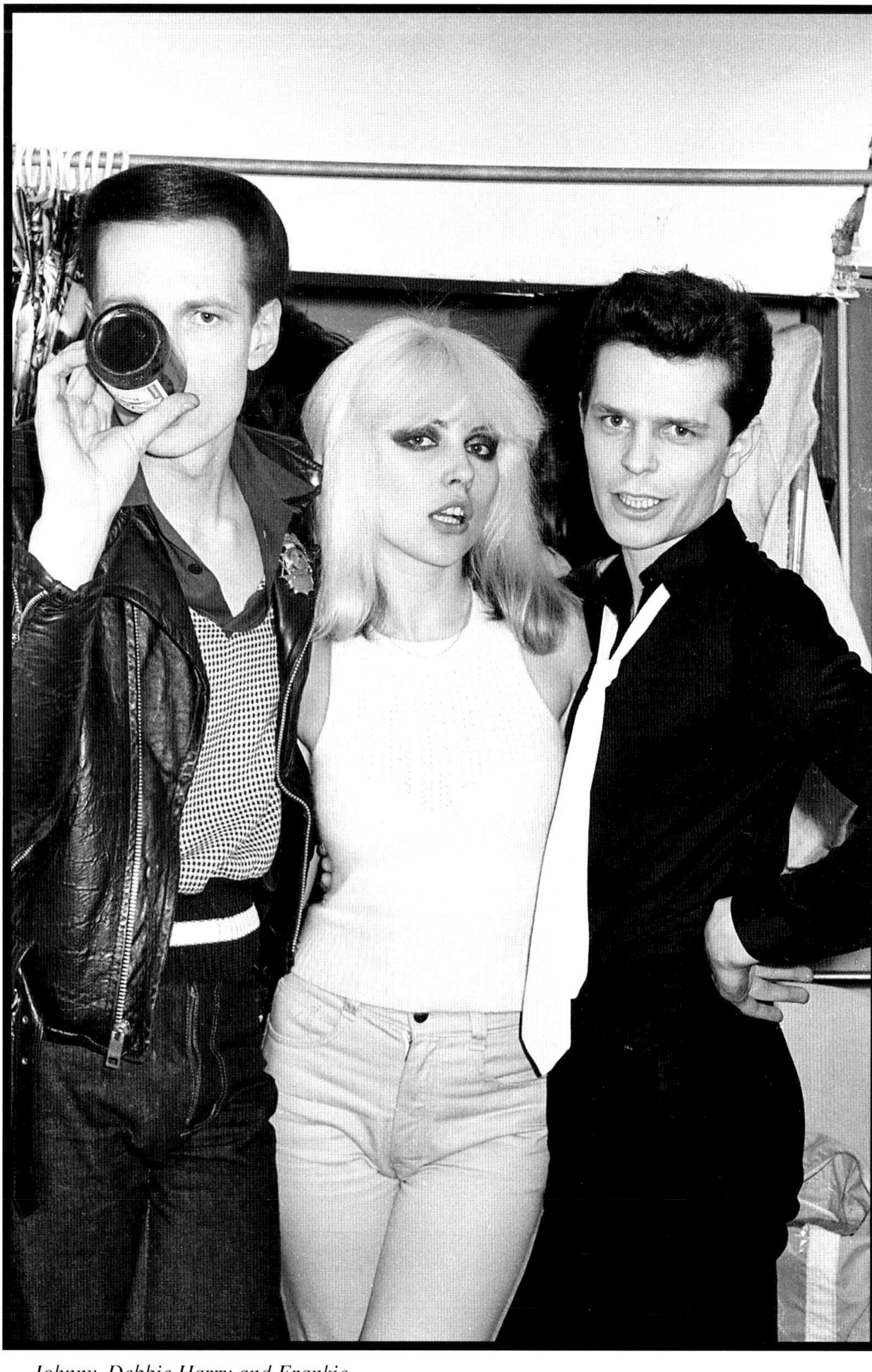

Johnny, Debbie Harry and Frankie
Blondie played the Mabuhay, March of 1977. Crime was the opening band.

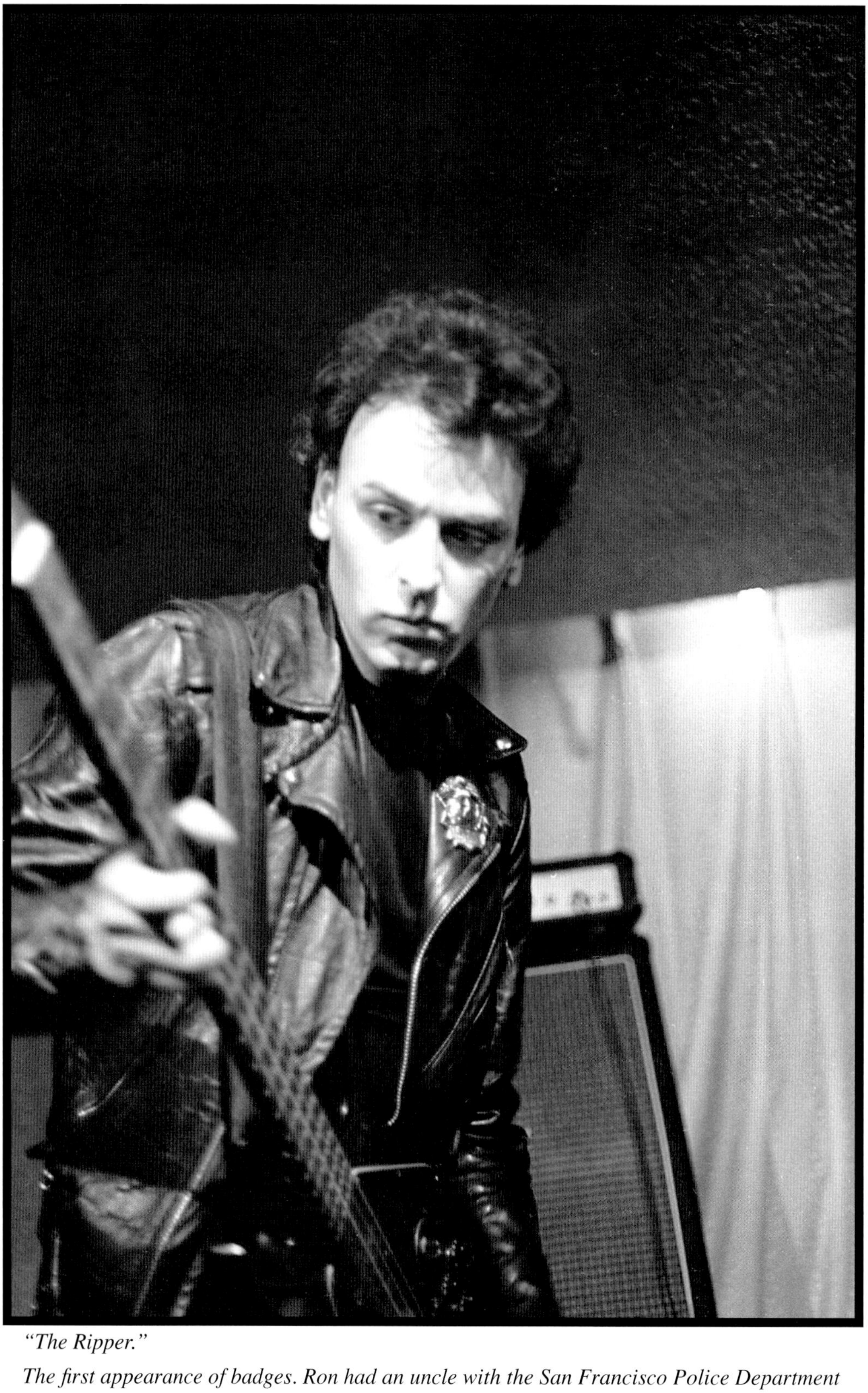

"The Ripper."

The first appearance of badges. Ron had an uncle with the San Francisco Police Department who let Ron borrow one of his badges.

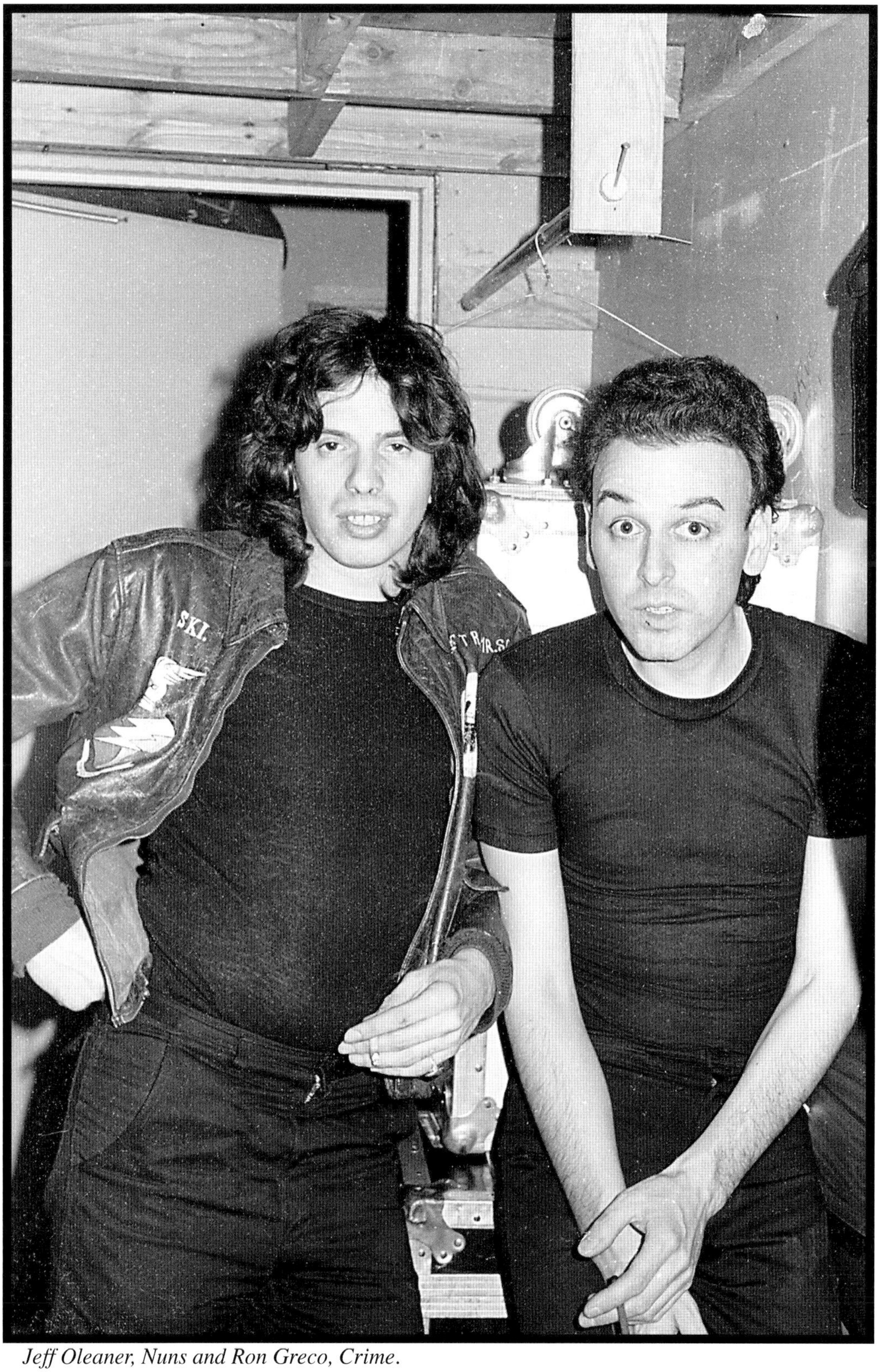

Jeff Oleaner, Nuns and Ron Greco, Crime.

The first big show of the early San Francisco Punk Scene was when the Nuns and Crime played the Mabuhay. The show was a big success, the Mabuhay sold out, but the billing was never repeated. Small bands, big egos.

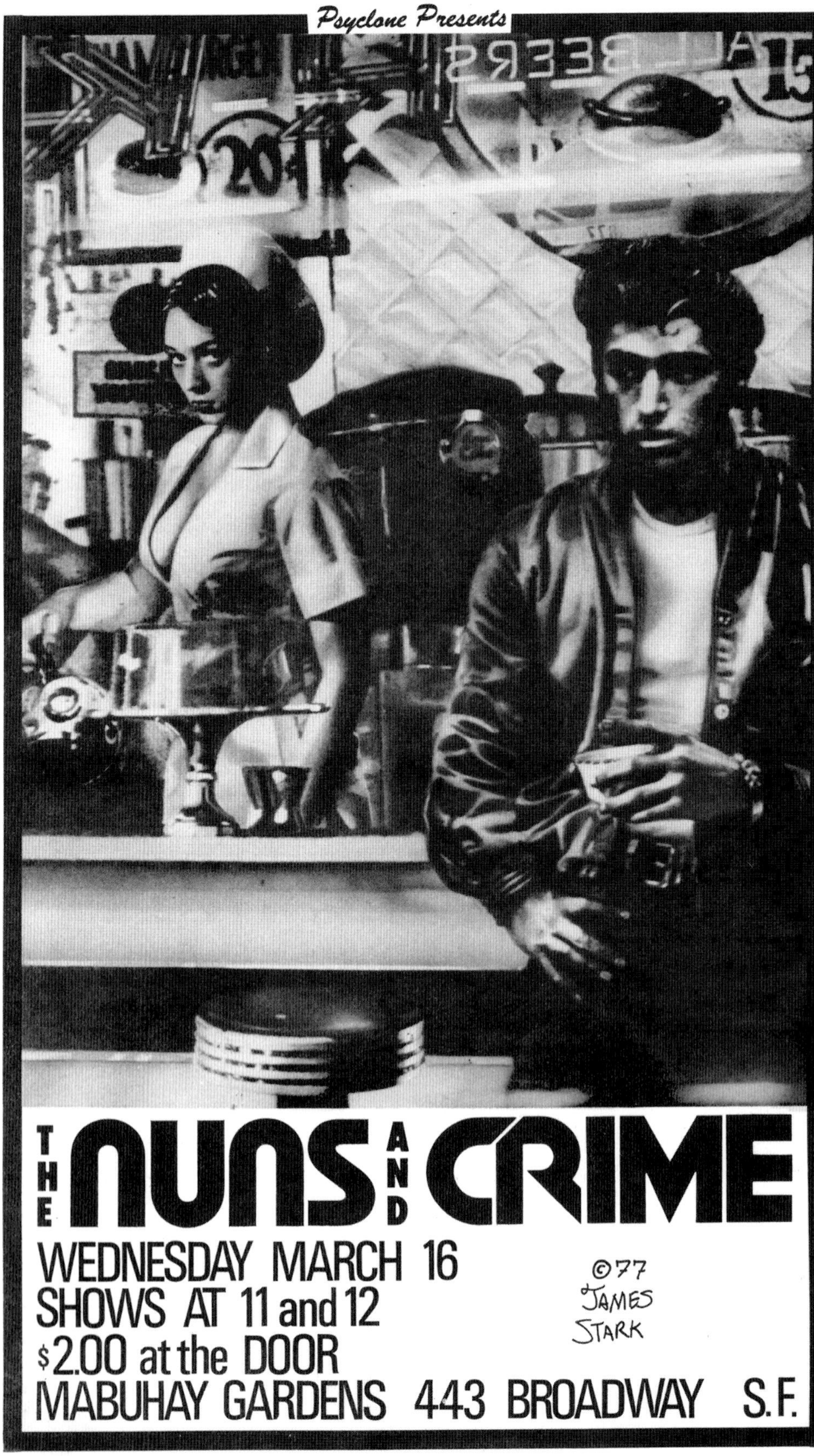
Psyclone Presents
THE NUNS AND CRIME
WEDNESDAY MARCH 16
SHOWS AT 11 and 12
$2.00 at the DOOR
MABUHAY GARDENS 443 BROADWAY S.F.
©77 JAMES STARK

Brittley Comes On the Scene

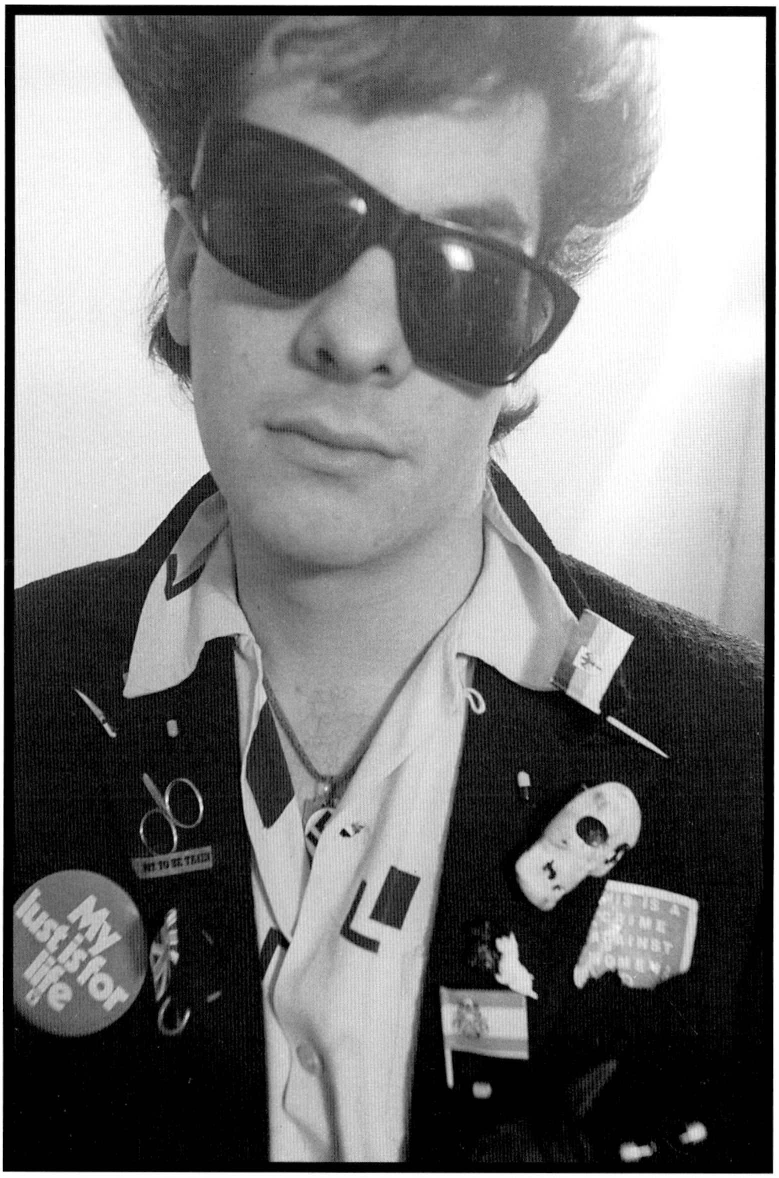

Brittley Black first showed up at the Mabuhay for the Blondie show March, 1977. He'd been in a band called the Circus Pimps, and his father, Dave Black, was a well-known big-band drummer. He had read about Crime in Rock Scene magazine and came to check out what was happening along with Pat Ryan, John Sanfilippo and Rabbit. (Later, Pat, John and Brittley would become part of the Bobby Death Band, and Pat eventually played bass for the Nuns.) By this time, Ricky was at the end of his Crime adventure and the band was looking for a new drummer. Johnny talked to Brittley about being in the band and invited him to come to the rehearsal space and check things out. Brittley loved Marshall stacks and loud music, and he and Ron hit it off from the start. With Ricky gone, the rhythm section kicked ass.

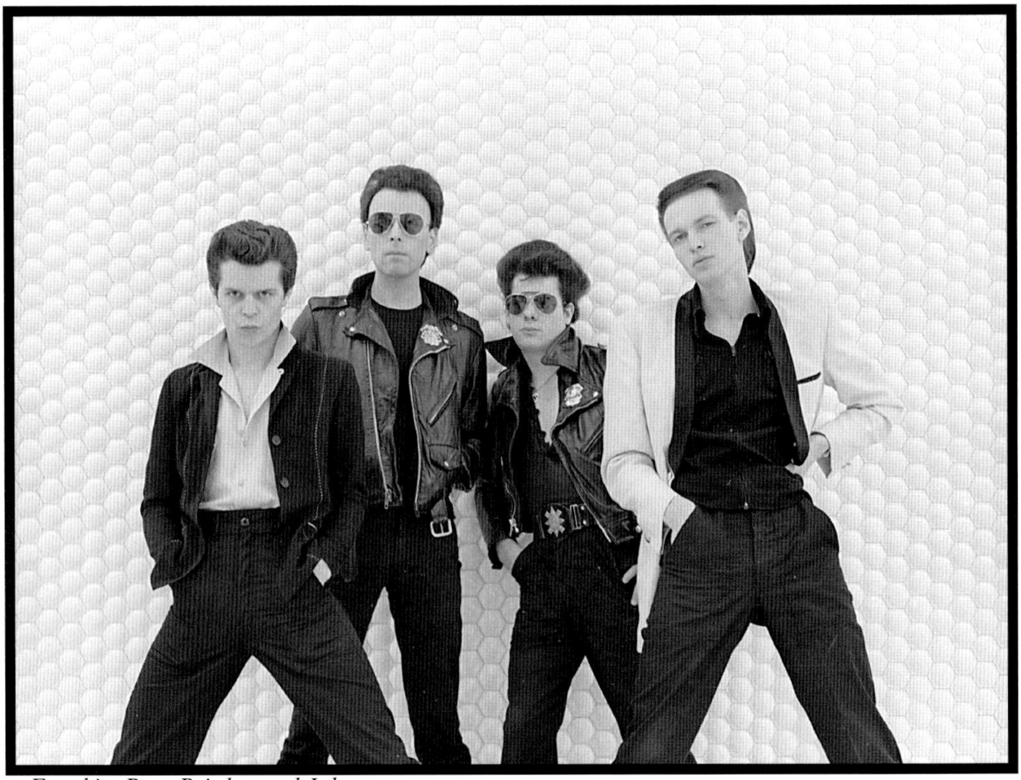

Frankie, Ron, Brittley and Johnny

I've always preferred shooting on the street, taking locations as they come. It also tended to keep everybody loose, making for more interesting photographs. In the mid-1970s the BART system began to operate in the San Francisco Bay Area. BART stations were slick and harshly modern. The Powell Street Station had shiny ceramic-tiled walls and bright fluorescent lighting that made for an interesting look. When these photos were taken, the station still had a lot of empty space, which would later be filled with different concessionaires. The photos seen here, pages 22 - 32 , stood in stark contrast to the usual band photography of the day, which required a lot of lights and makeup. The whole point of punk was to get away from the commercial look and strip it down to the basics. Let it all hang out and go.

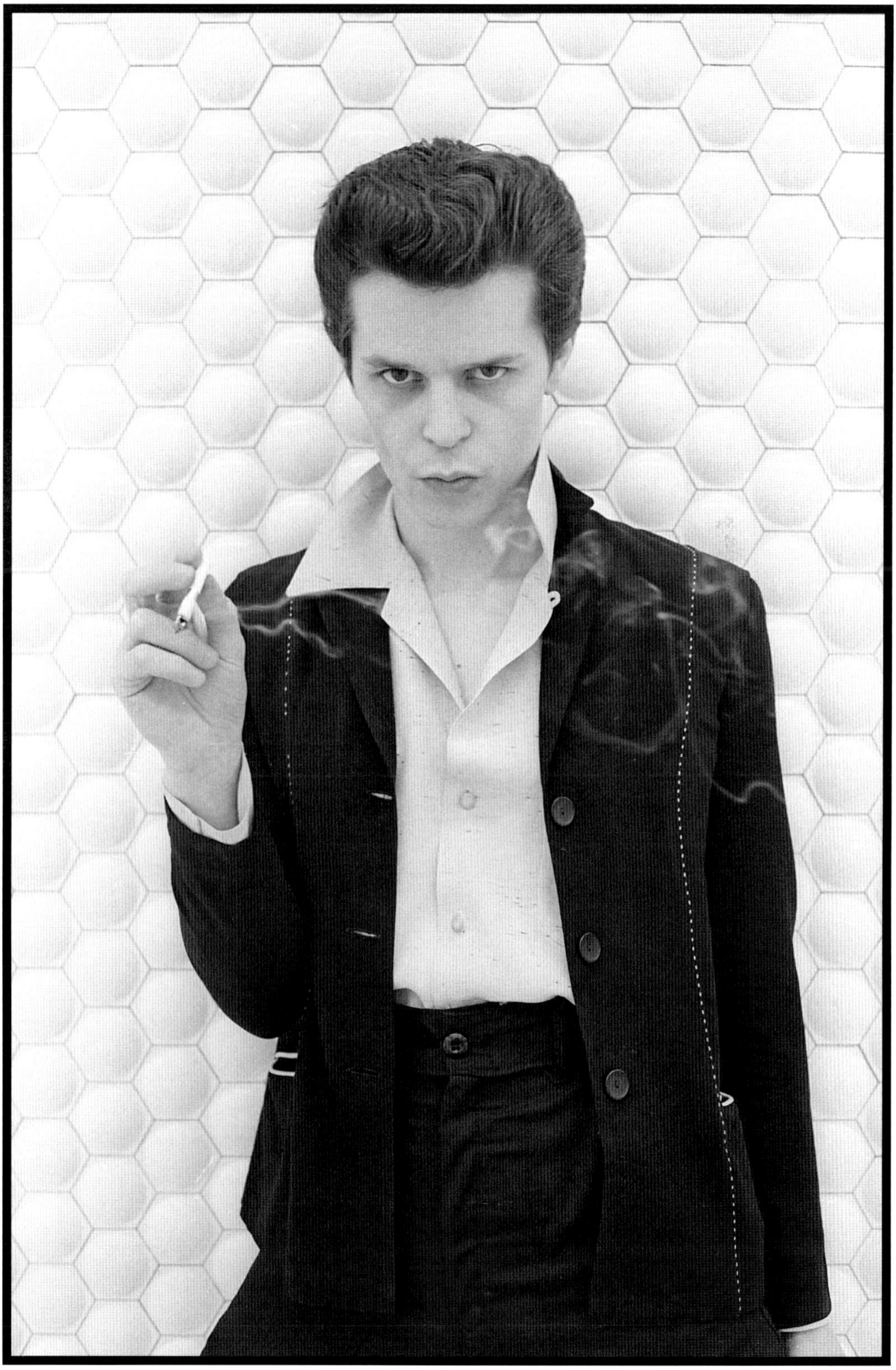

Frankie Fix

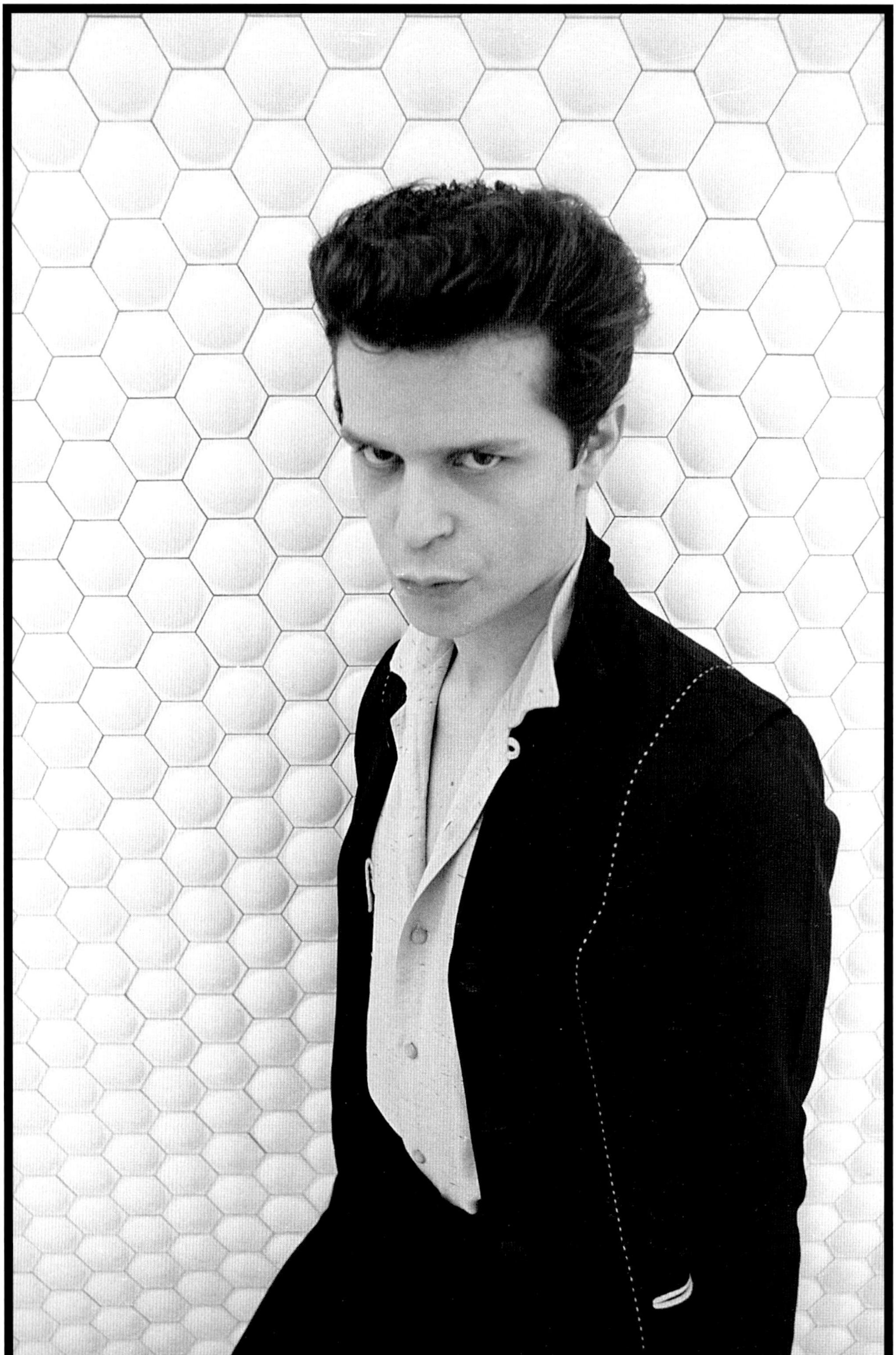

Frankie Fix

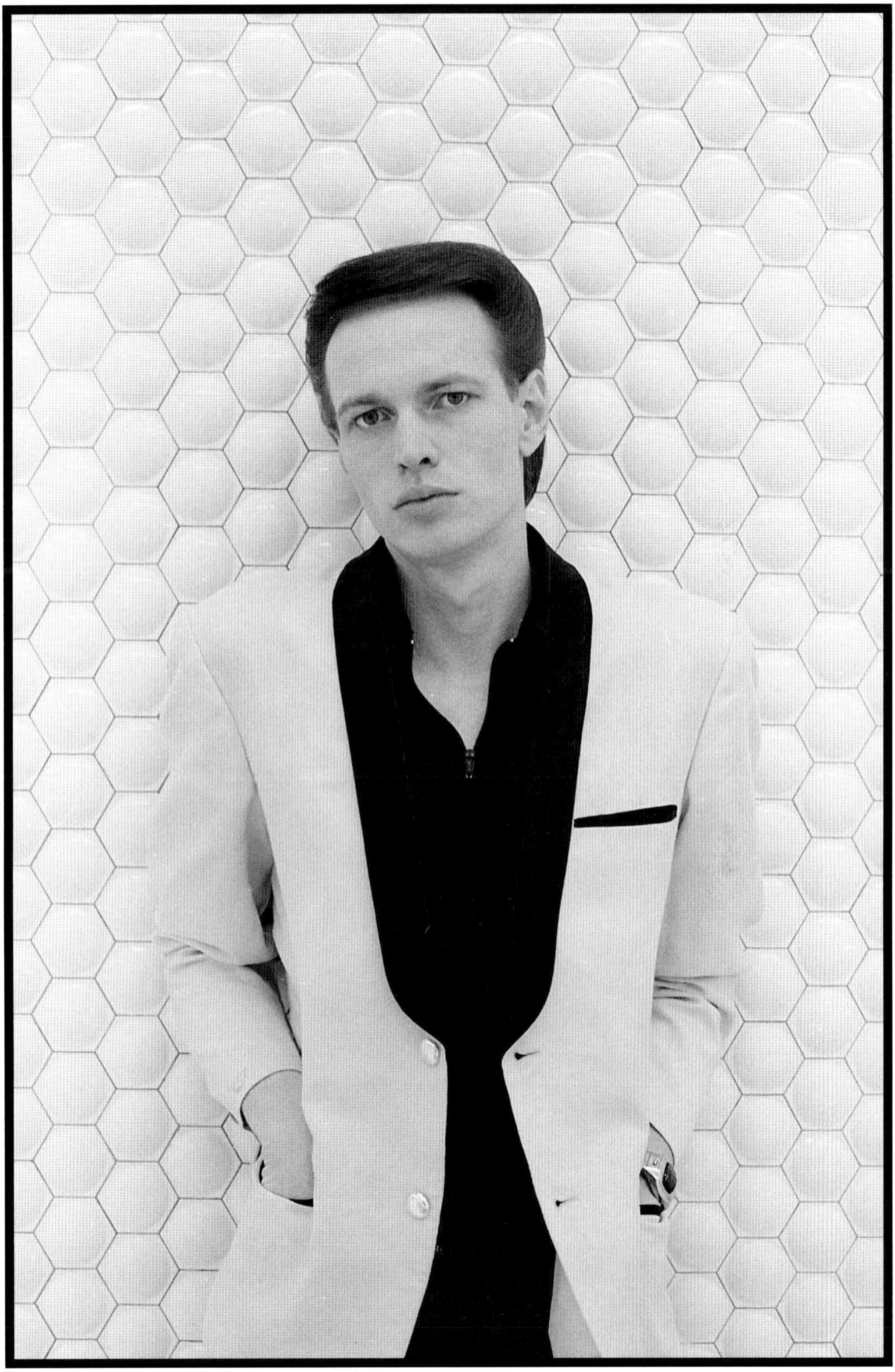

Johnny Strike

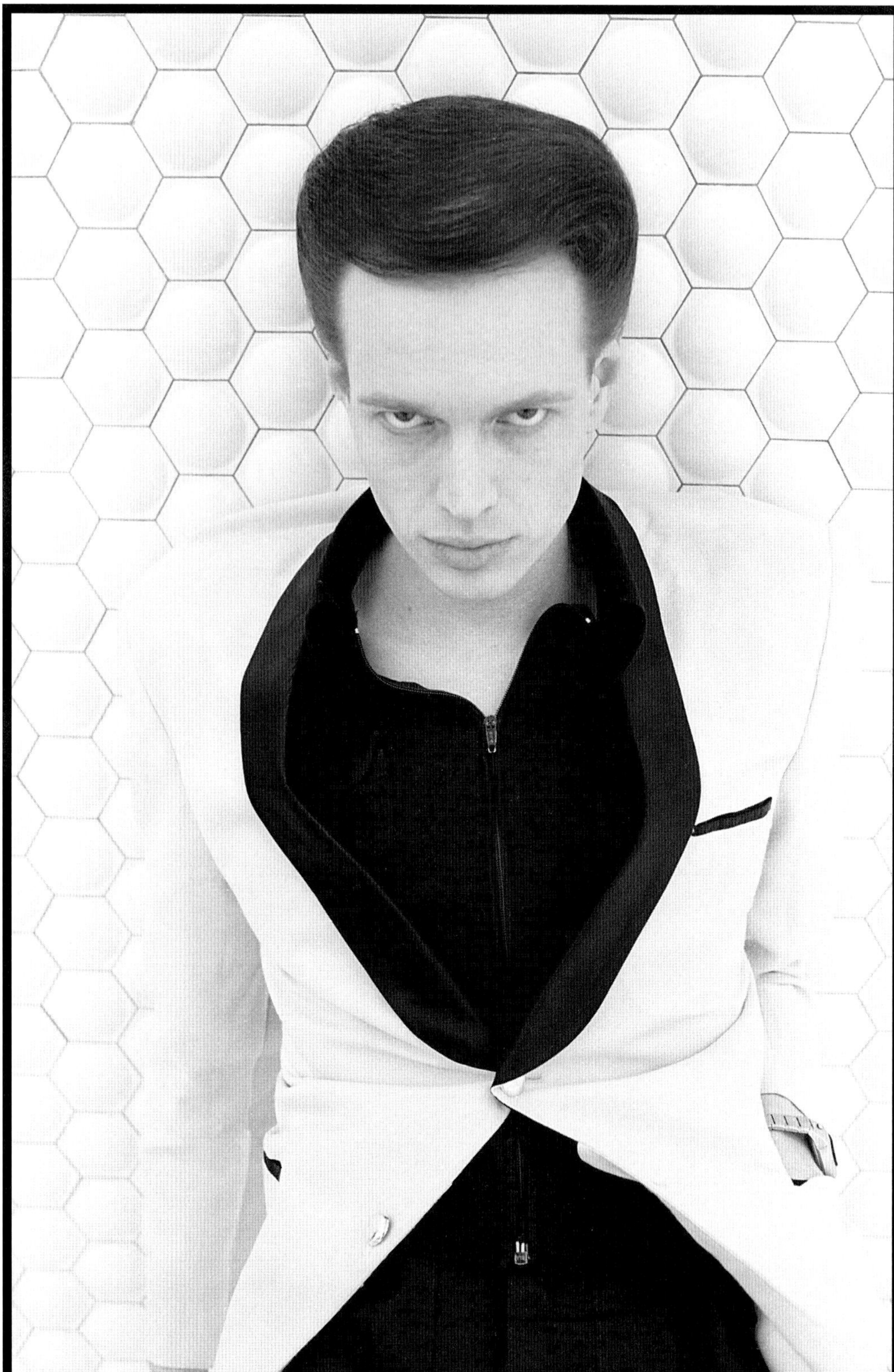

Johnny Strike

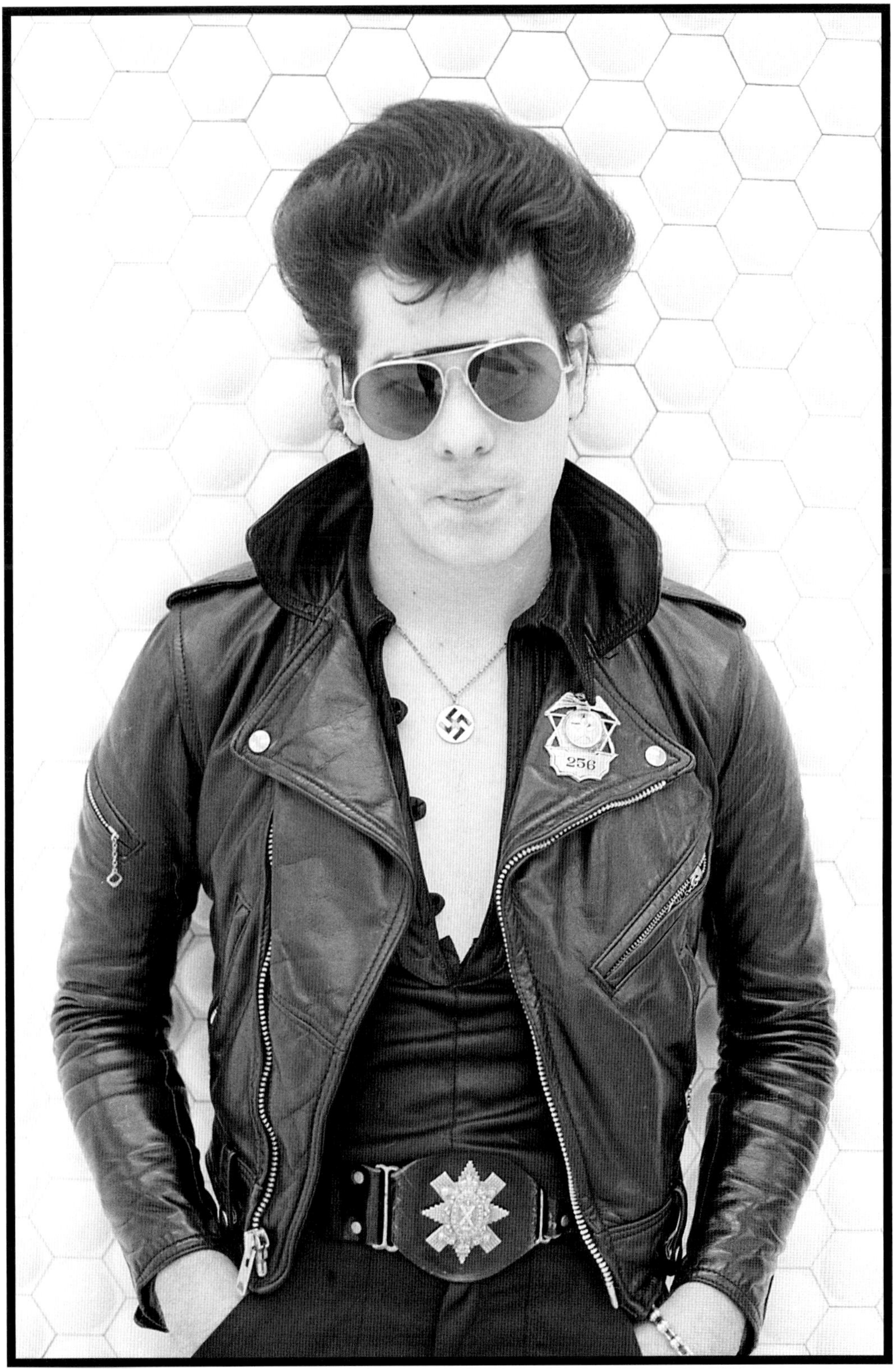

Brittley Black

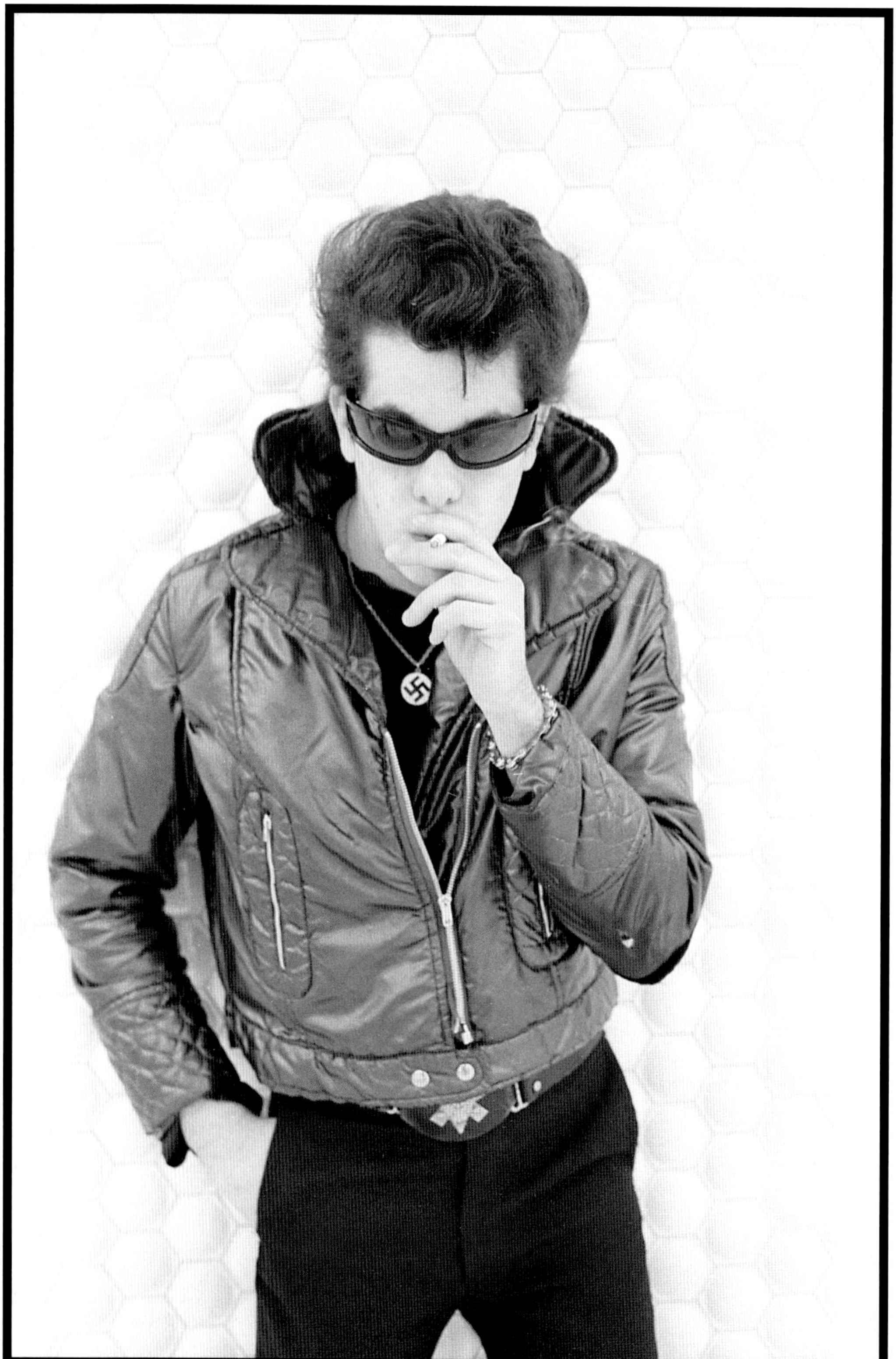

Brittley Black

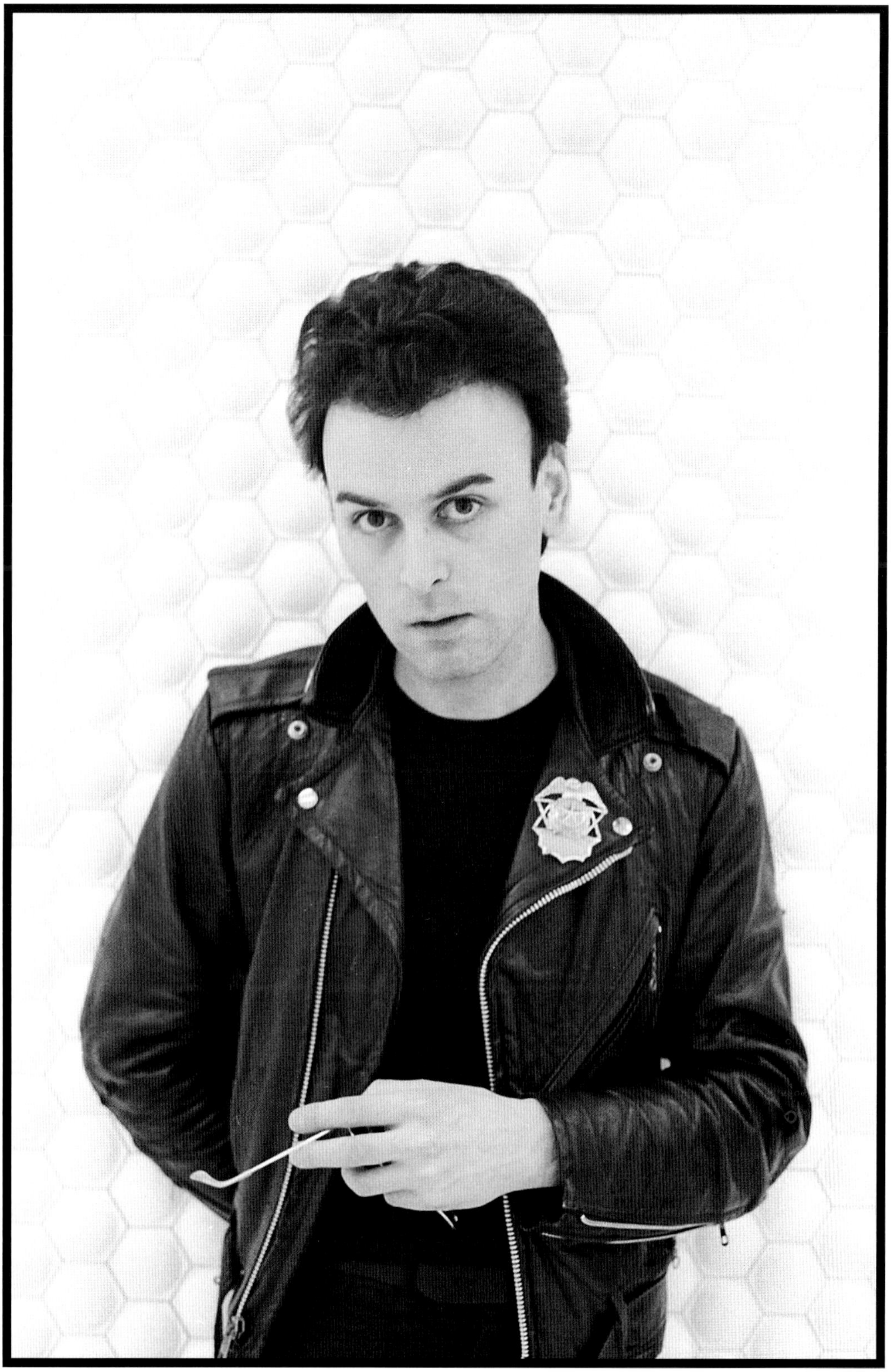

Ron "The Ripper" Greco

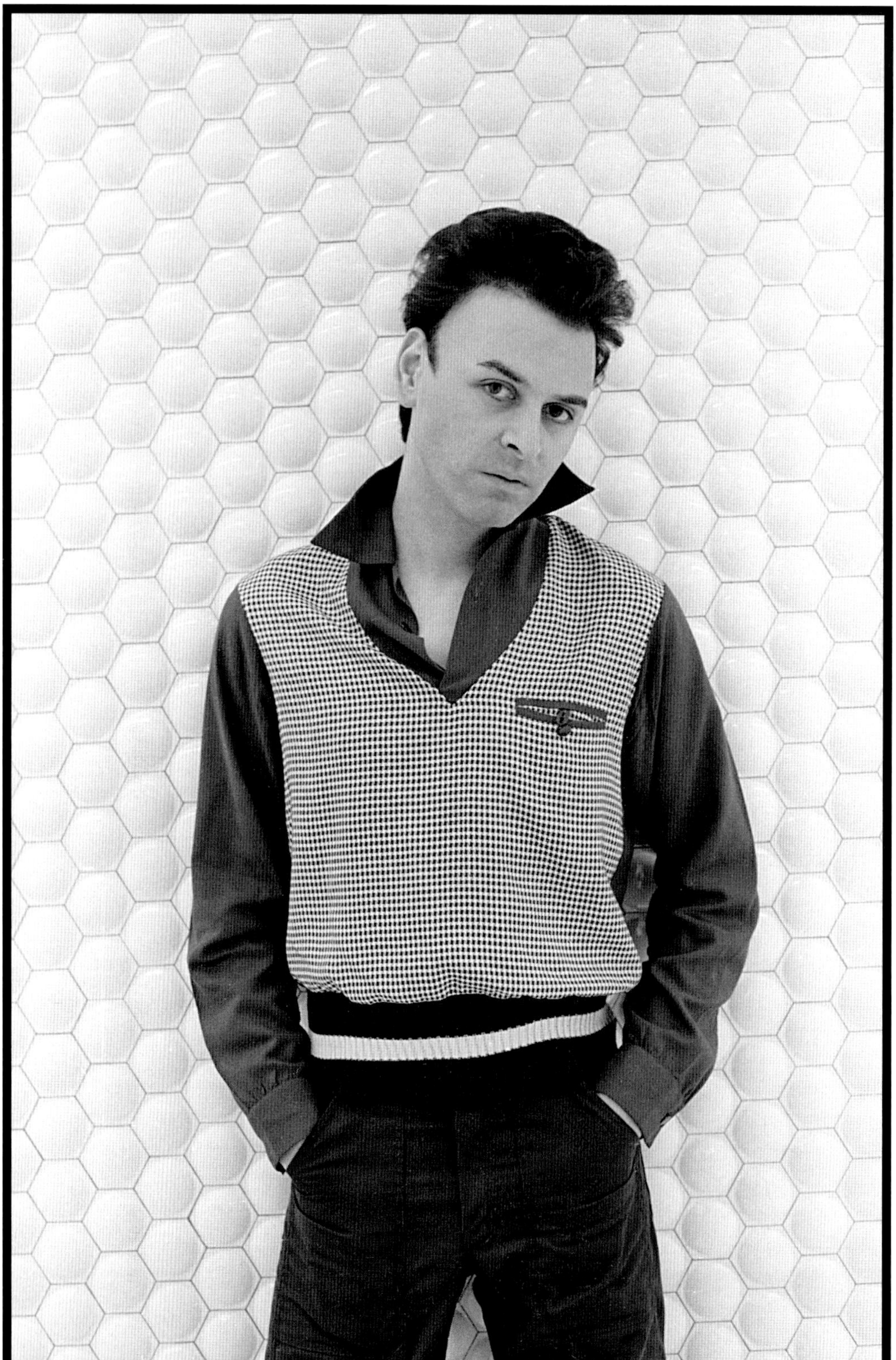

Ron Greco

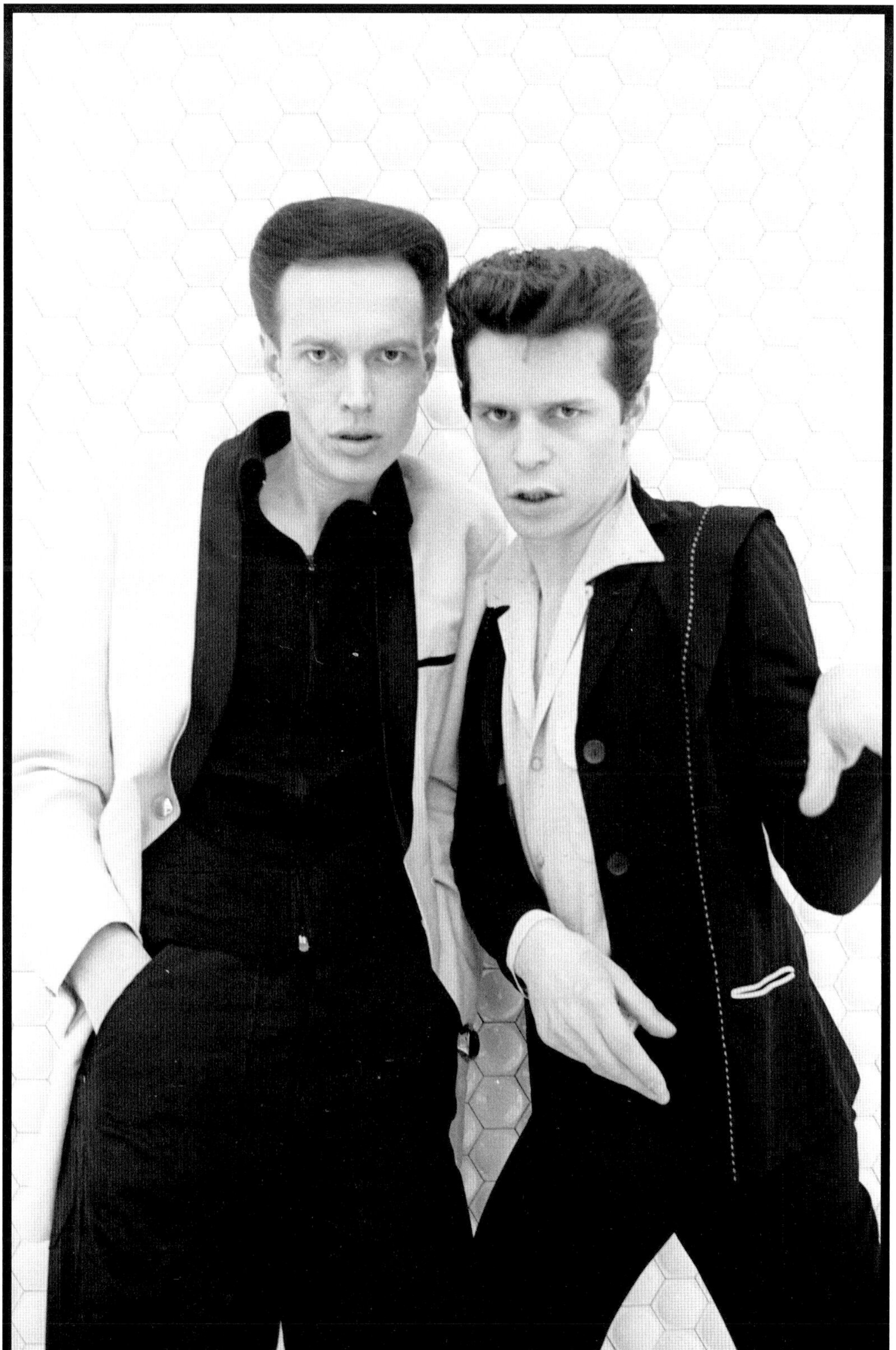

Johnny and Frankie

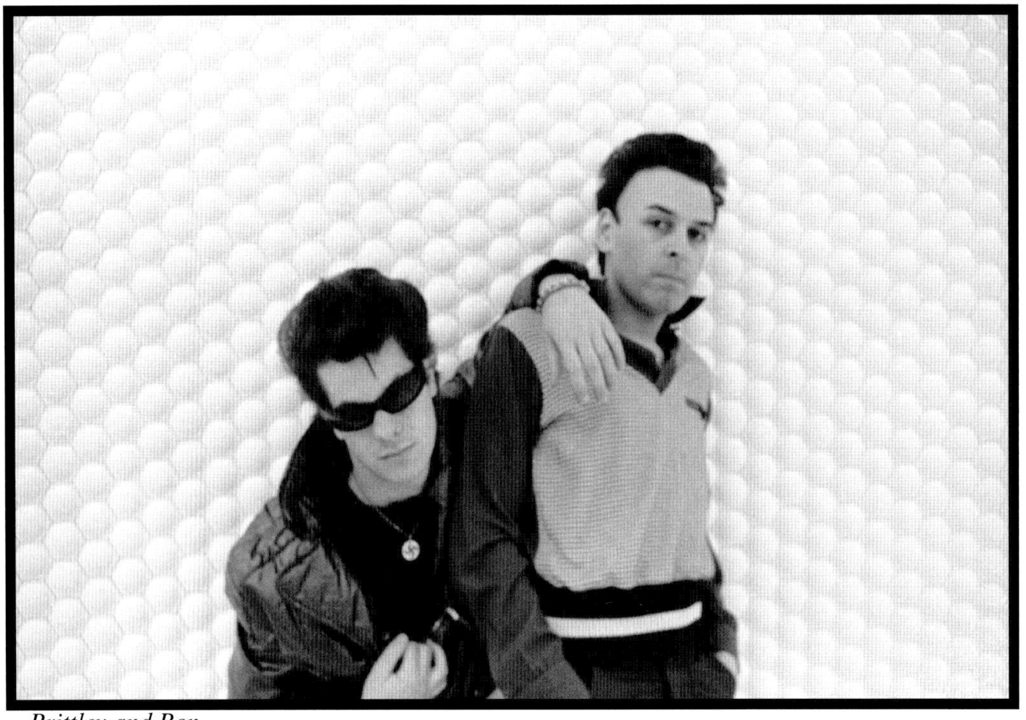

Brittley and Ron

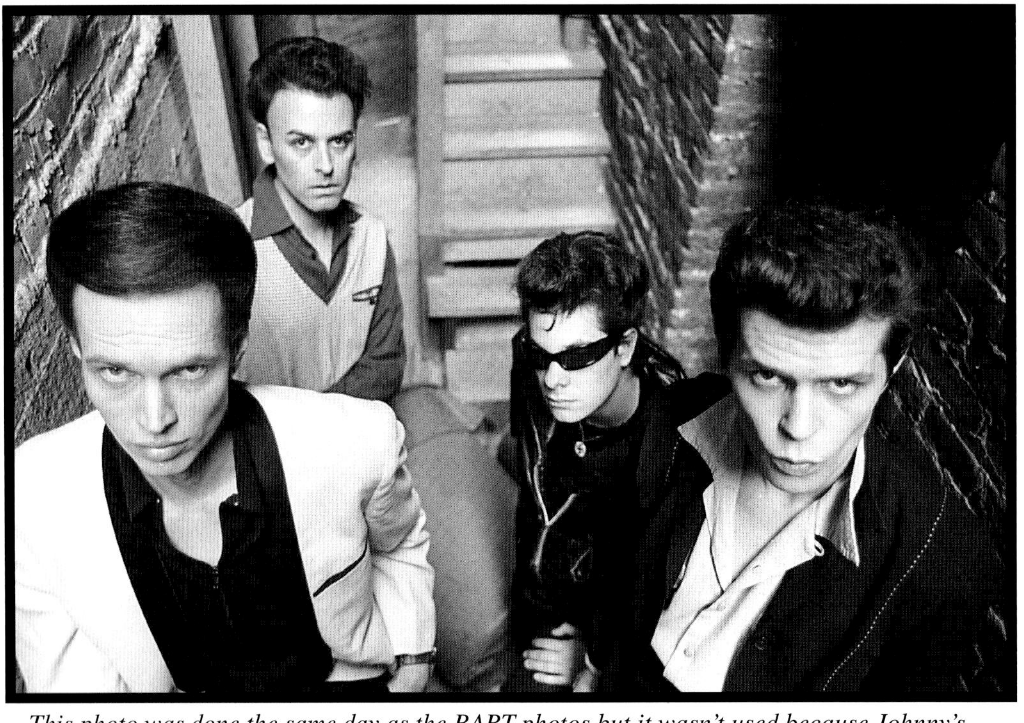

This photo was done the same day as the BART photos but it wasn't used because Johnny's bald spot was showing.

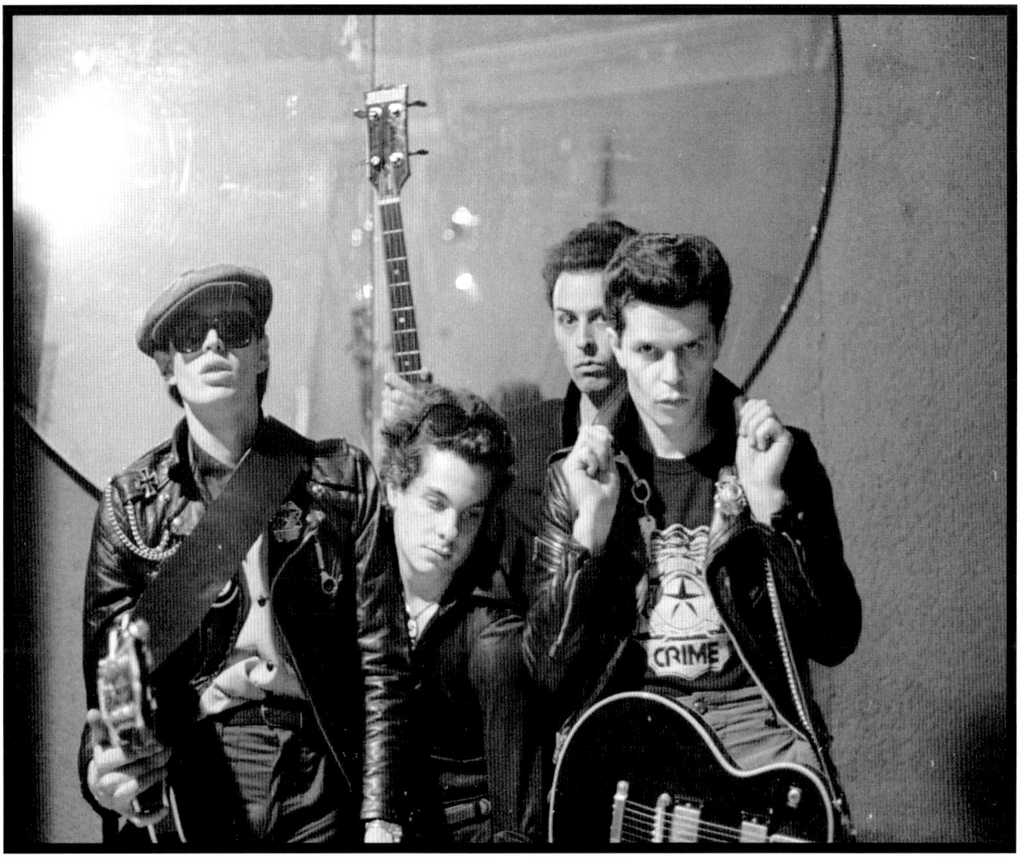

Johnny, Brittley, Ron and Frankie

By mid-1977, Time and Space rehearsal studios moved from Howard Street to Natoma Street, behind the Chronicle Building where the photos on this page and page 34 were taken. This band shot and the following four used about a dozen frames. The individual photos were one frame each. This photograph was done on the spur of the moment, street clothes and flash on camera in front of a piece of mylar. It was rare to get Frankie and Johnny to pose in this kind of situation. Usually they liked to have more control over their look.

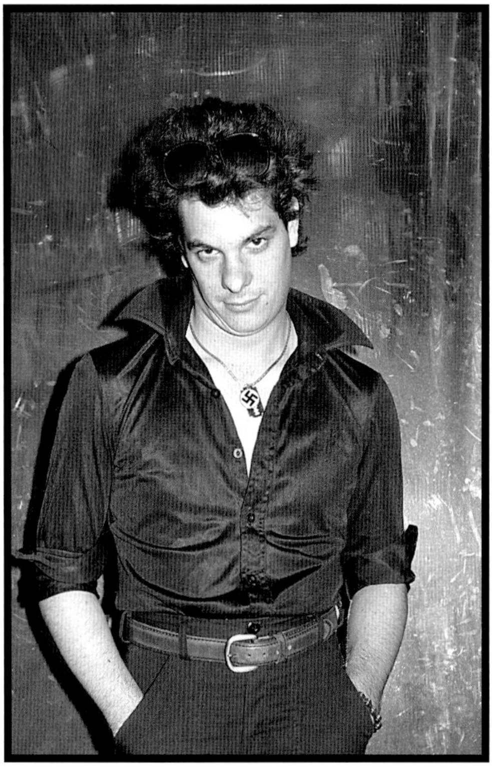

Brittley

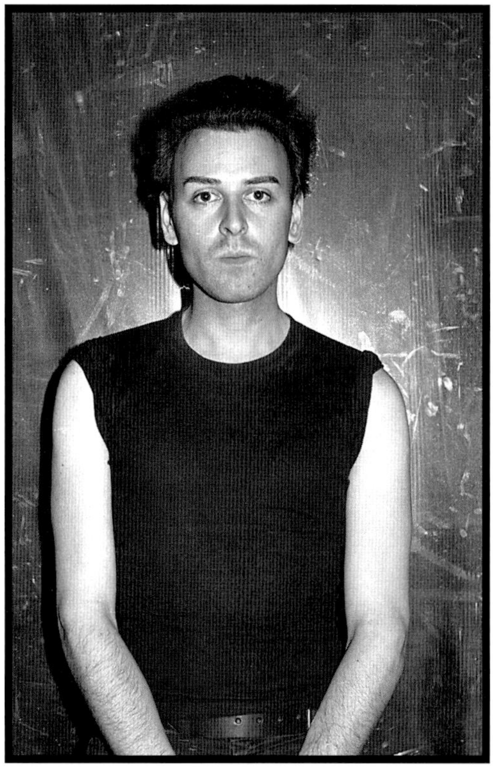

Ripper

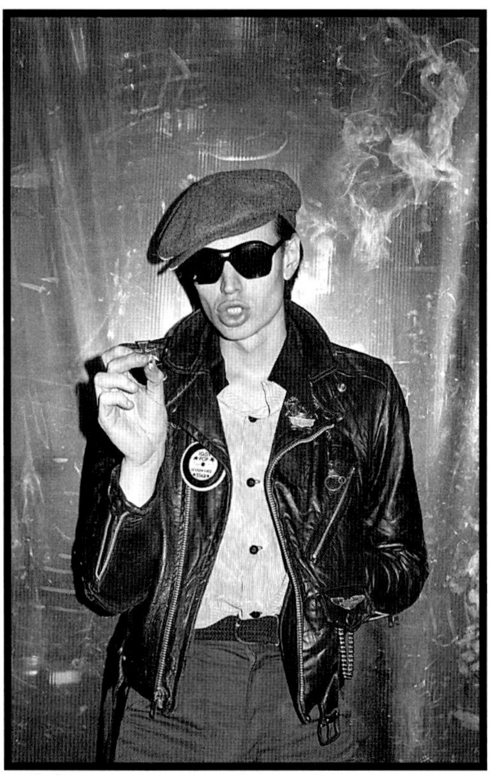

Johnny

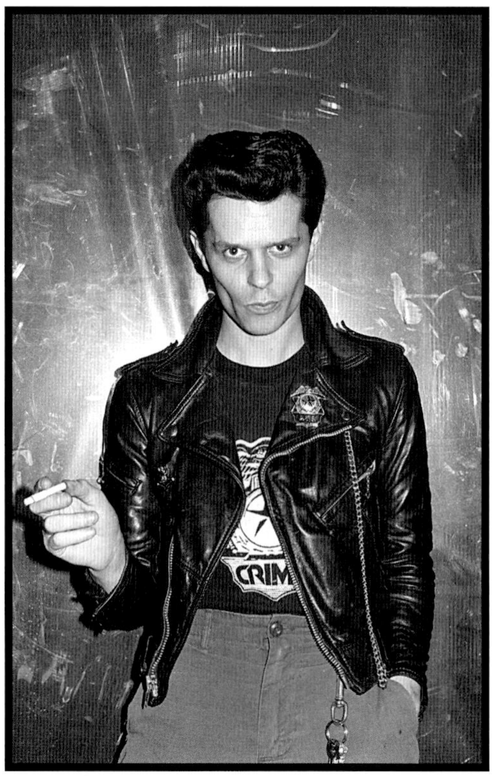

Frankie

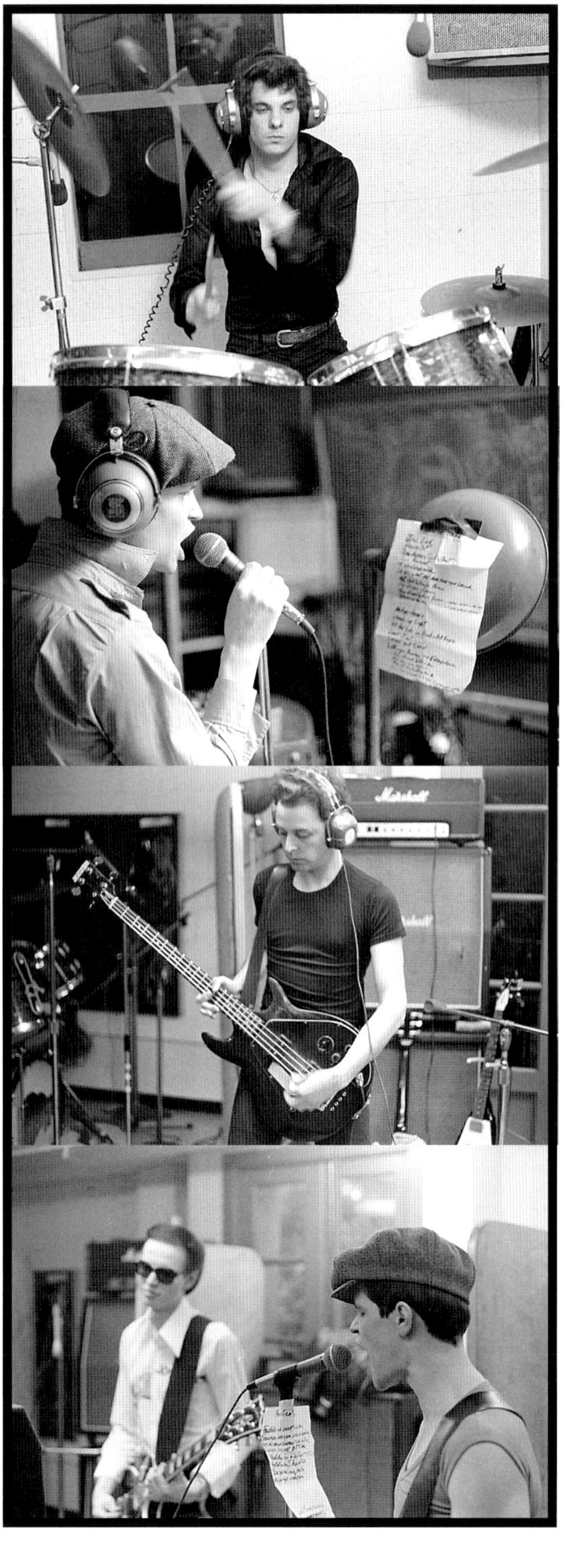

Crime went into the recording studio in mid-May 1977 to record "Murder by Guitar" and "Frustration" for their second single. Novak had done some demos for the Nuns and offered to do the recording in a studio at Mills College, where he was a graduate student. This time, things were more controlled, and the recording took two or three days to complete. The result is considered Crime's best. During this session, Crime also recorded "San Francisco Doomed" and "Gangster Funk."

Recording consists of short spurts of work with long periods of waiting.

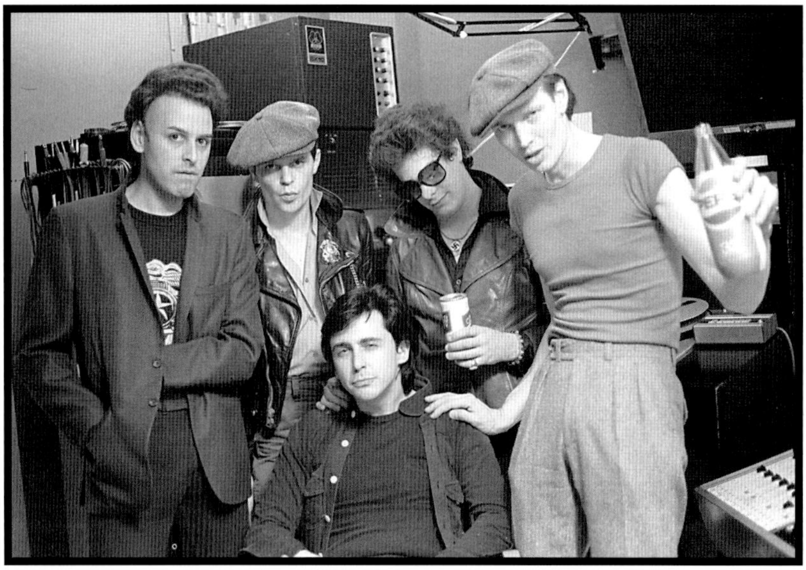

Ron, Frankie, Novak, Brittley and Johnny

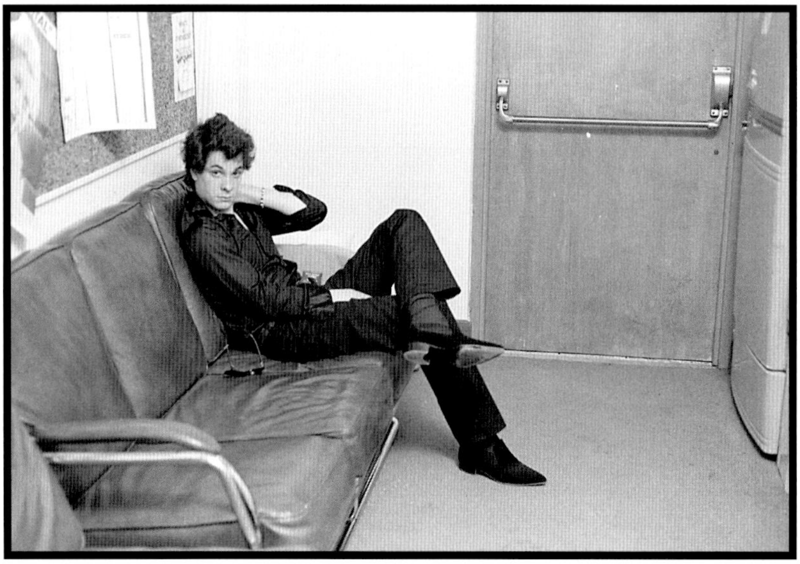

Brittley waiting in the hall.

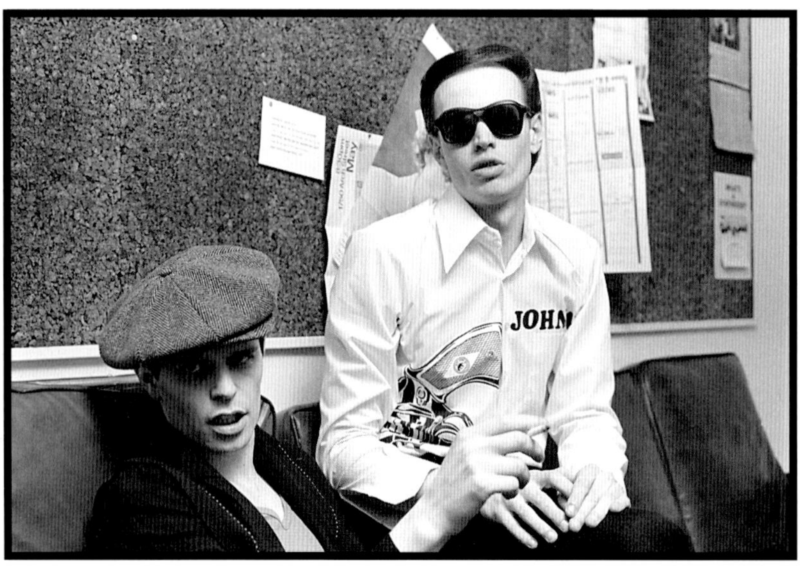

Frankie and Johnny

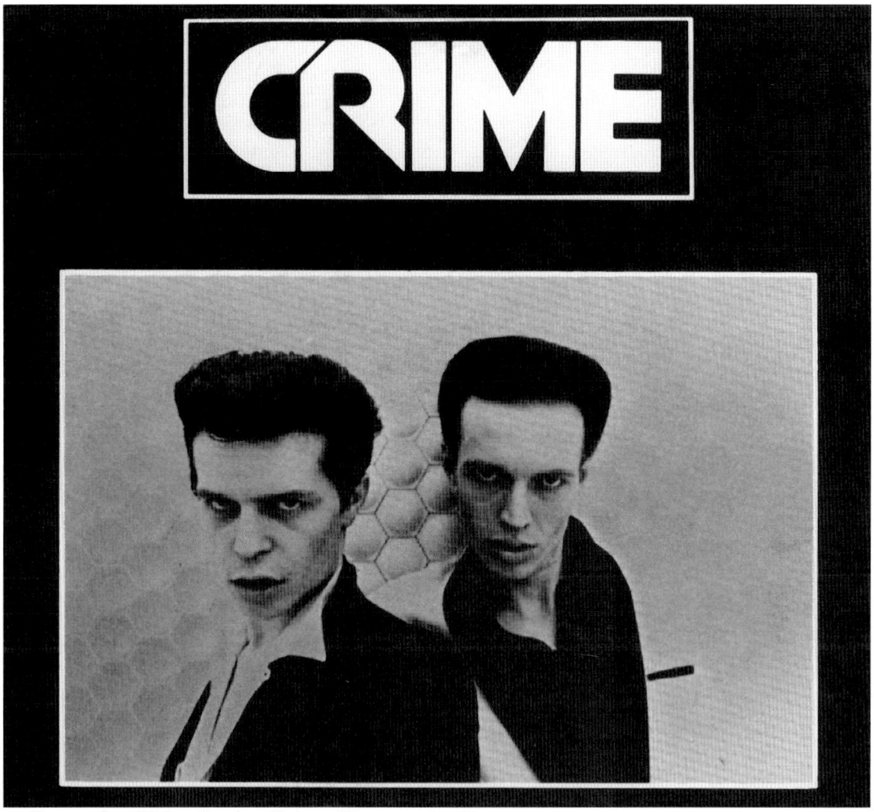

Cover for "Murder by Guitar/Frustration".

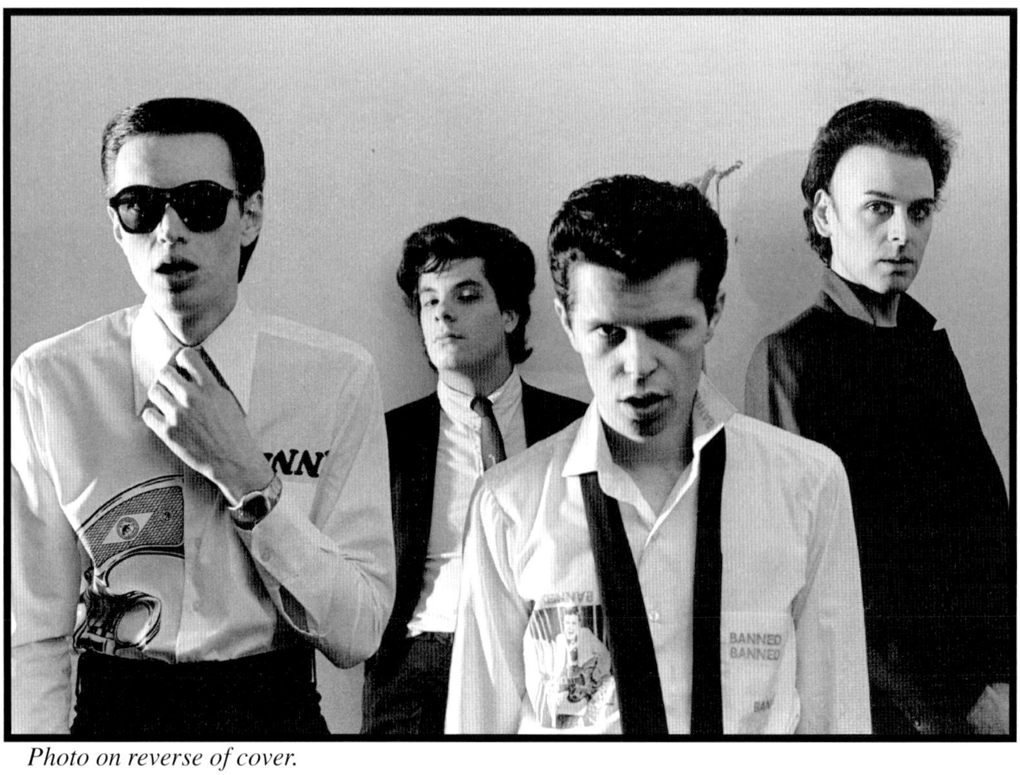

Photo on reverse of cover.

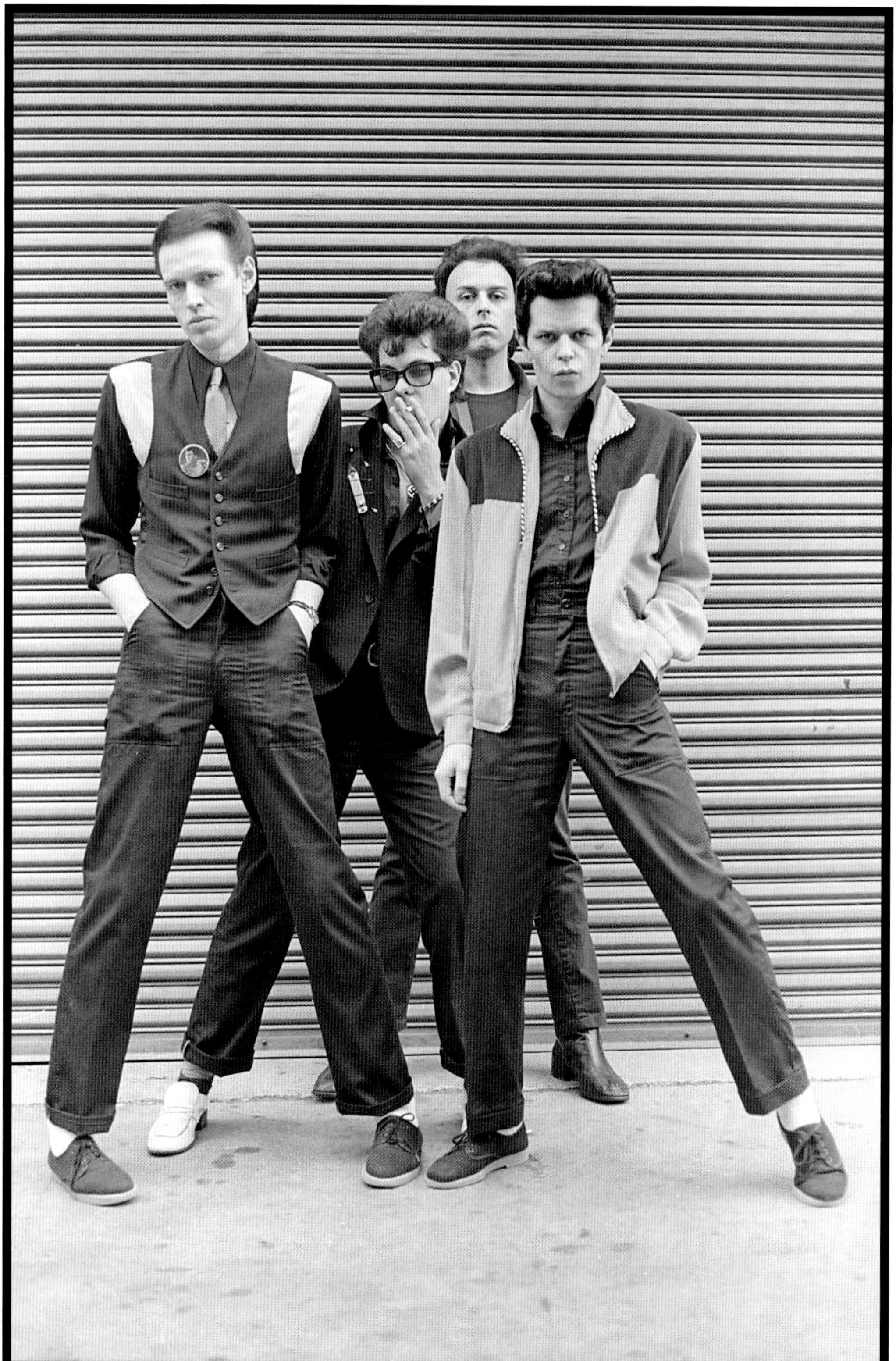

Johnny, Brittley, Ron and Frankie. The boys have moved to a more '50s kind of street drag.

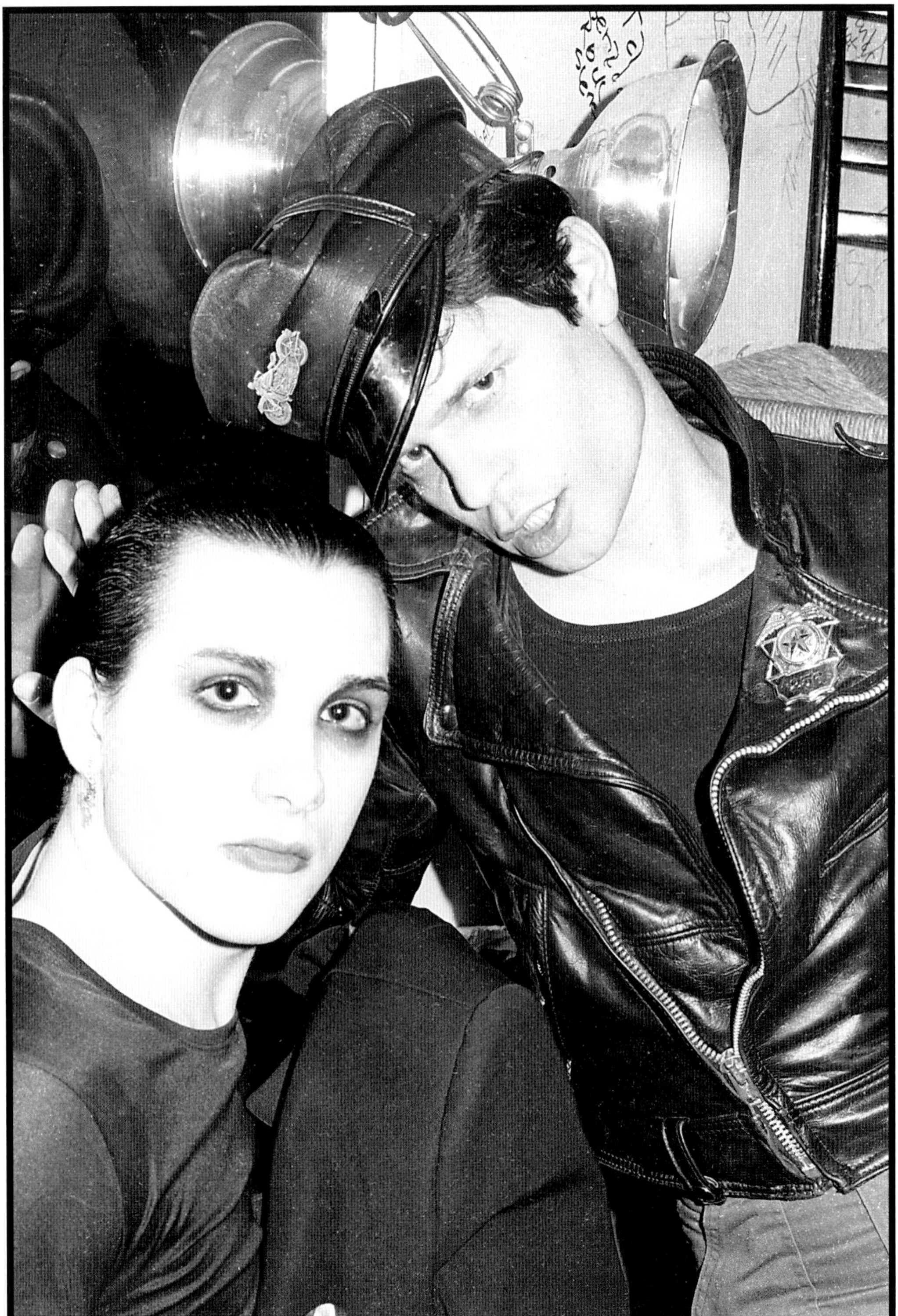

Frankie and Dave Vanian, The Damned

The Damned were the first English punk band to tour America. They played the Mabuhay in San Francisco on April 21, 1977 with Crime as the opening act. Some of these photos later appeared in File magazine, with fake captions about a large international party where The Damned were hanging out.

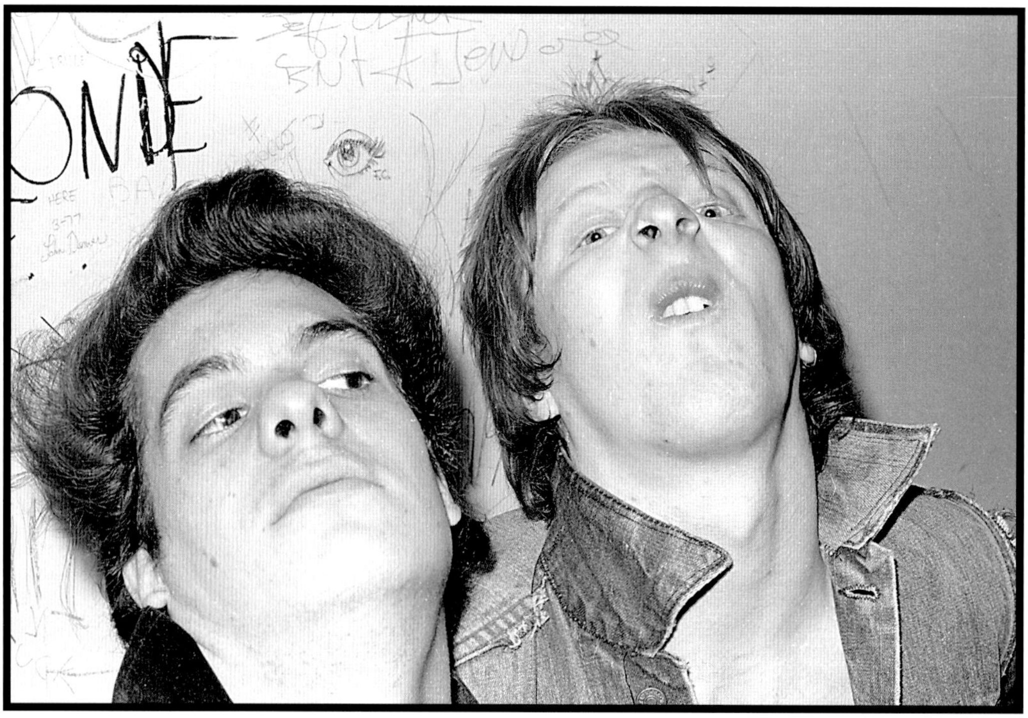

Brittley Black, Crime and Rat Scabies, The Damned.

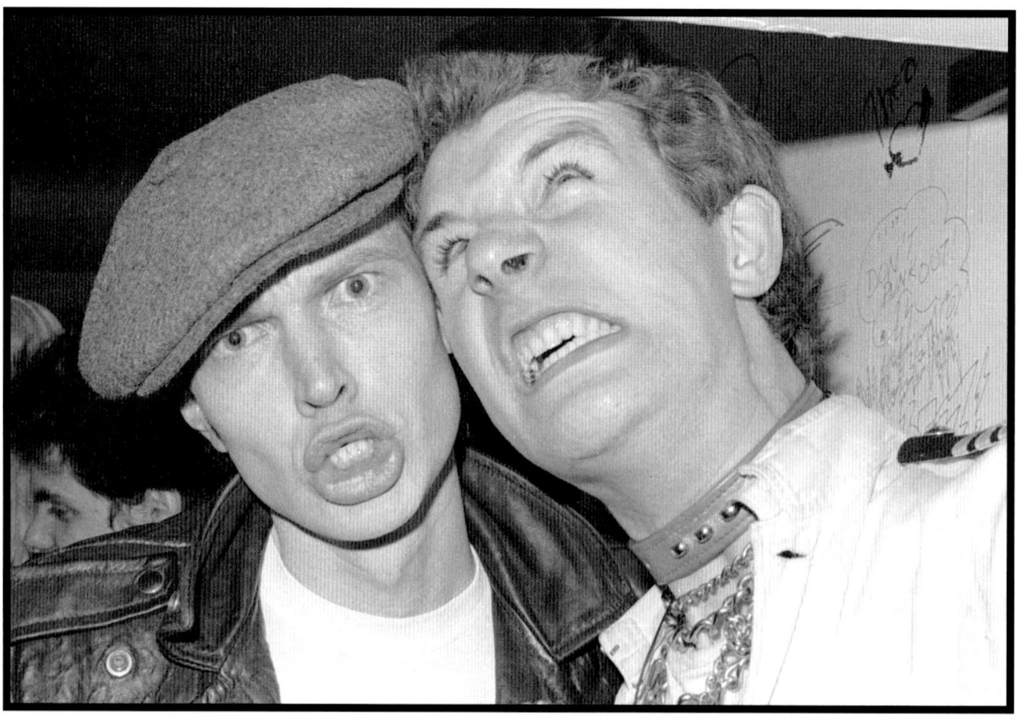

Johnny with Captian Sensible, The Damned.

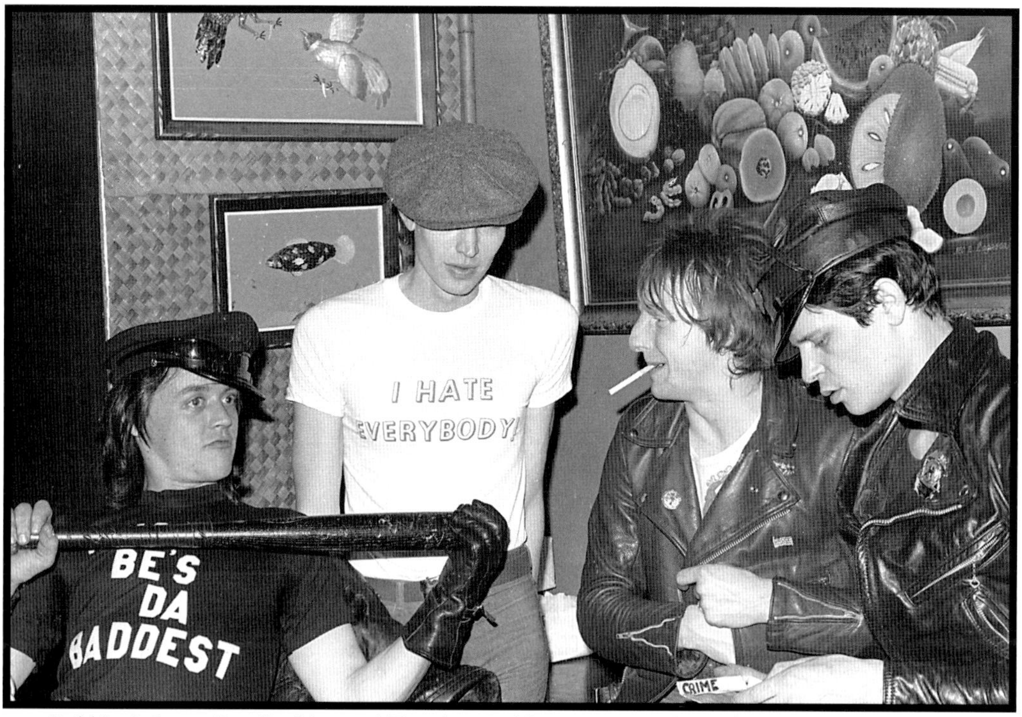

Rabbit, Johnny, Rat Scabies and Frankie. Rabbit was part of Brittley's group when they showed up for the Blondie show. Later he was a Crime roadie, Mab door person, MC and general on "the" scene guy.

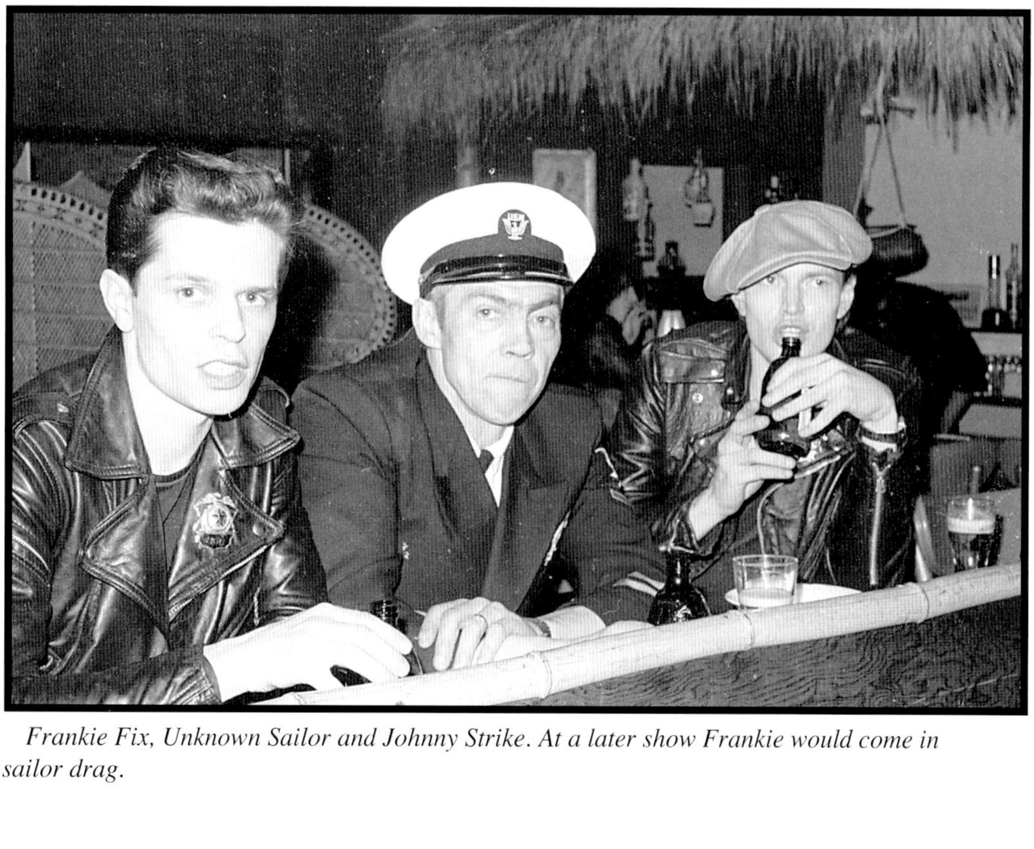

Frankie Fix, Unknown Sailor and Johnny Strike. At a later show Frankie would come in sailor drag.

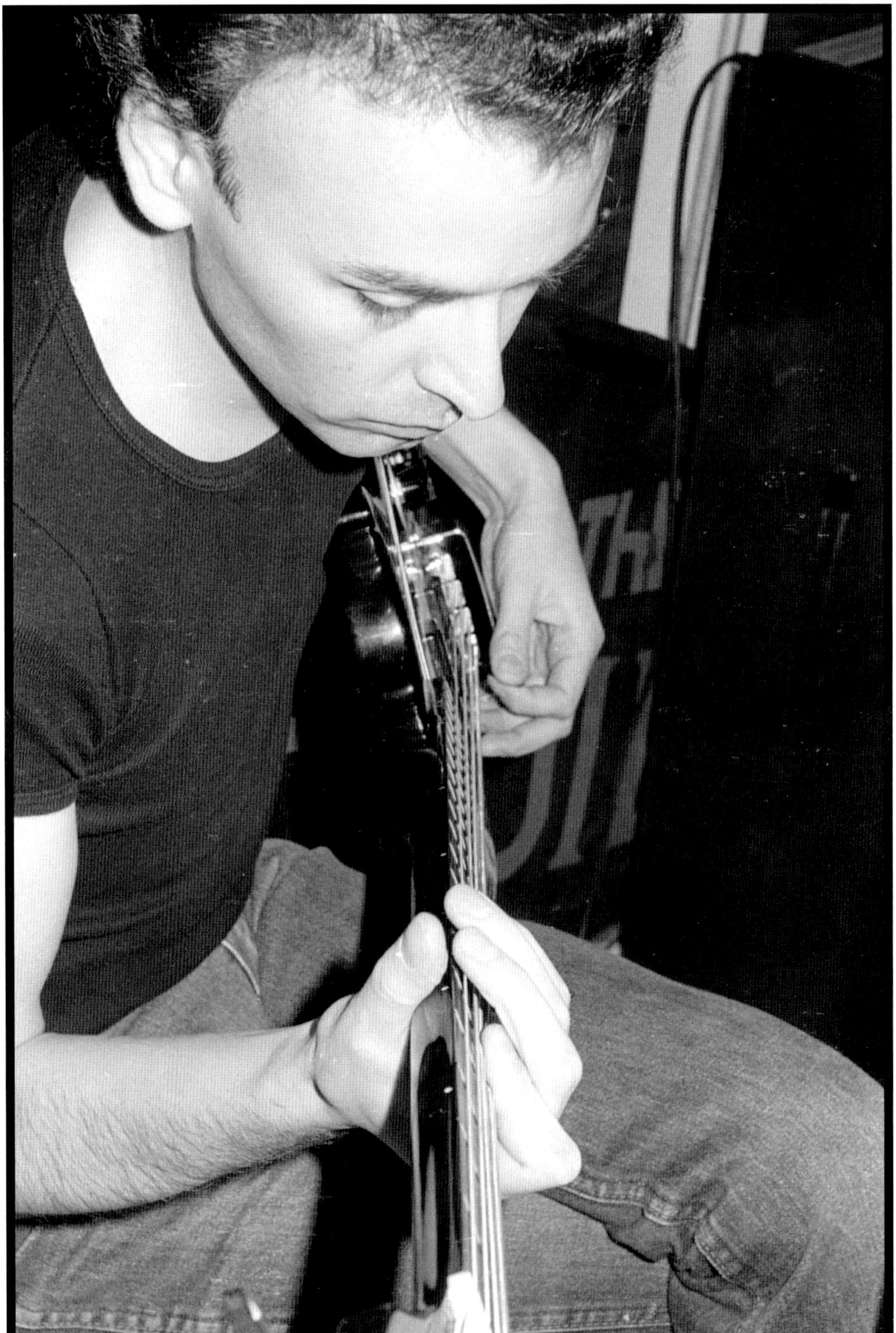

Ron "The Ripper" Greco

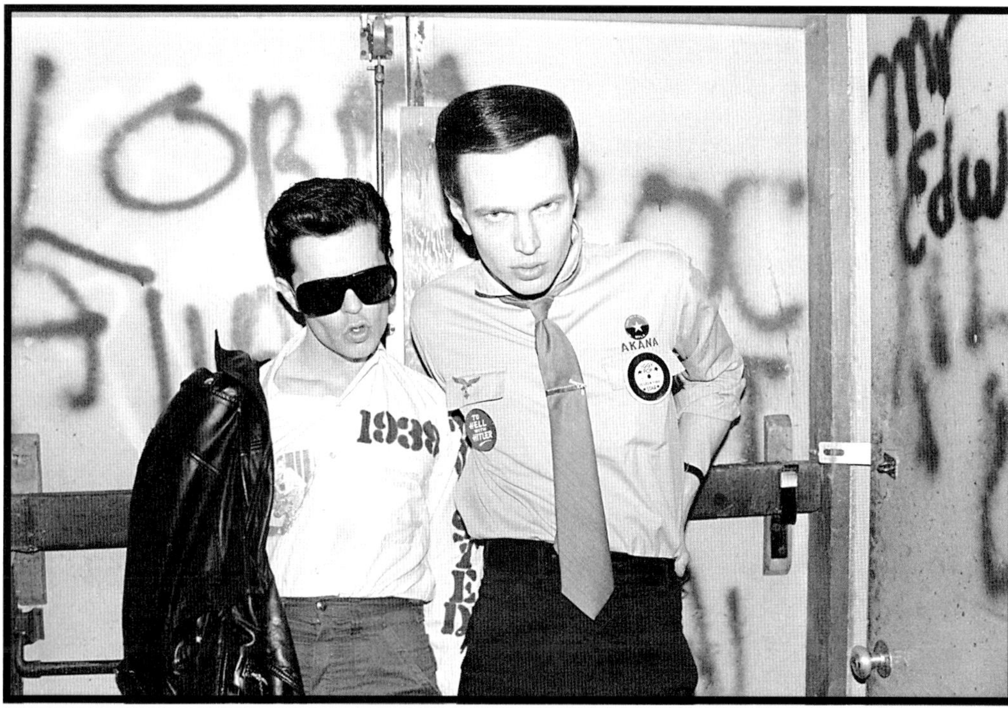

Frankie and Johnny

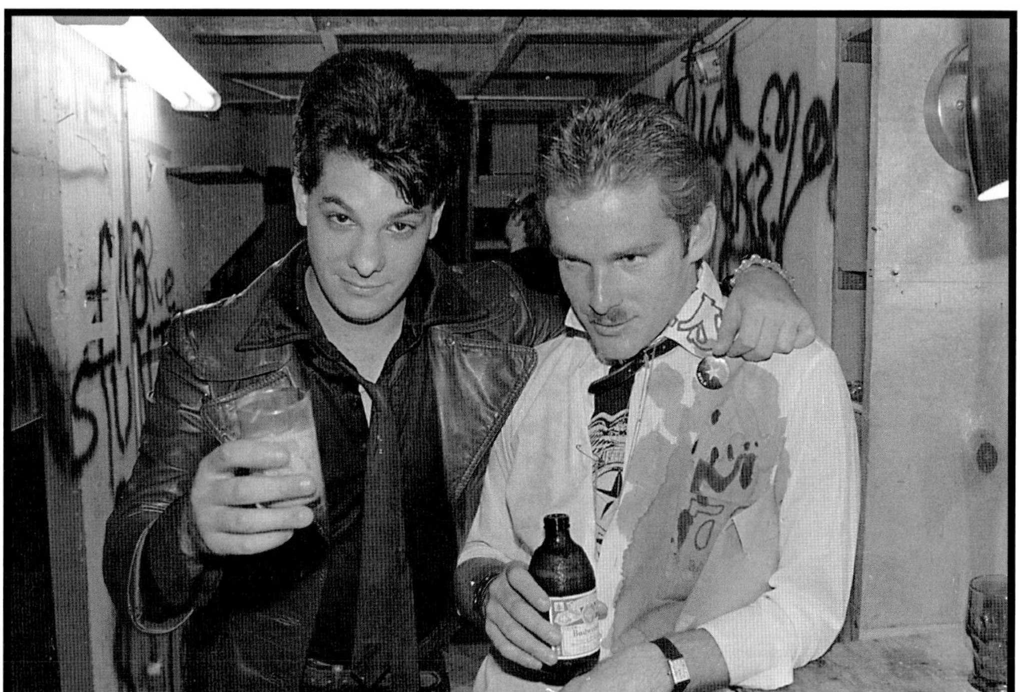

Brittley Black and Tony Steel. Tony was one of the many gays who were part of the mix.

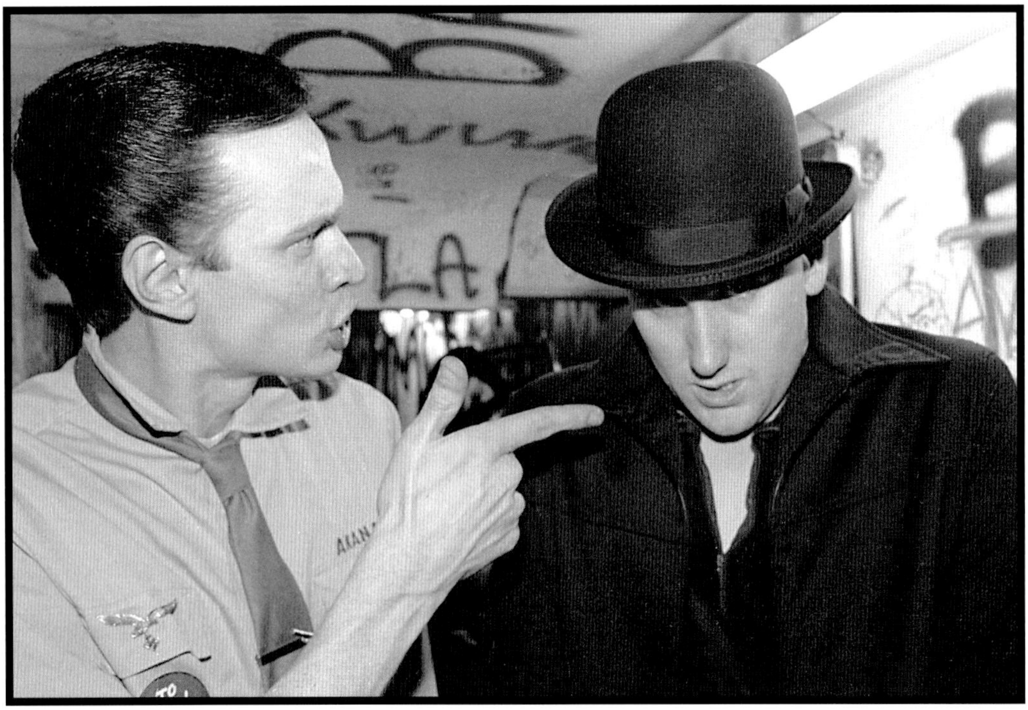

Johnny and Bobby Death

Bobby was one of the early inhabitants of South Park in San Francisco's SOMA district. He and members of his band were big into guns. They had a firing range in their loft and when they wanted people to leave they would start blasting away and that would clear out the crowd. One night Bobby came to the Mab, bleeding, claiming he was a victim of a drive-by shooting. Turns out he shot himself in the leg.

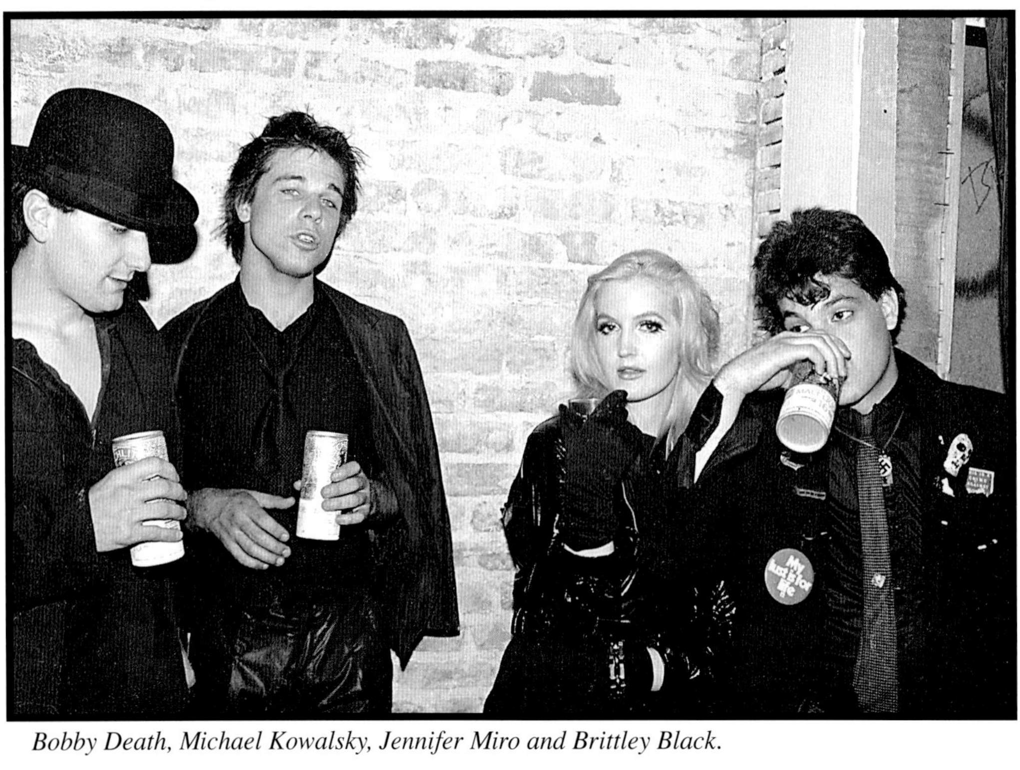

Bobby Death, Michael Kowalsky, Jennifer Miro and Brittley Black.

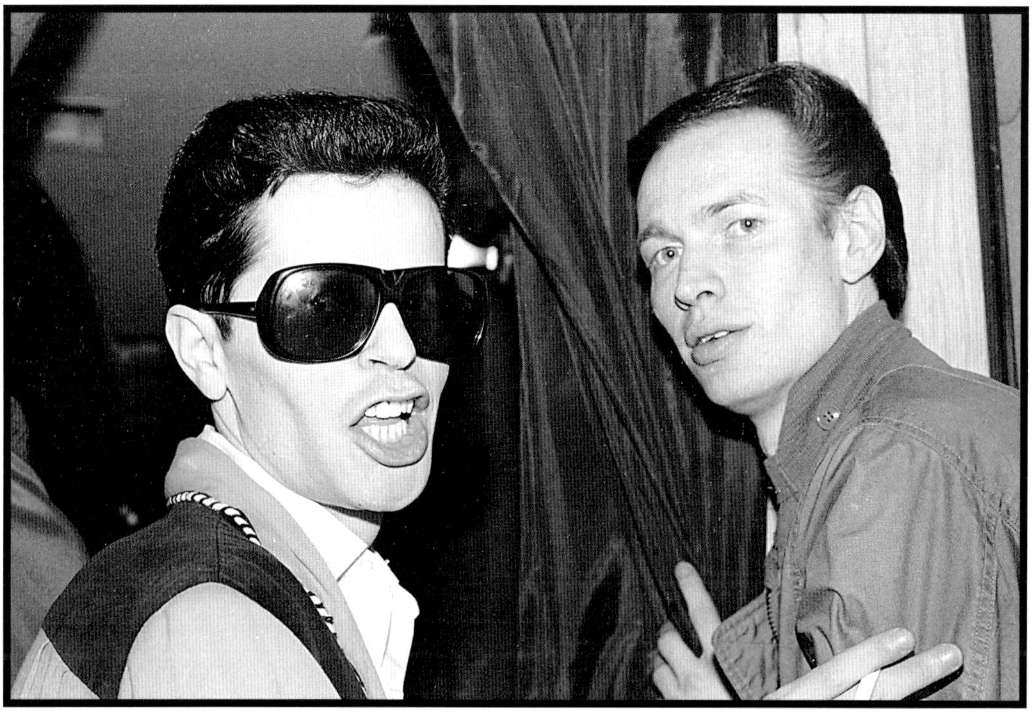

Frankie Fix and Johnny Strike

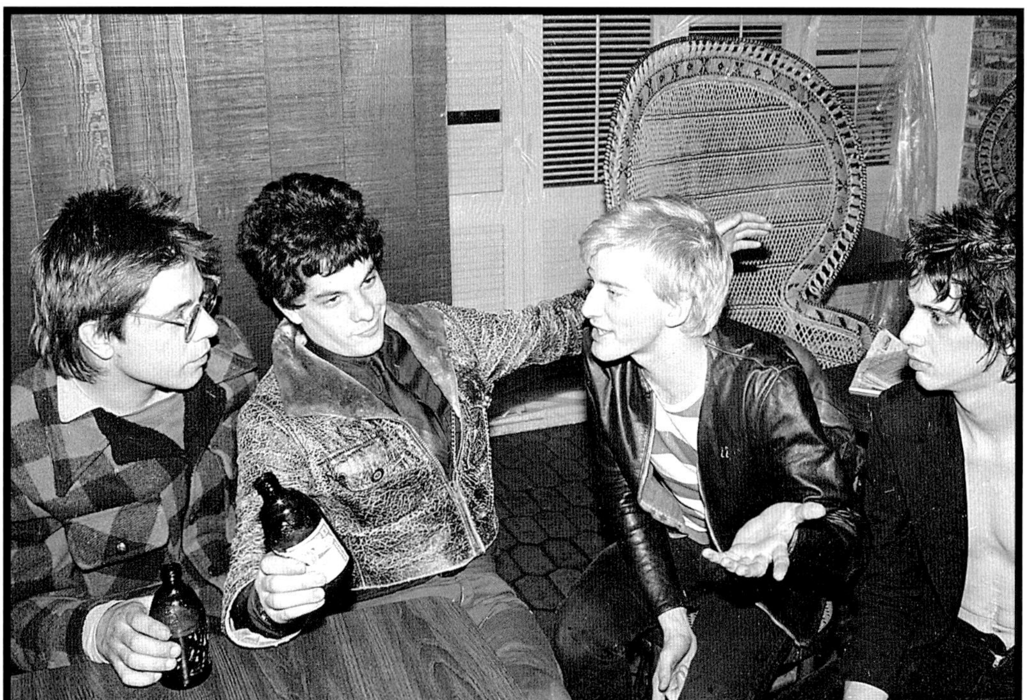

Michael Kowalsky, Brittley Black, Jimmy Wilsey and Ricky Williams.

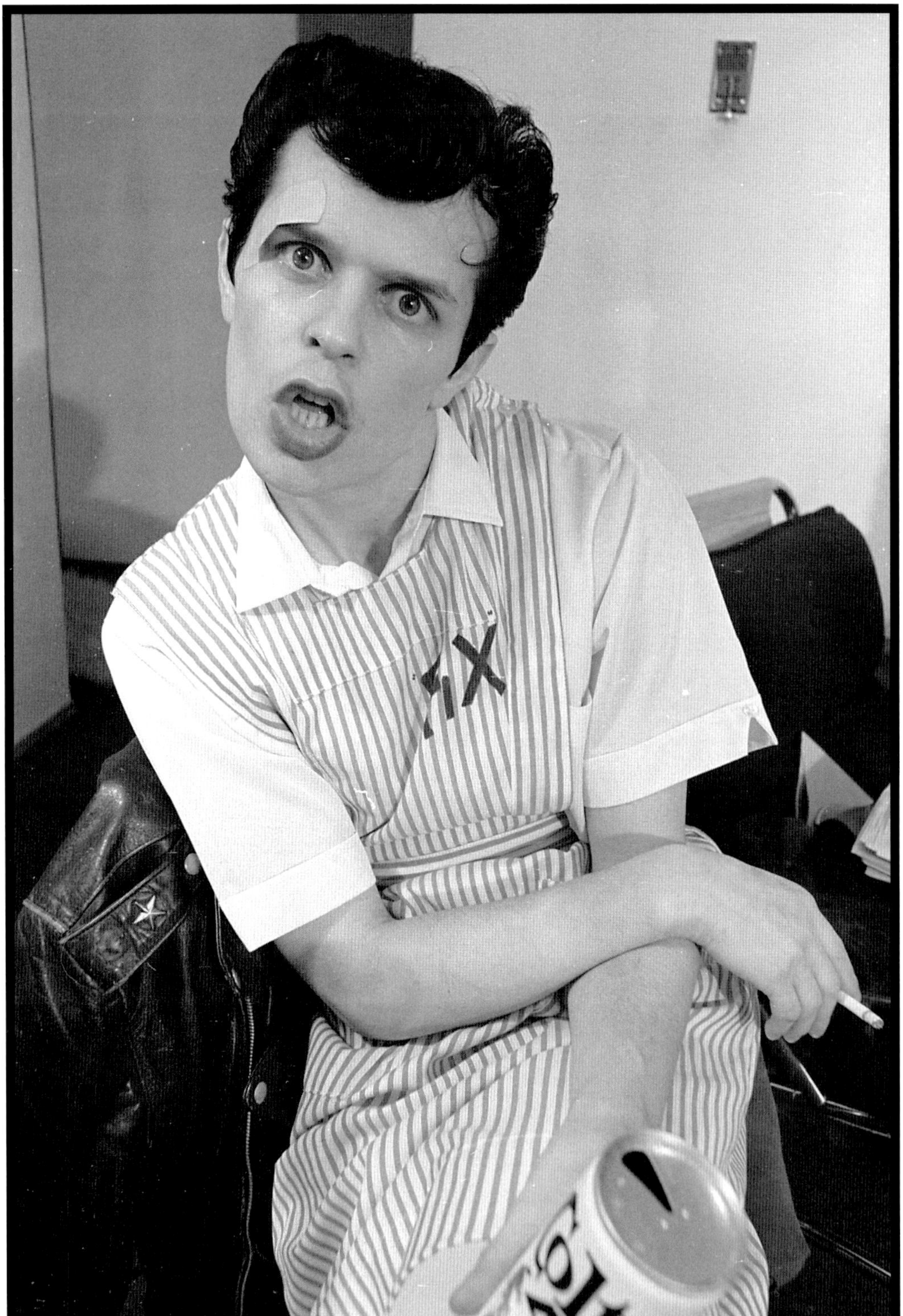

Frankie in nurse's drag.

Ricky Williams would have his own nurse —or a girl who claimed to be one— accompany him to shows to take care of him so he could perform. Johnny wrote "I Knew This Nurse" based on that, and Frankie wore the nurse's uniform for the song's first performance.

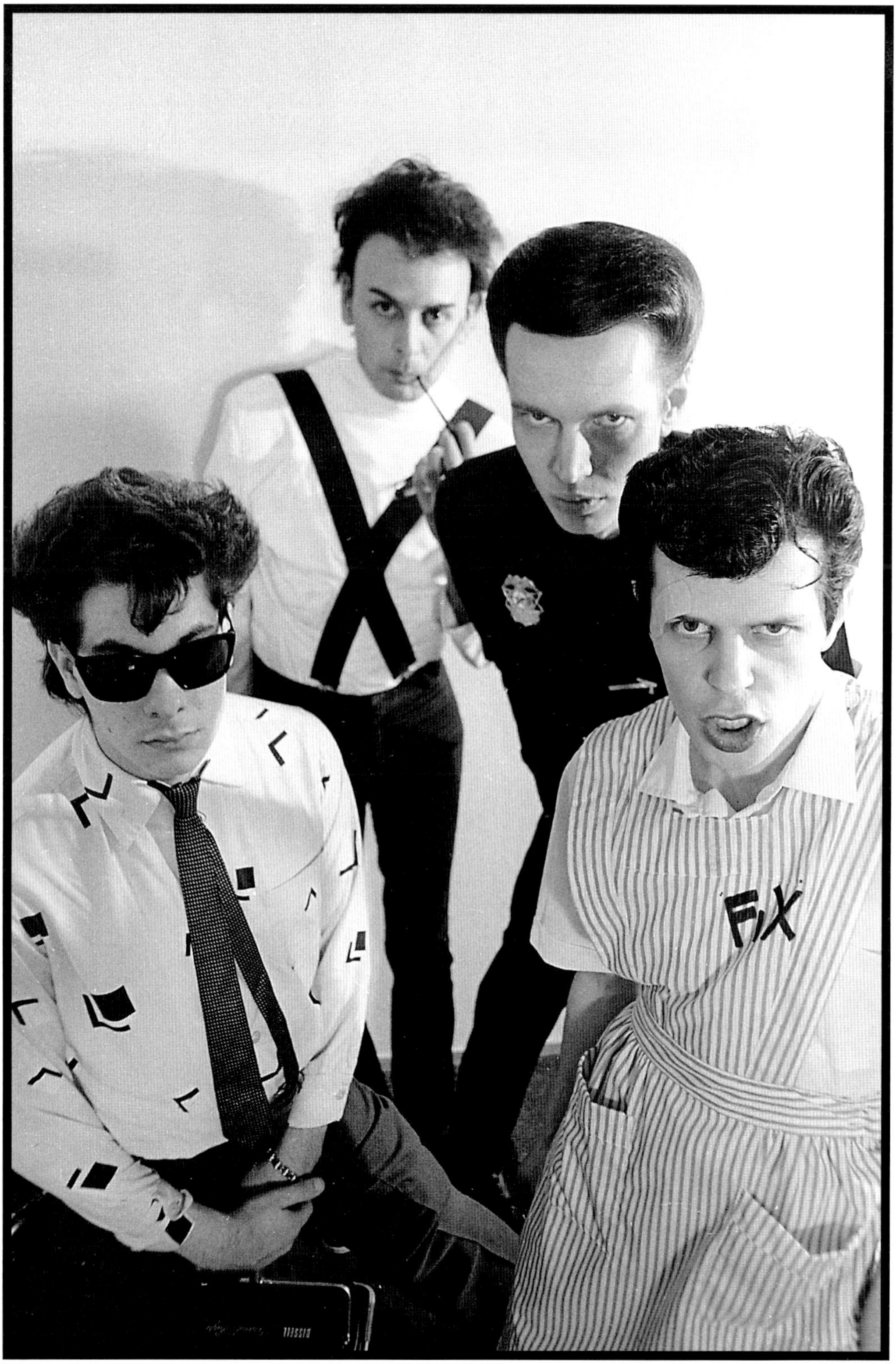

Brittley, Ron, Johnny and Frankie

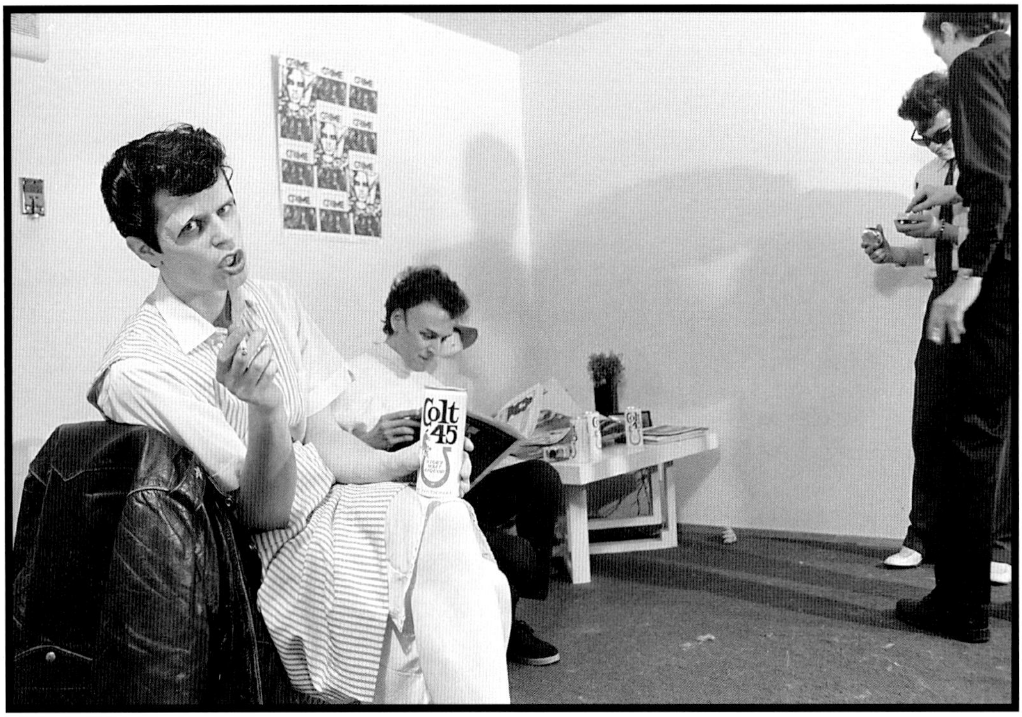

Getting ready for a photo shoot at Frankie's apartment

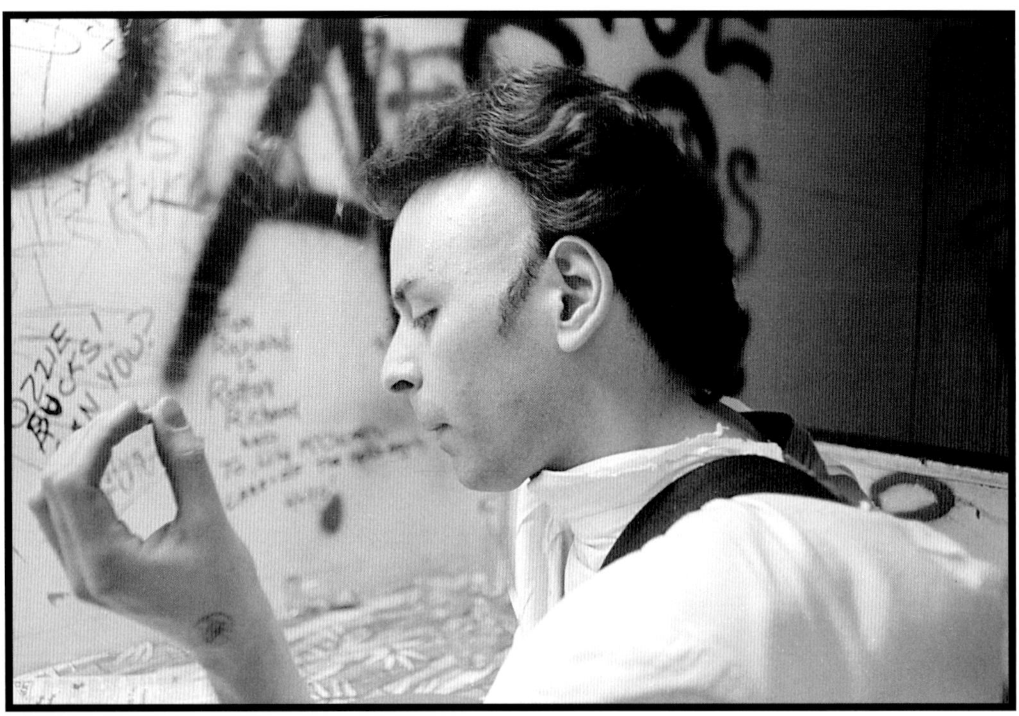

Ron

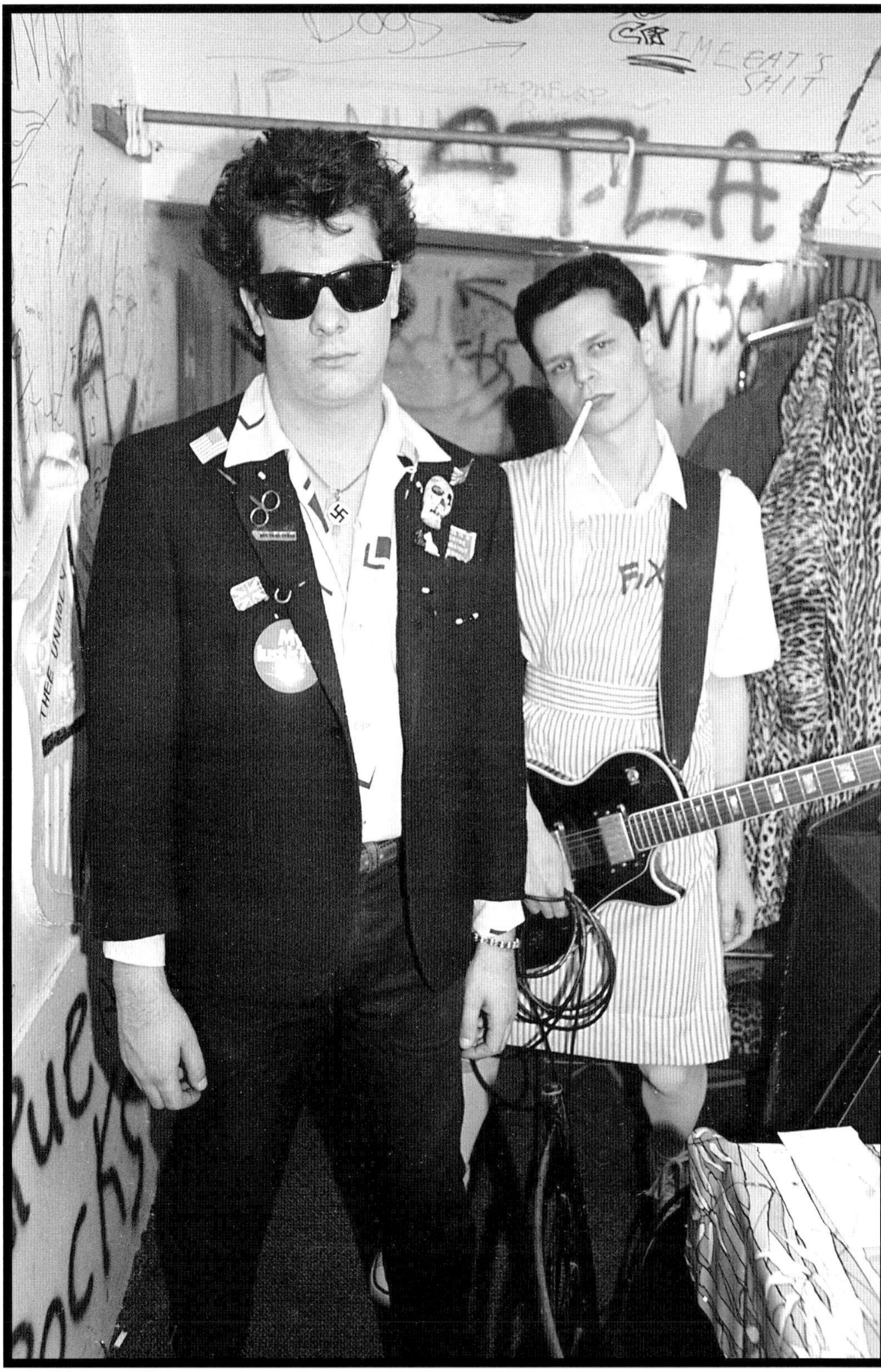

Brittley and Frankie

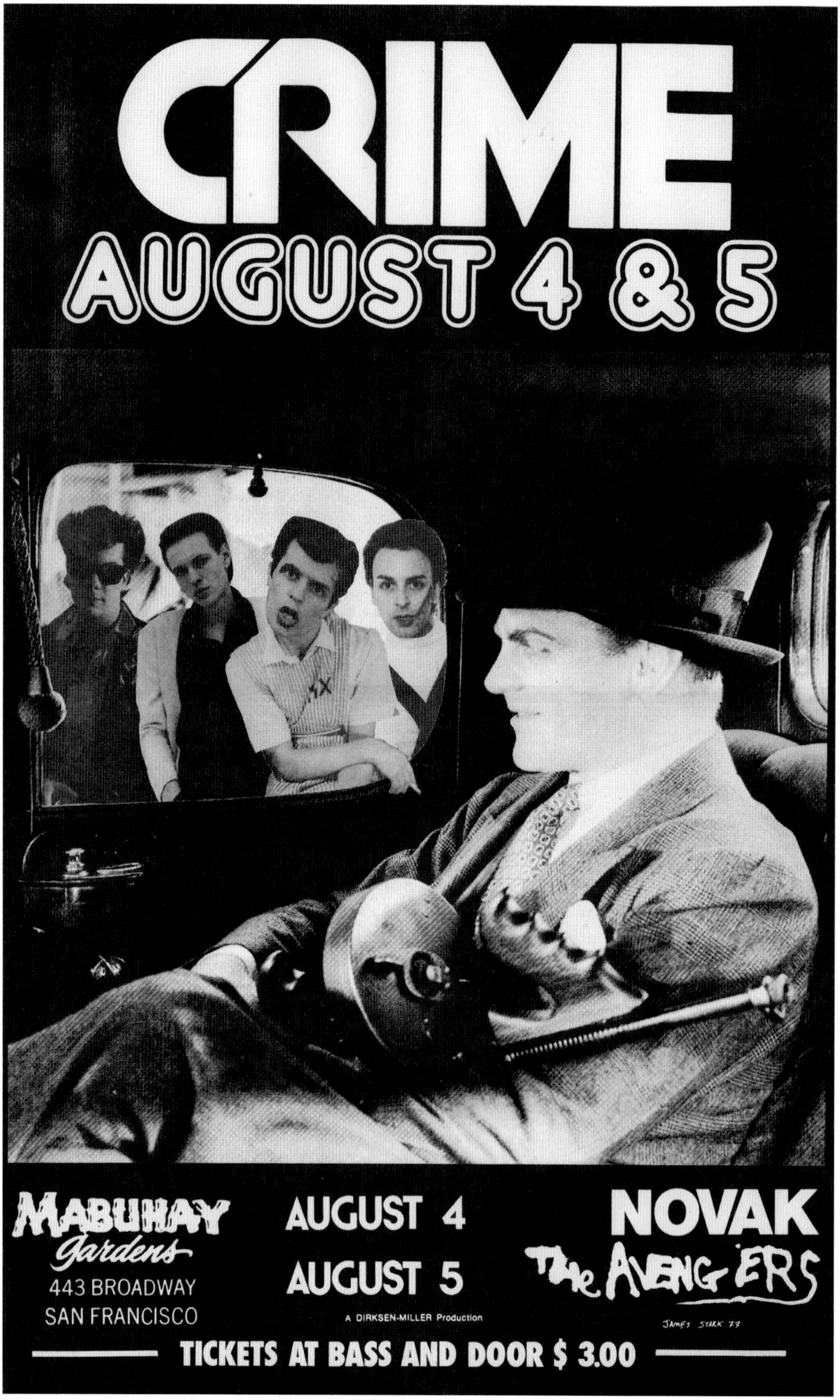
CRIME
AUGUST 4 & 5
MABUHAY
Gardens
443 BROADWAY
SAN FRANCISCO
AUGUST 4
AUGUST 5
A DIRKSEN-MILLER Production
NOVAK
The AVENGERS
JAMES STARK 77
TICKETS AT BASS AND DOOR $ 3.00

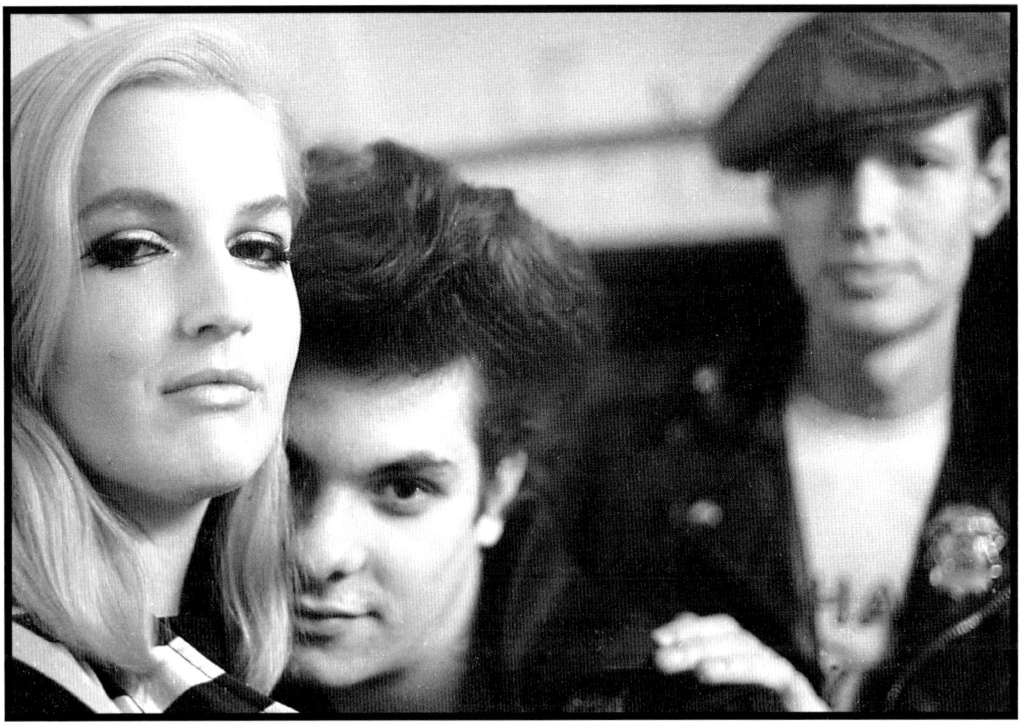

Jennifer Miro, Nuns with Brittley Black and Johnny Strike in background.

Crime and The Nuns were the two hottest bands in San Francisco during the early punk era, and they had an intense rivalry. A couple of times, band members nearly came to fisticuffs before cooler heads prevailed. Jennifer Miro was the Nuns' keyboard player, singer and songwriter; Brittley was Crime's drummer.

When Jennifer and Brittley hooked up, Jennifer would hang out with Crime instead of the Nuns. Jennifer felt that love affairs were more important than bands and more fun. Brittley would play Frank Sinatra records for her and take her out in his Cadillac for cocktails at the Hyatt Regency Hotel.

Frankie was married to Carla, a nice Italian girl whose family owned a vineyard in Napa. She worked a straight job while Frankie played rock and roll star. In a couple of years she left.

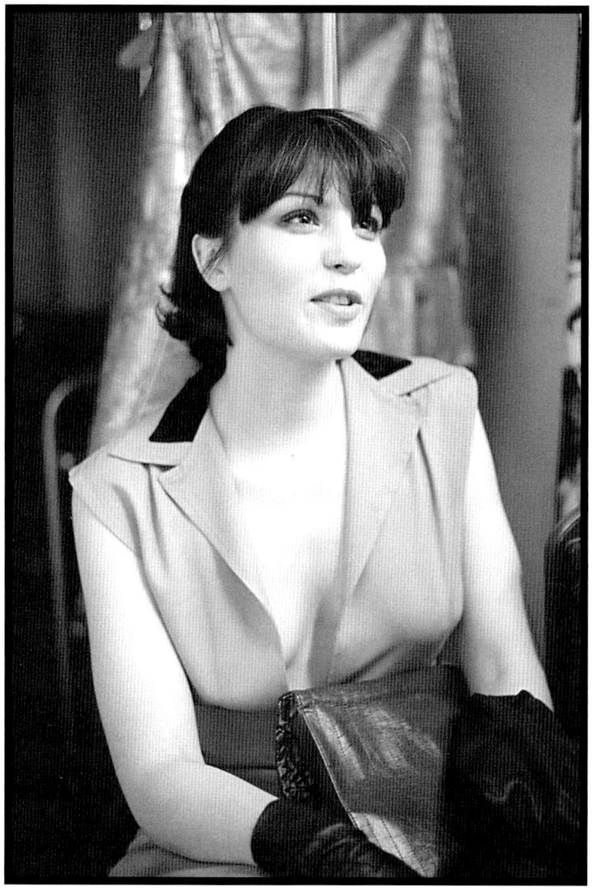

Carla

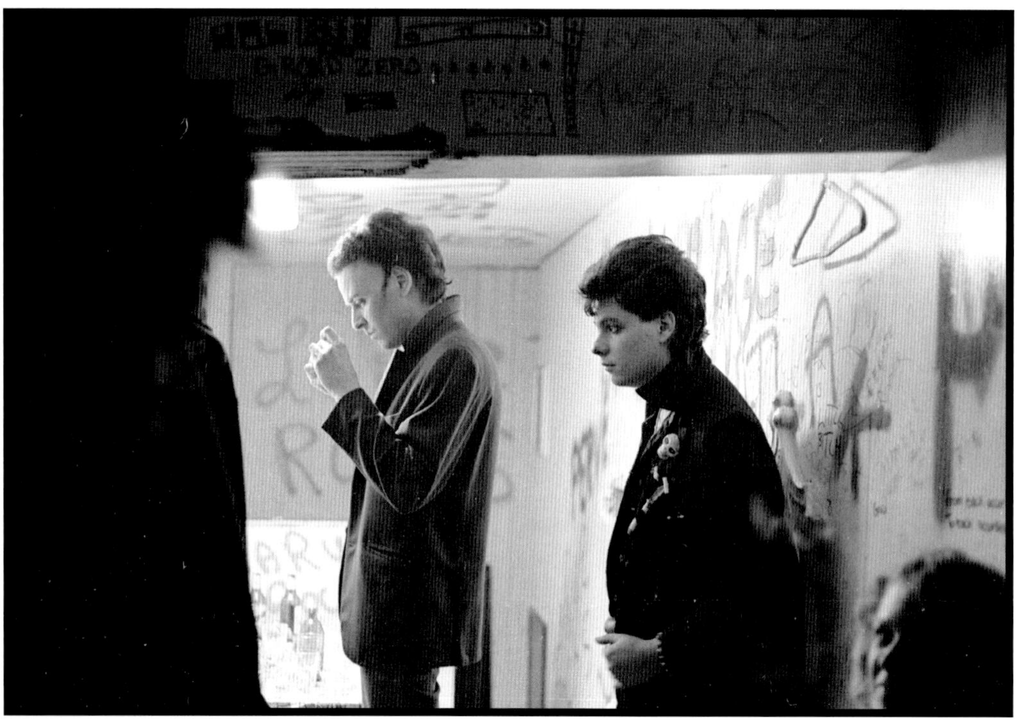

Ron and Brittley, backstage, Mabuhay.

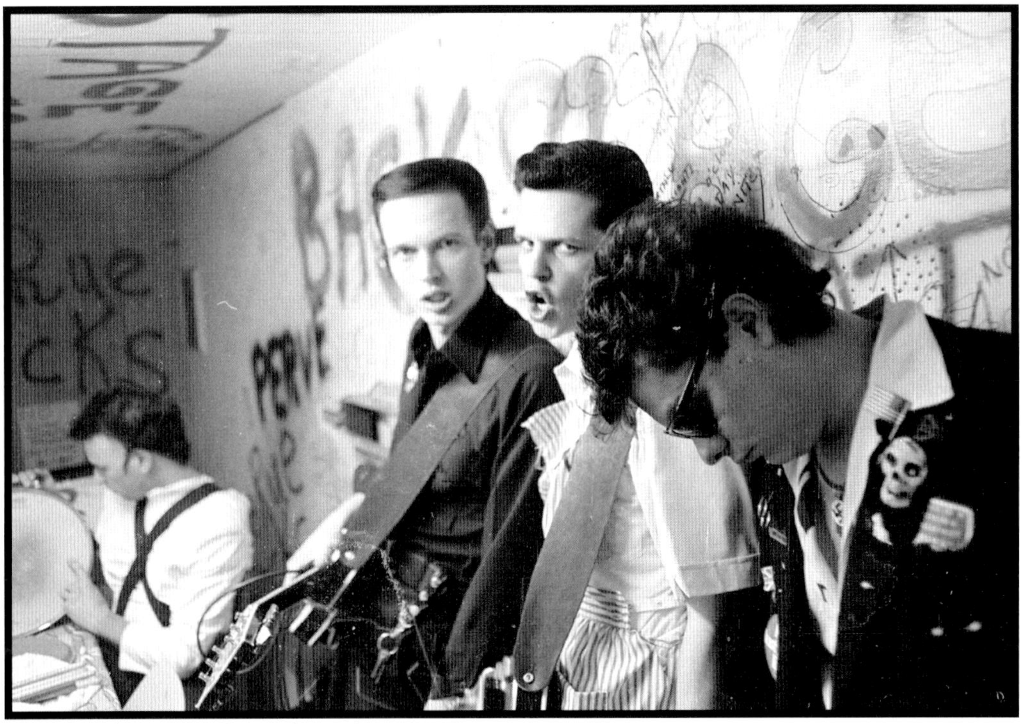

Ron, Johnny, Frankie and Brittley

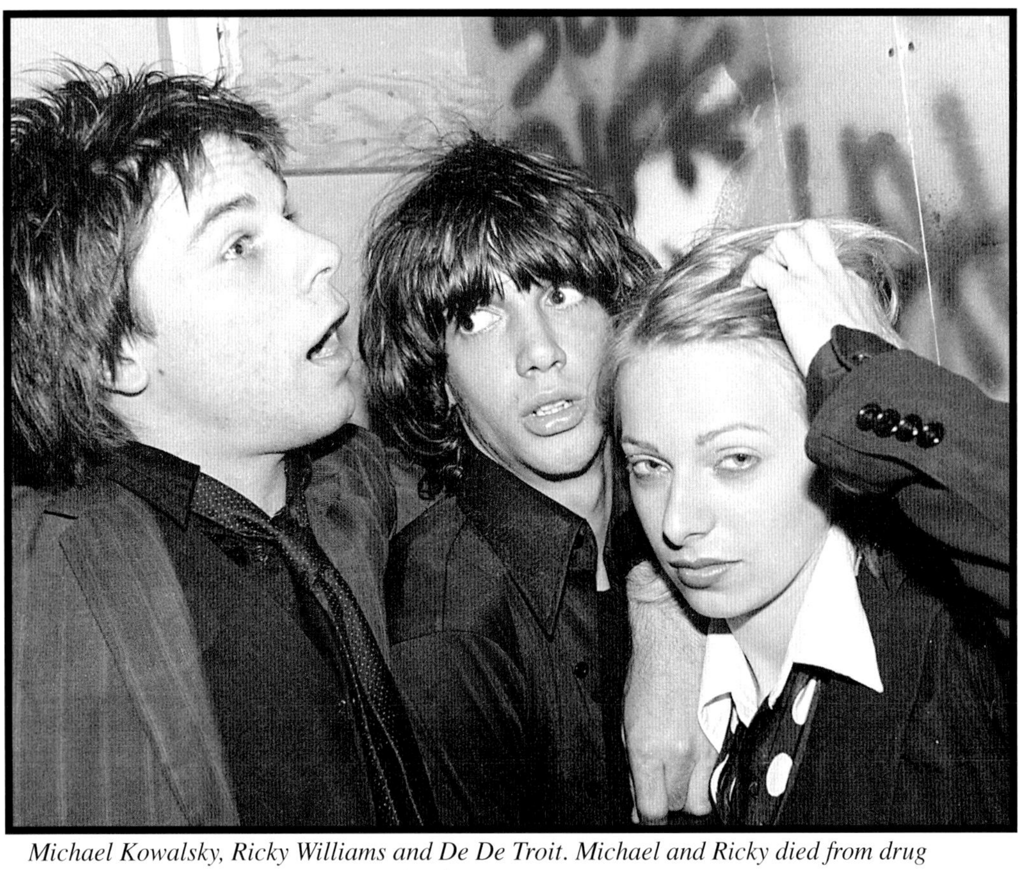

Michael Kowalsky, Ricky Williams and De De Troit. Michael and Ricky died from drug overdoses and De De lives in LA with her band UXA.

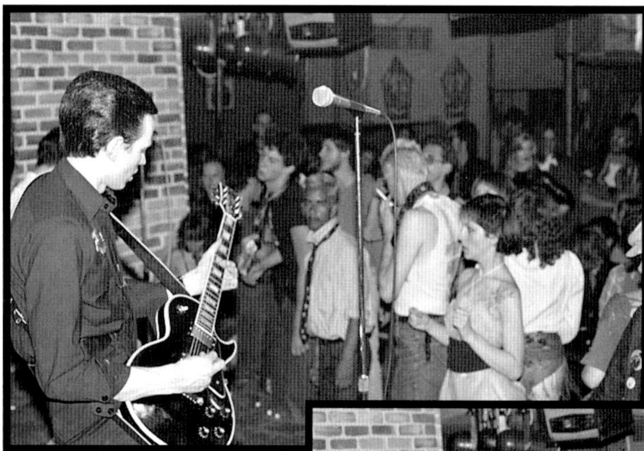

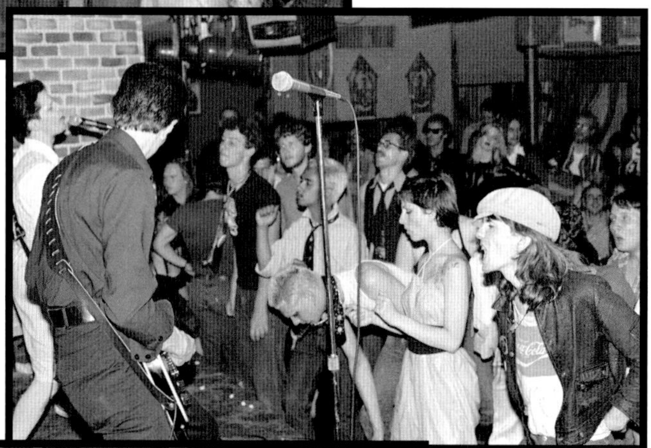

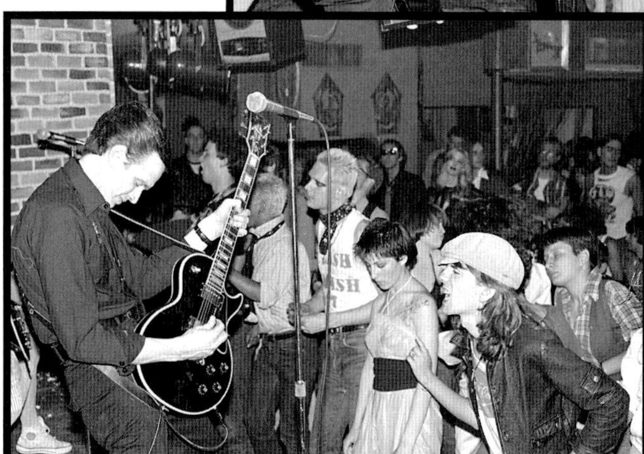

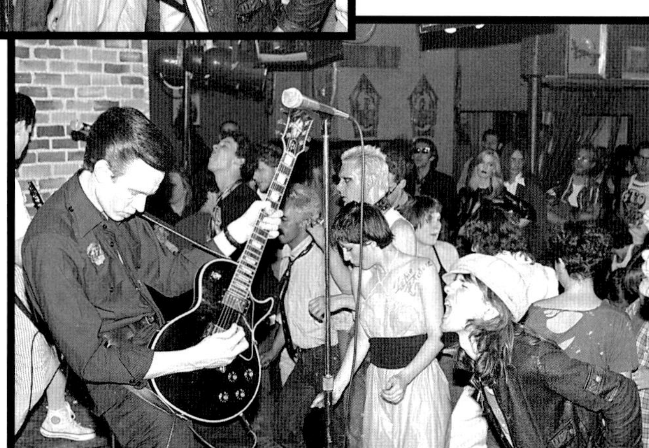

Crime on stage at the Mabuhay.

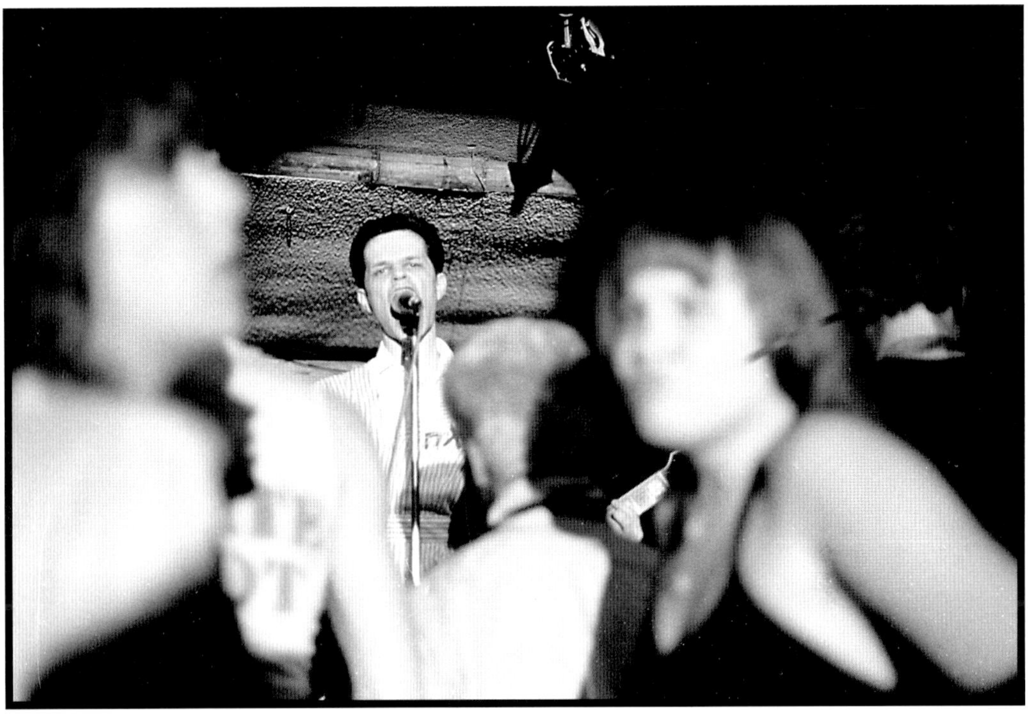

Frankie at the Mab.

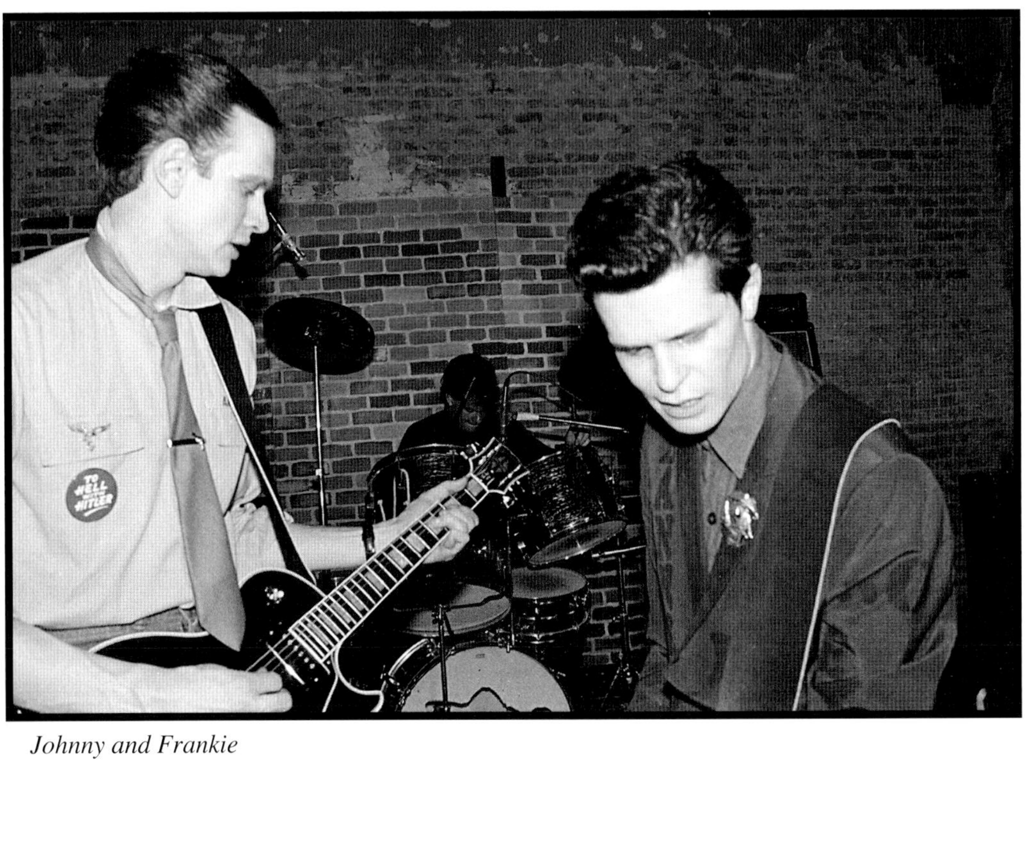

Johnny and Frankie

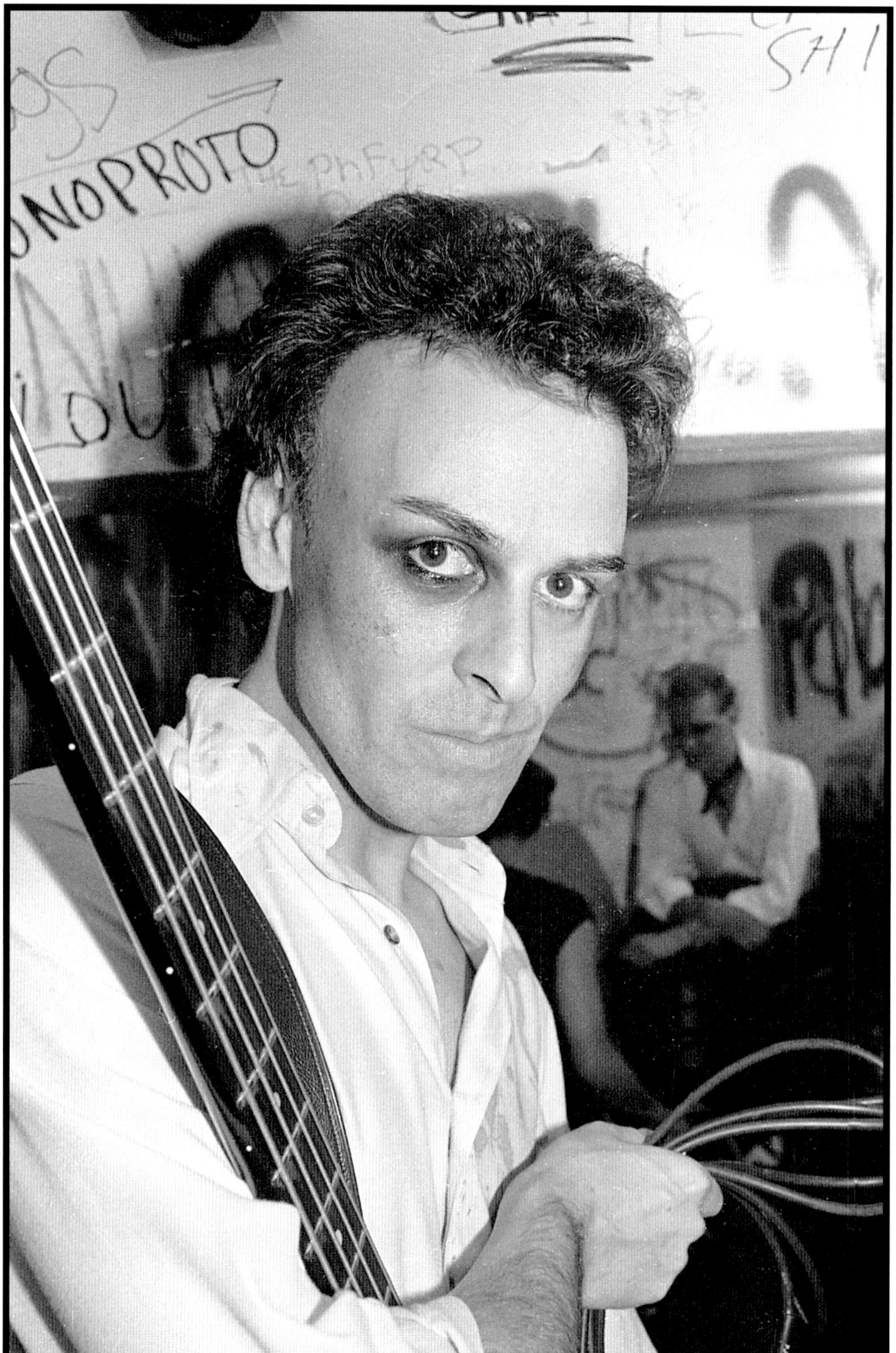

Ron

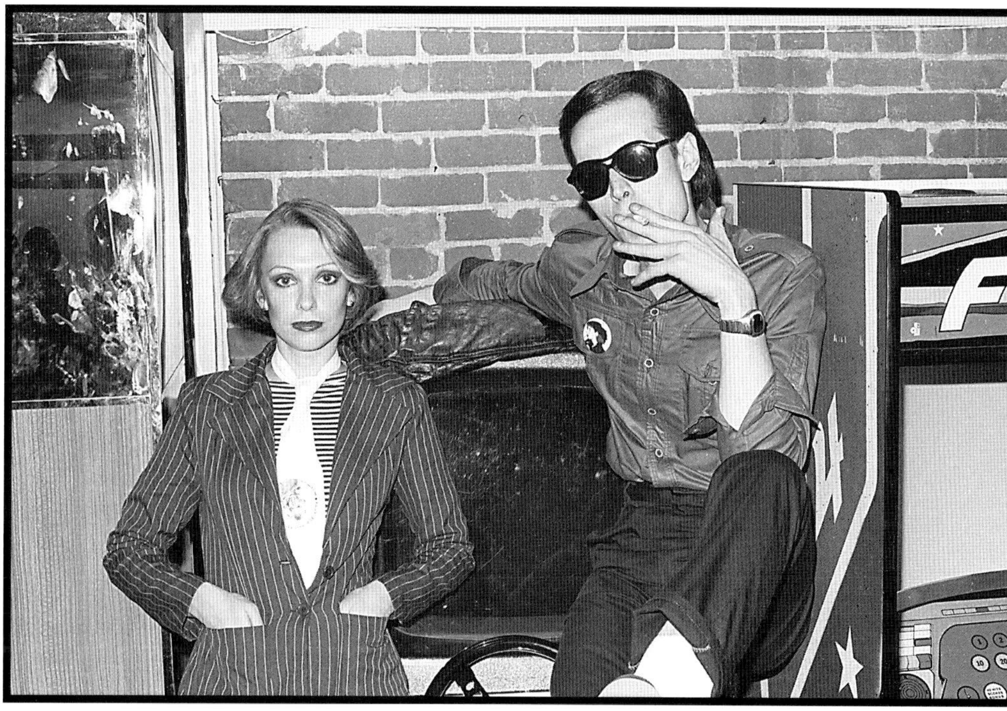

Johnny with his wife Jane.

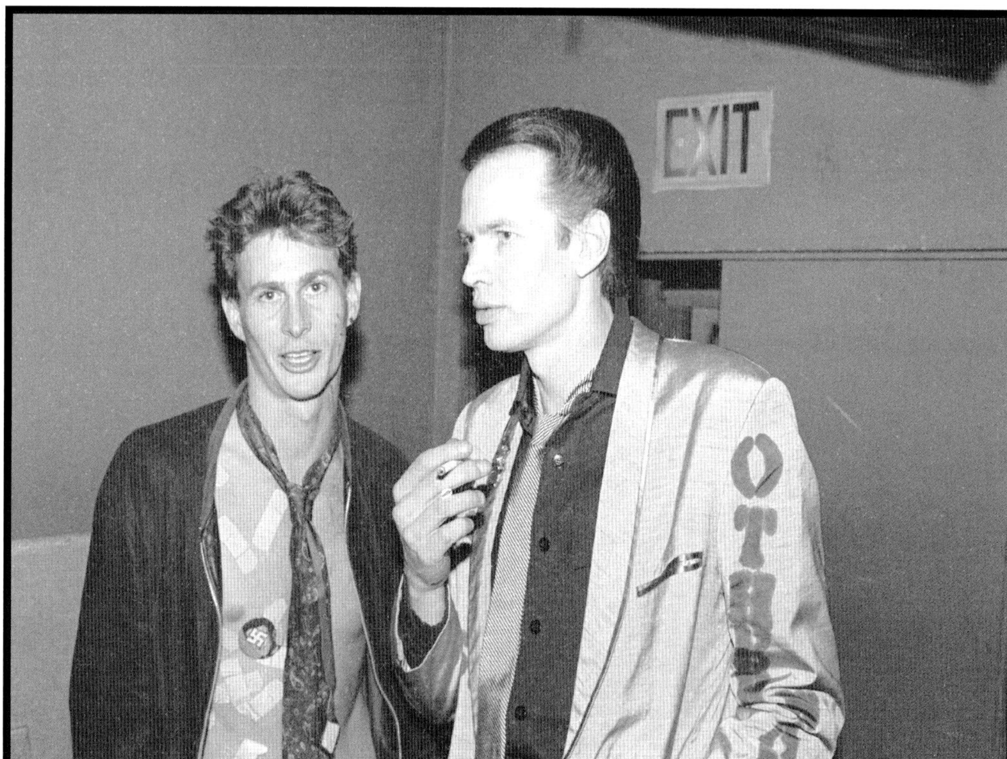

Danny Furious, The Avengers, and Johnny.

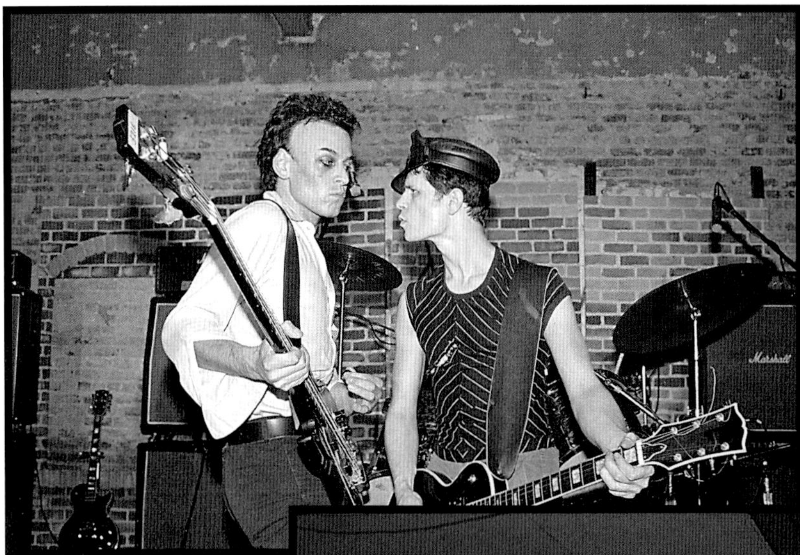

Ron and Frankie

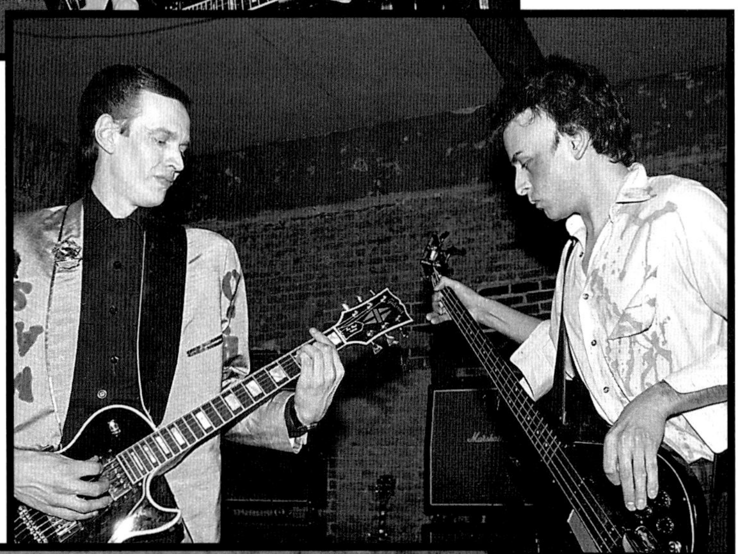

Johnny and Ron

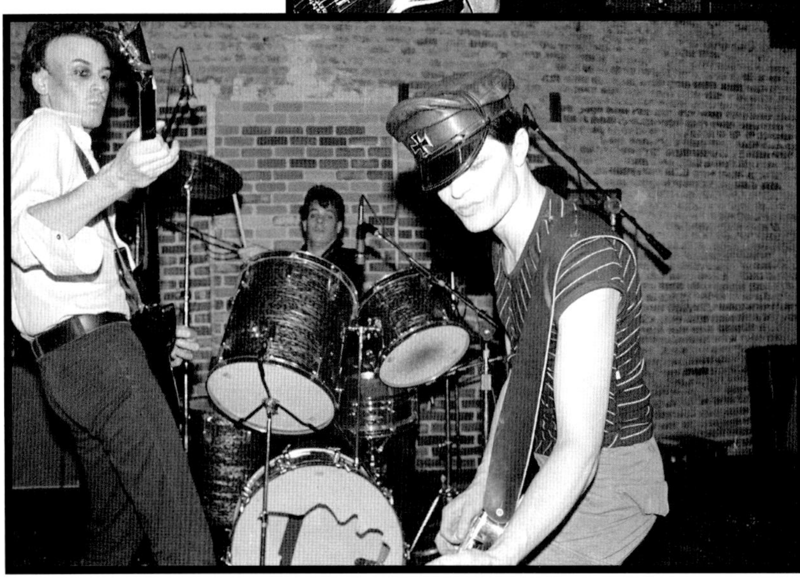

Ron, Brittley and Frankie

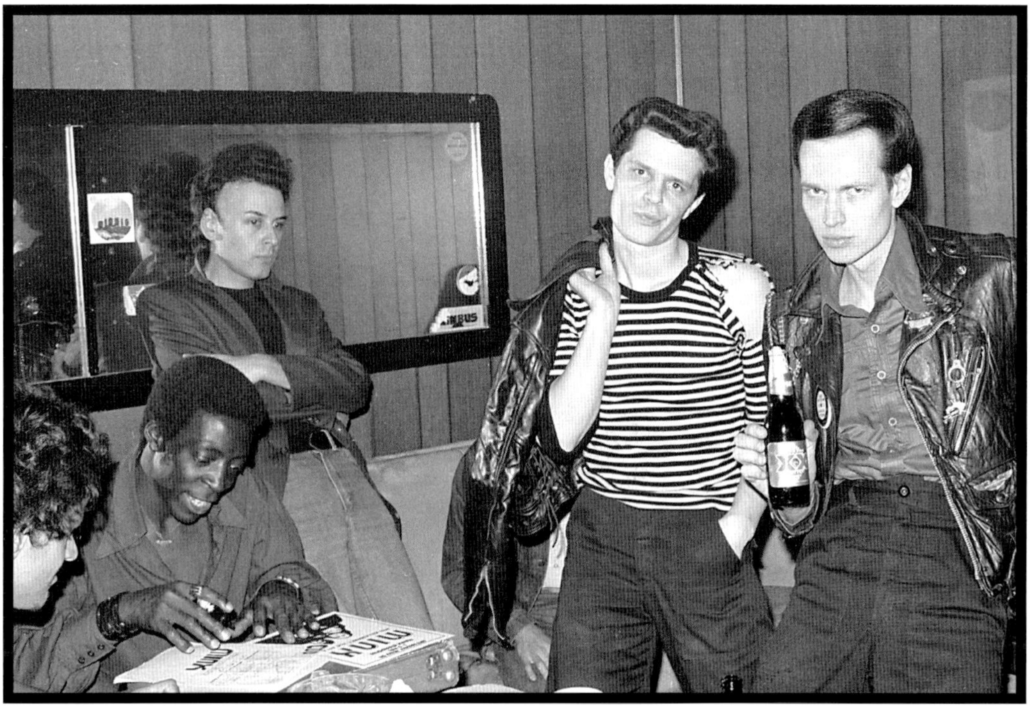

Crime with JB Hutto in North Beach. He was a classic Chicago blues player. Frankie and Johnny were into old blues guys. JB would play in North Beach when touring. He had a long cord hooking up his guitar to an amp and he would walk out into the audience while playing.

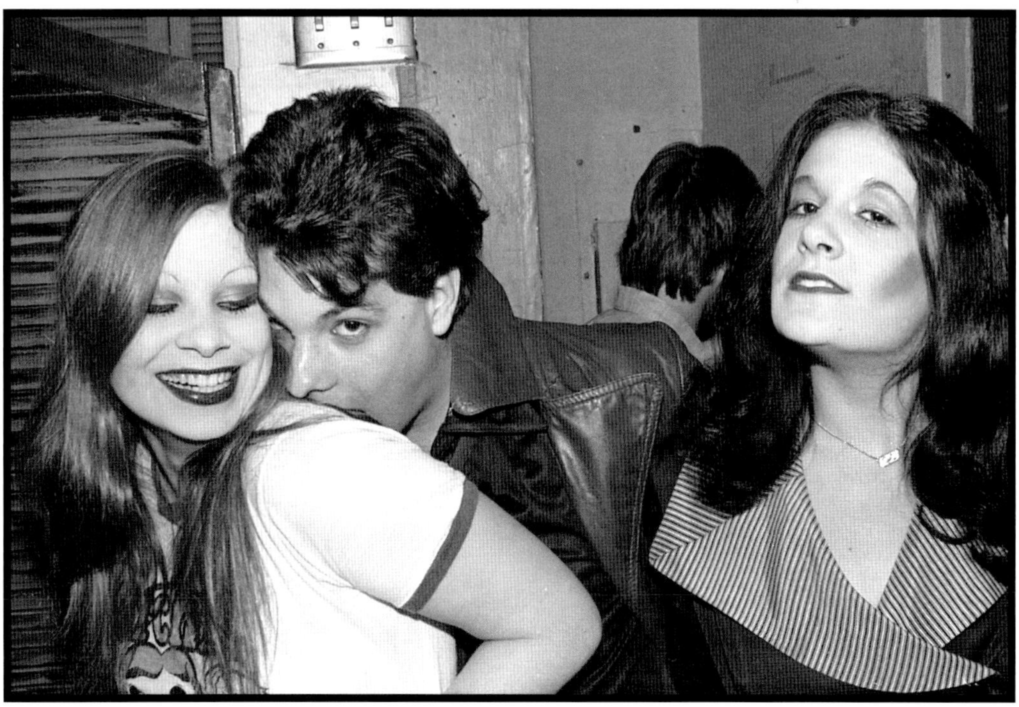

Brittley with Tracy and Jeanette. He always had girls around.

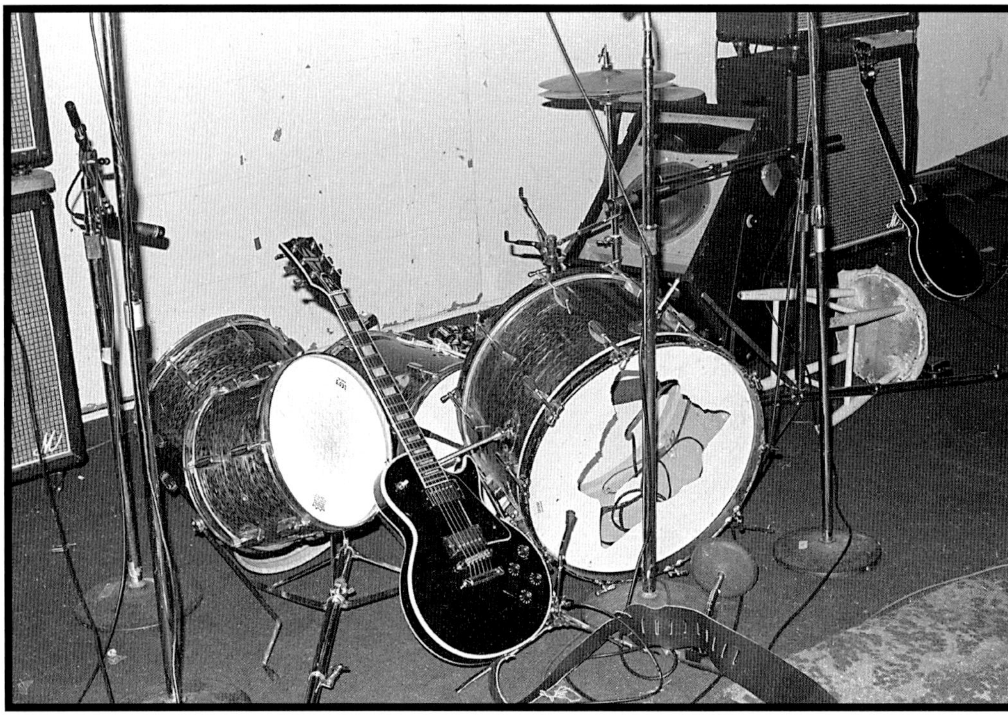

After a typical Crime set.

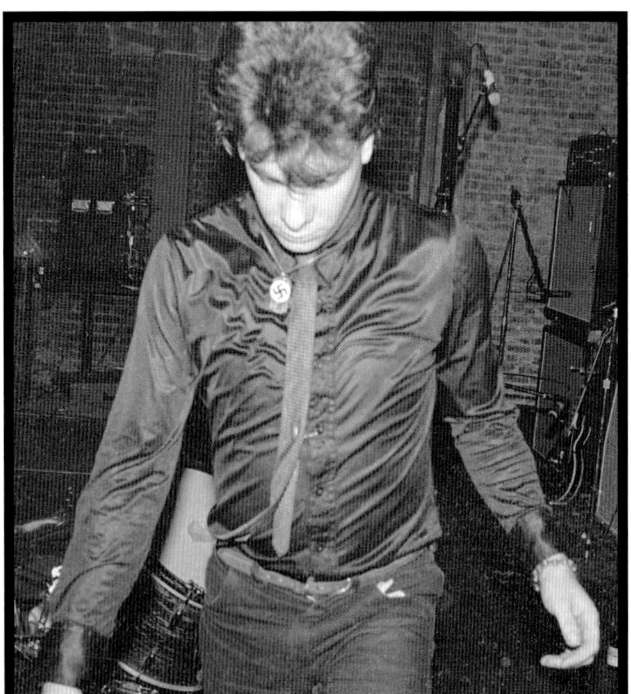

Brittley leaving.

End of the Brittley era.

Brittley left Crime in the latter part of 1977 to join the "Readymades," a band put together by Howie Klein and Sandy Pearlman with ex-Avenger bass player Jonathan Postal as front person. Commerce beat art.

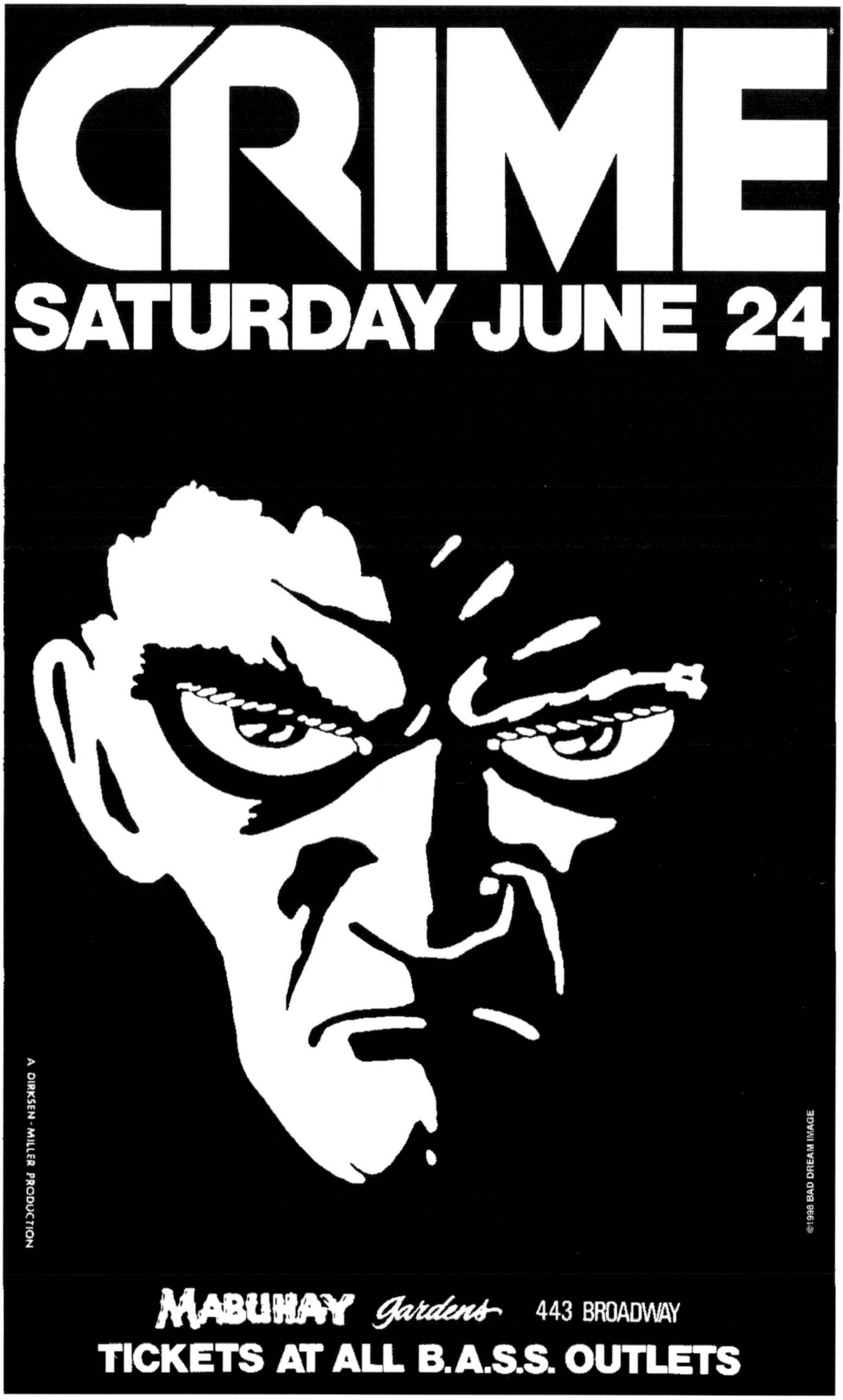
CRIME
SATURDAY JUNE 24
A DIRKSEN-MILLER PRODUCTION
©1998 BAD DREAM IMAGE
MABUHAY Gardens 443 BROADWAY
TICKETS AT ALL B.A.S.S. OUTLETS

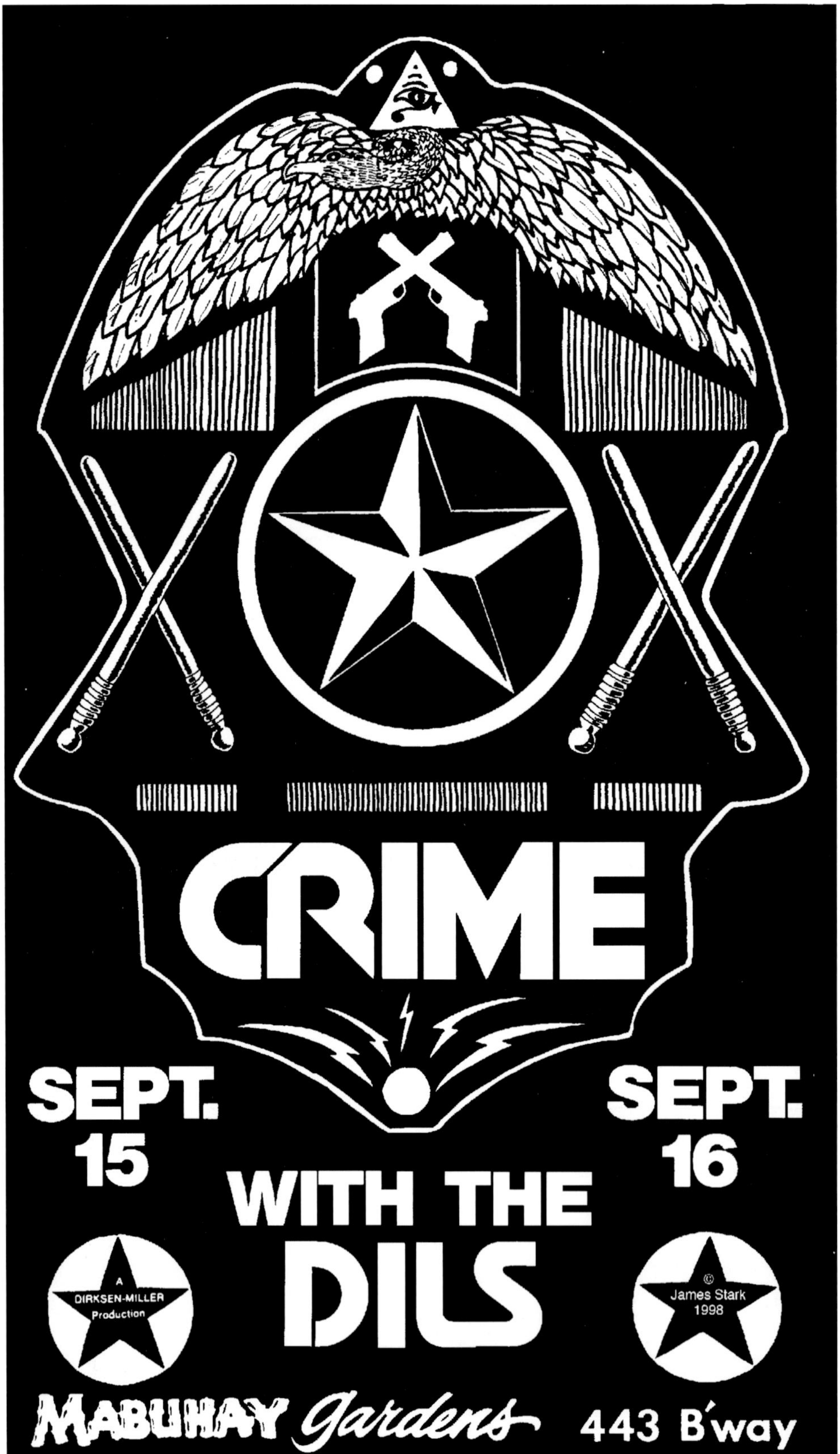
CRIME
SEPT.
15
SEPT.
16
WITH THE
DILS
A
DIRKSEN-MILLER
Production
©
James Stark
1998
MABUHAY Gardens
443 B'way

Hank Rank Comes In

After Brittley Black left Crime to join the Readymades, the word got out that the band was looking for a drummer. They received a very clever package of photos and other artifacts from Henry Rosenthal, who wanted to be the new Crime drummer. He had very little experience as a drummer, and none as a rock and roll drummer. Drummers being hard to come by, they decided to give him a shot at the position. He bought a drum kit, practiced a lot and became Crime's drummer.

At the same time that Hank joined the band, Crime started wearing full-blown police uniforms, which got them a lot of publicity.

The mood around the band changed when Hank became part of Crime. As he became more involved, he took on a leadership role. I didn't get along all that well with him, as he seemed like a spoiled rich kid, so I moved on to other things. Hank is the only living Crime drummer.

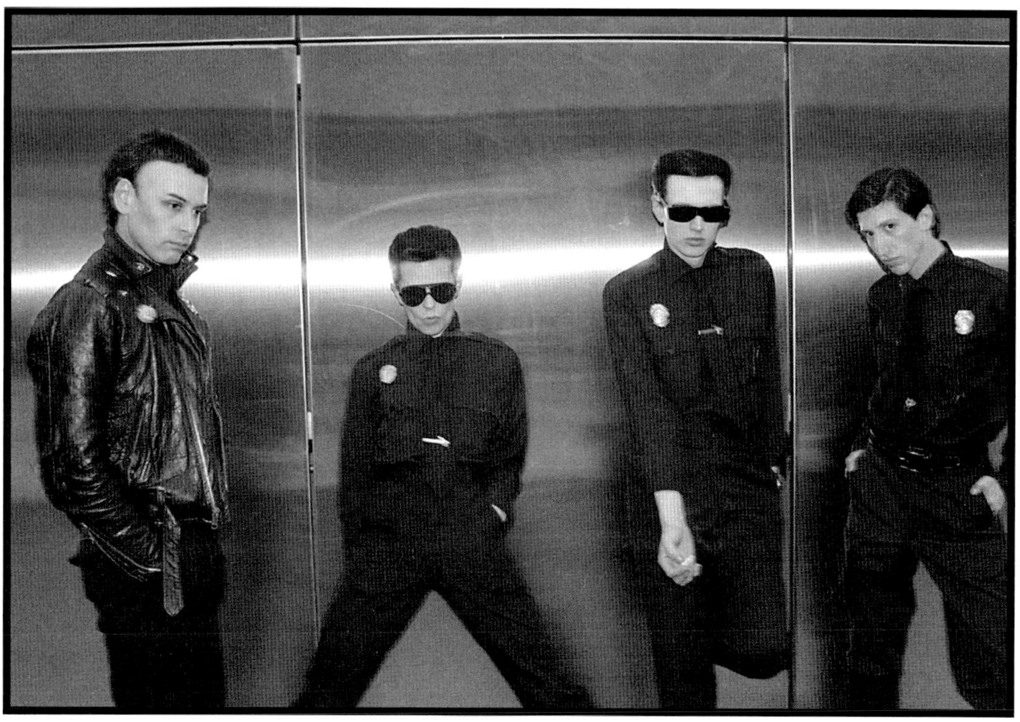

Ron "The Ripper" Greco, Frankie Fix, Johnny Strike and Hank Rank in a BART station. The background was a wall of stainless steel panels. I always liked the way light comes out of Frankie's head.

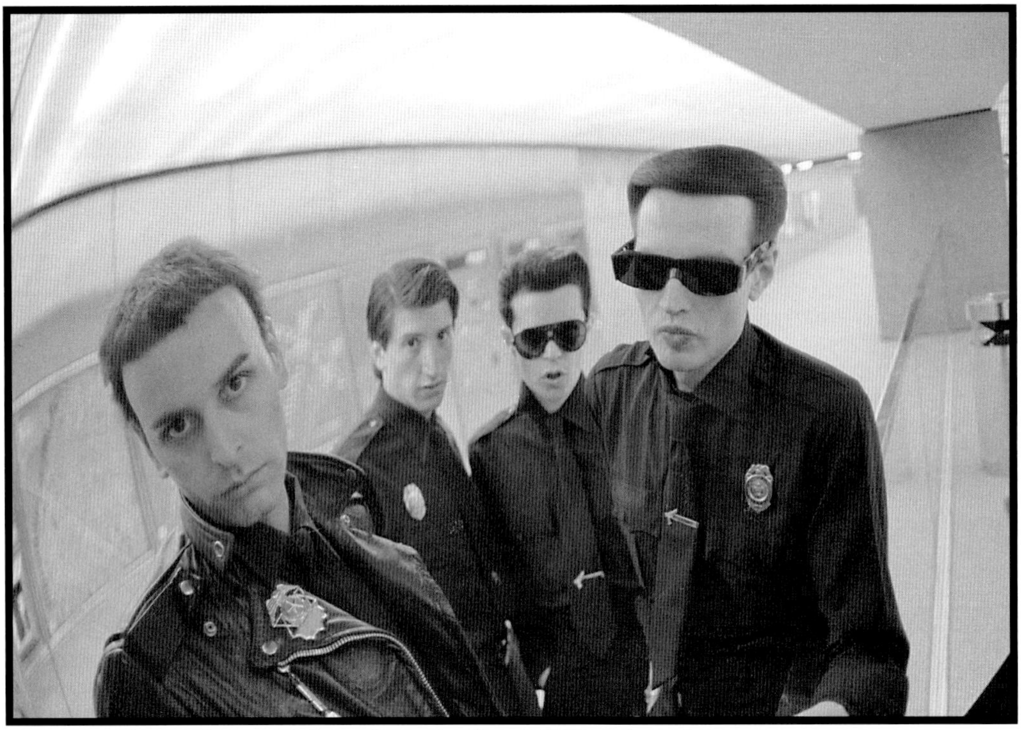

Ron, Hank, Frankie and Johnny. Refection in a BART station mirror.

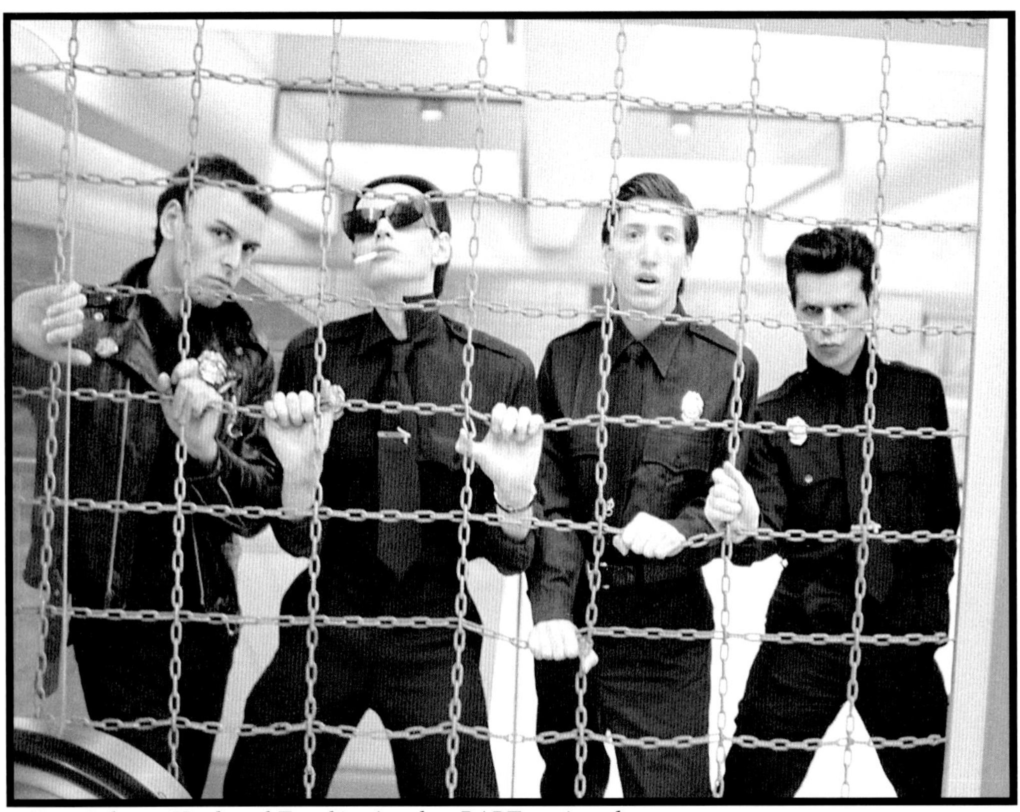

Ron, Johnny, Hank and Frankie. Another BART station shot.

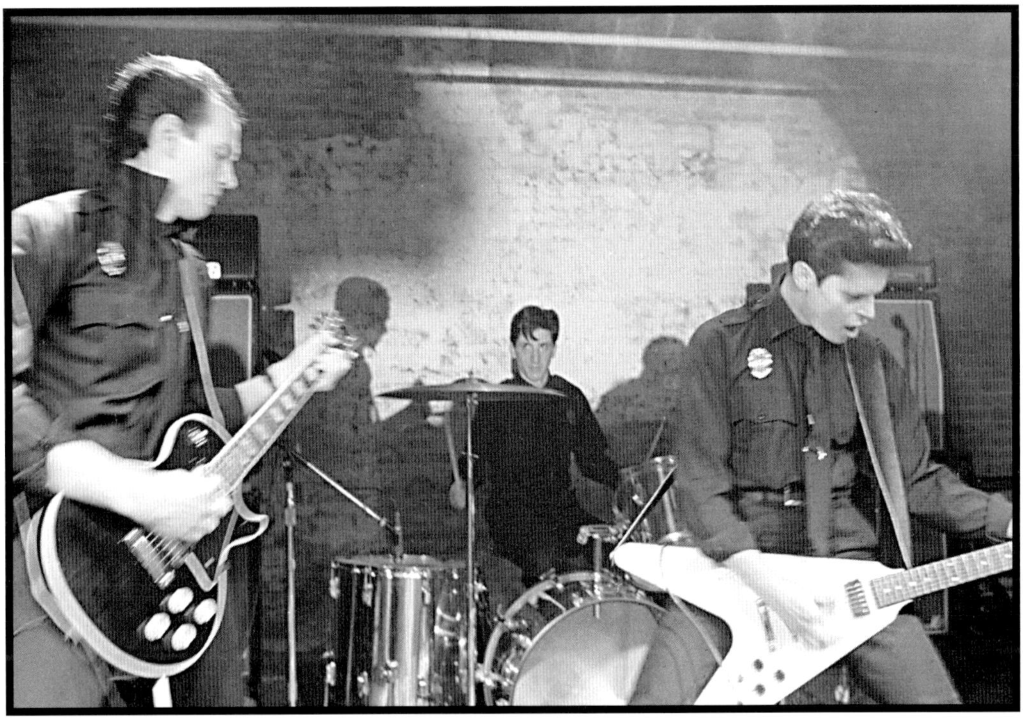

Johhny, Hank and Frankie

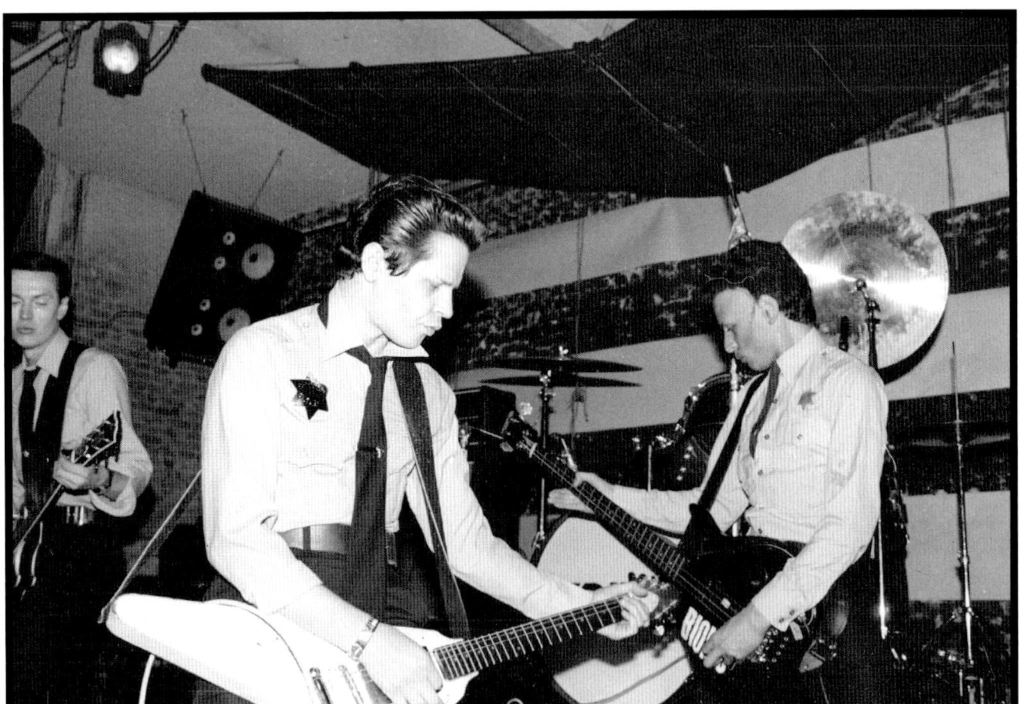

Johnny, Frankie and Ron

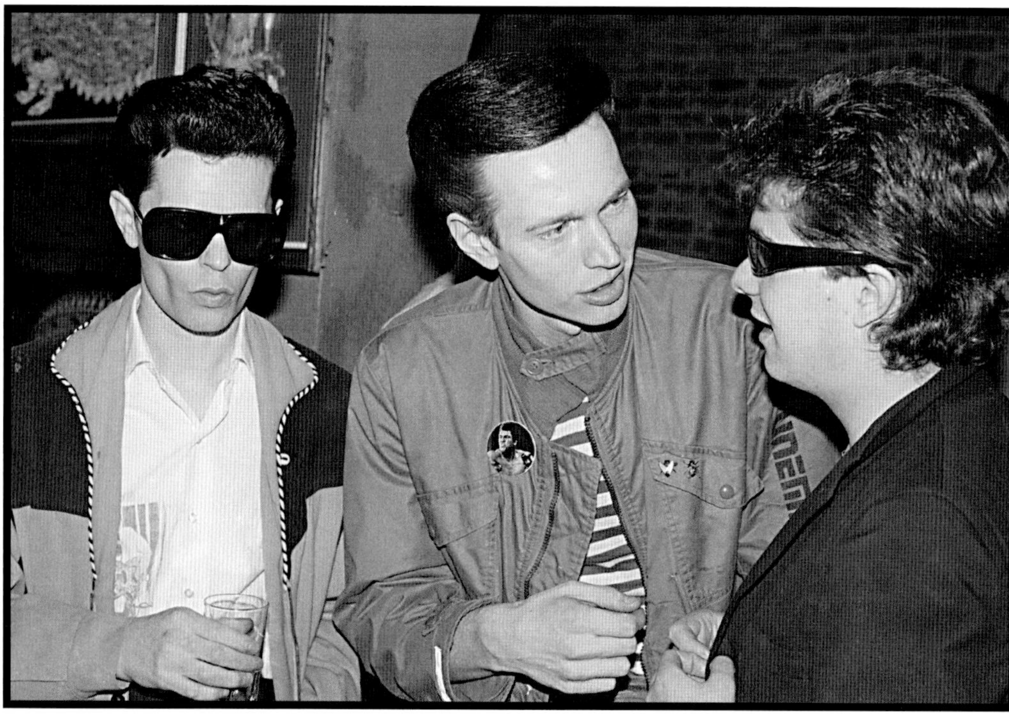

Frankie, Johnny and Brittley

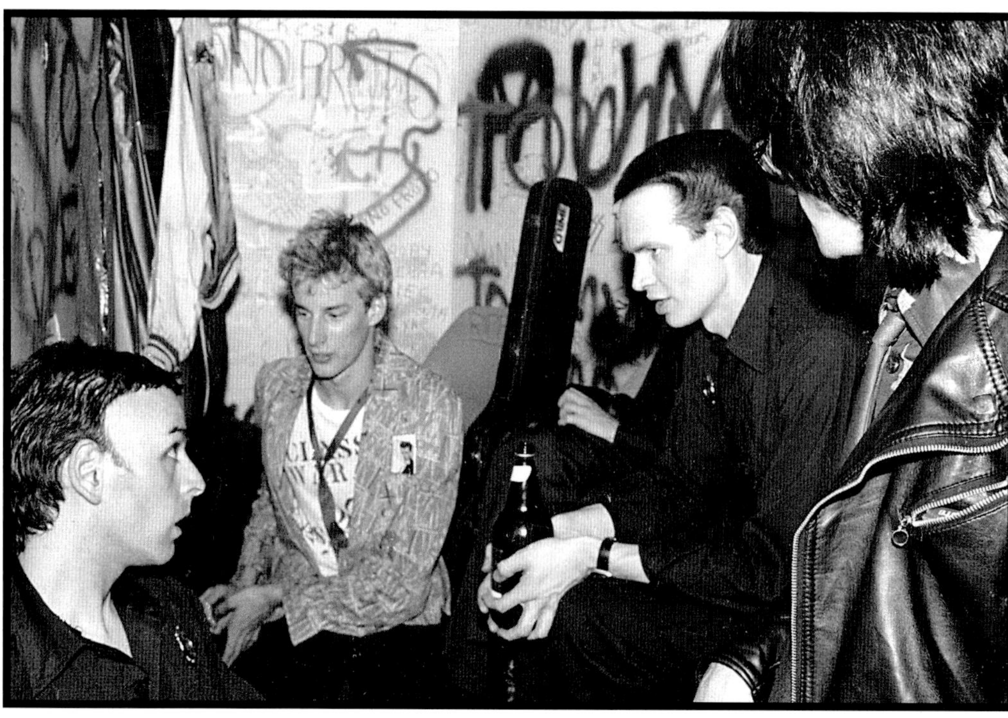

Ron, Chip Kinman of The Dils, and Johnny with future Crime member Joey Swails looking on. Joey was a Nuns roadie and later when Ron left he became a member of Crime, playing bass. When Ron returned, Joey switched to keyboards.

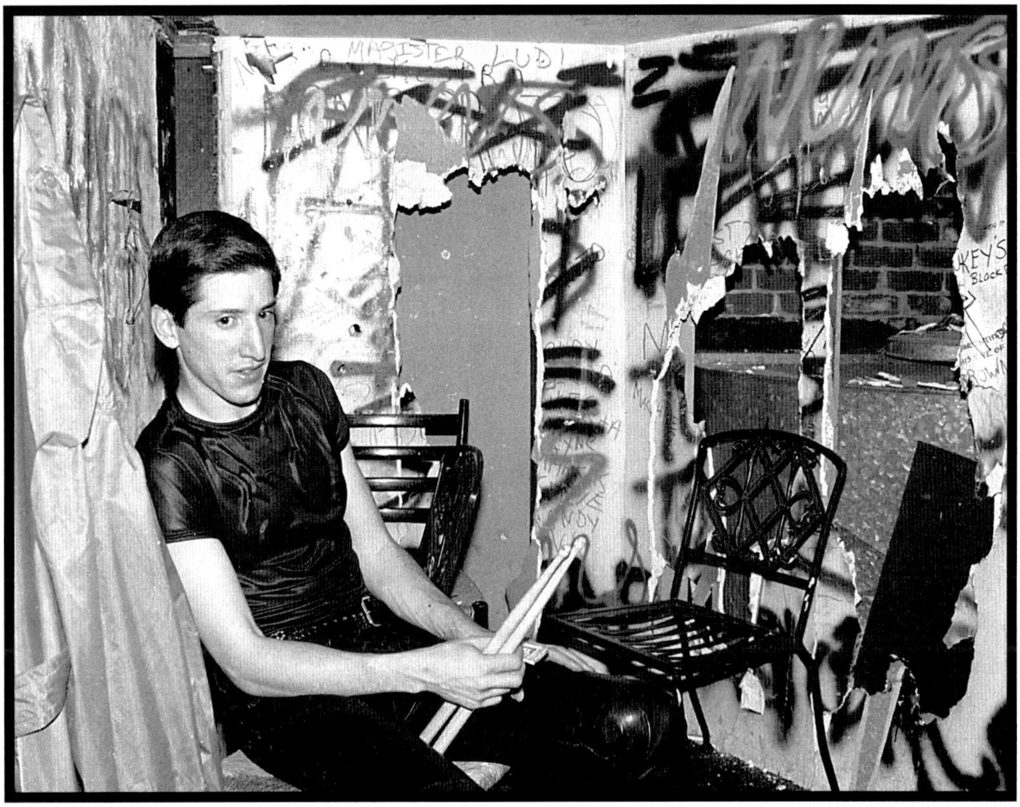

Hank waiting backstage at the Mabuhay Gardens

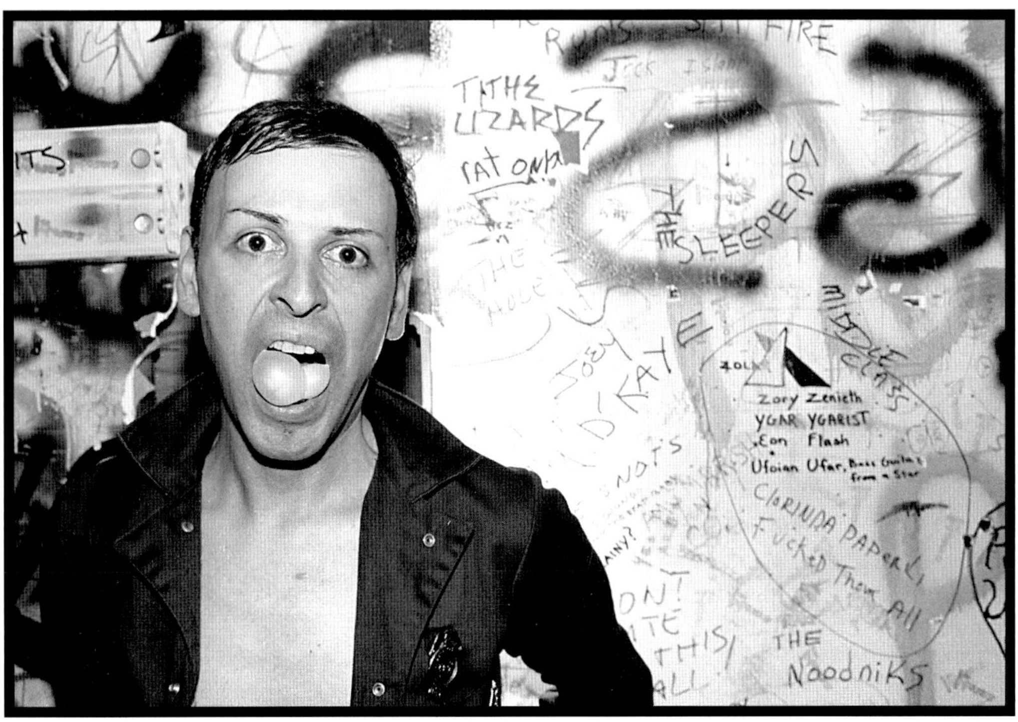

Ron with a wall of the ever-present grafitti

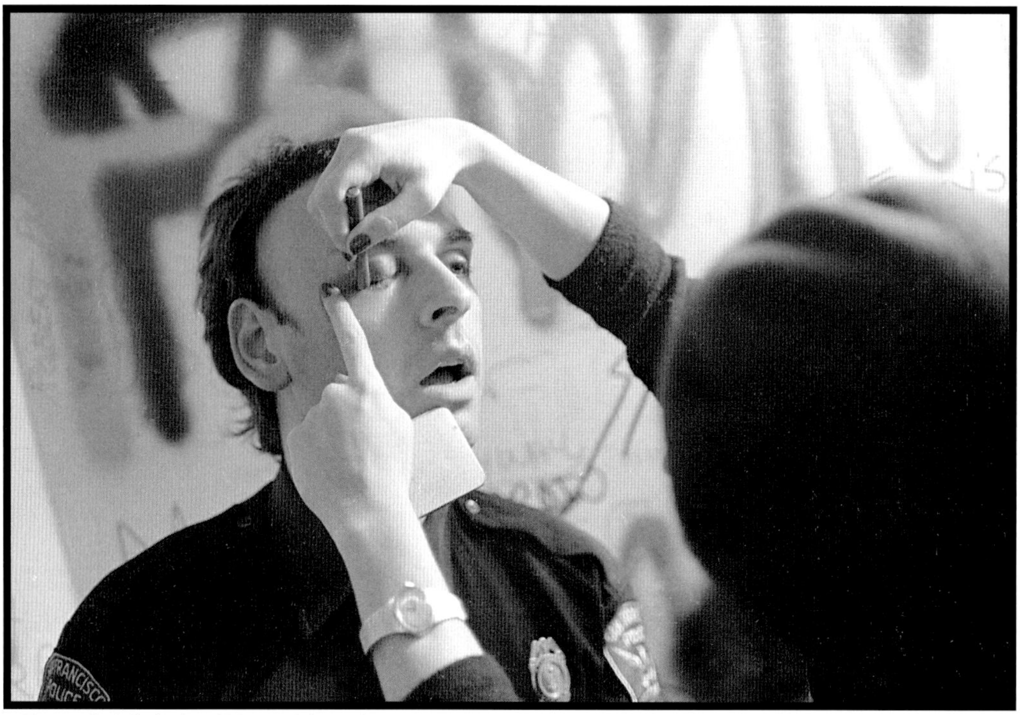

Lots of girls helped Ron with makeup.

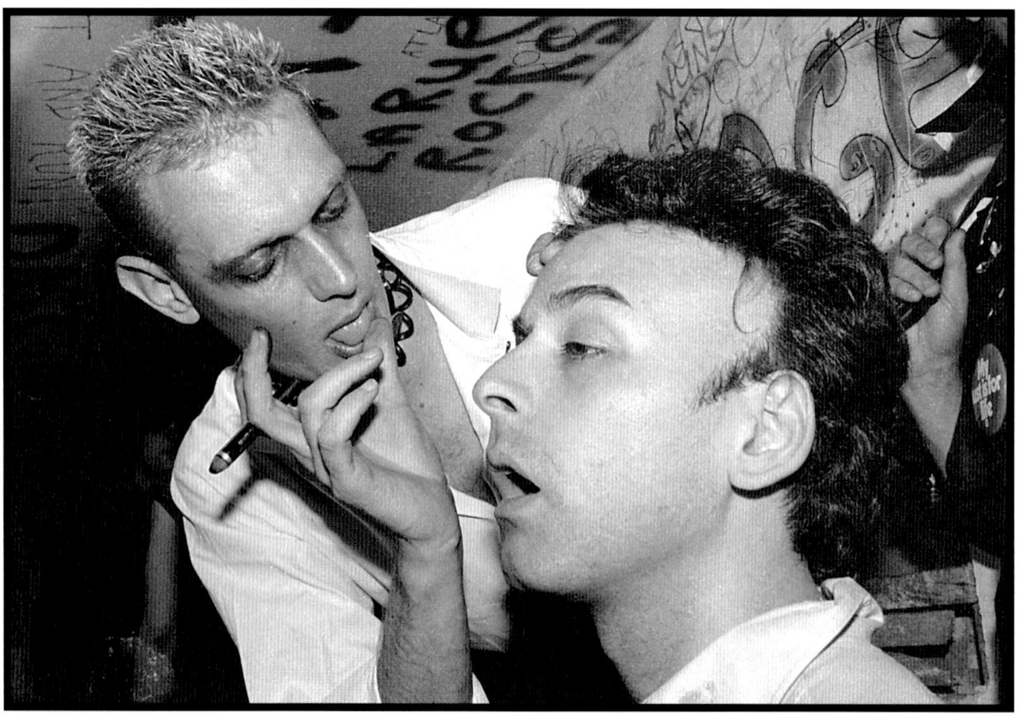

Don Vinyl applying makeup to Ron. Later Don founded the Offs, one of the great punk Ska bands.

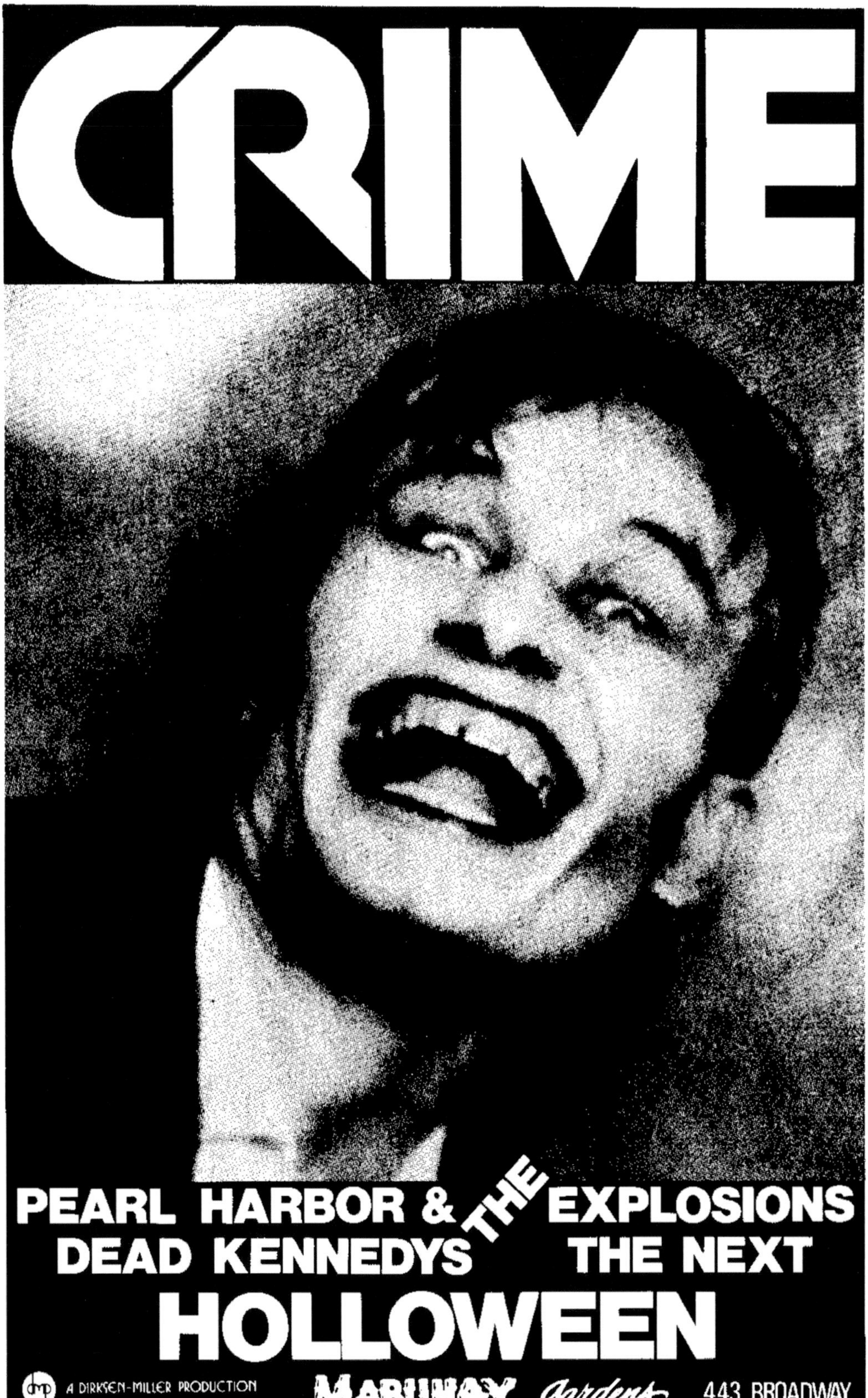
CRIME
PEARL HARBOR & THE EXPLOSIONS
DEAD KENNEDYS THE NEXT
HOLLOWEEN
A DIRKSEN-MILLER PRODUCTION
© 1978 BAD DREAM IMAGE
MABUHAY Gardens 443 BROADWAY

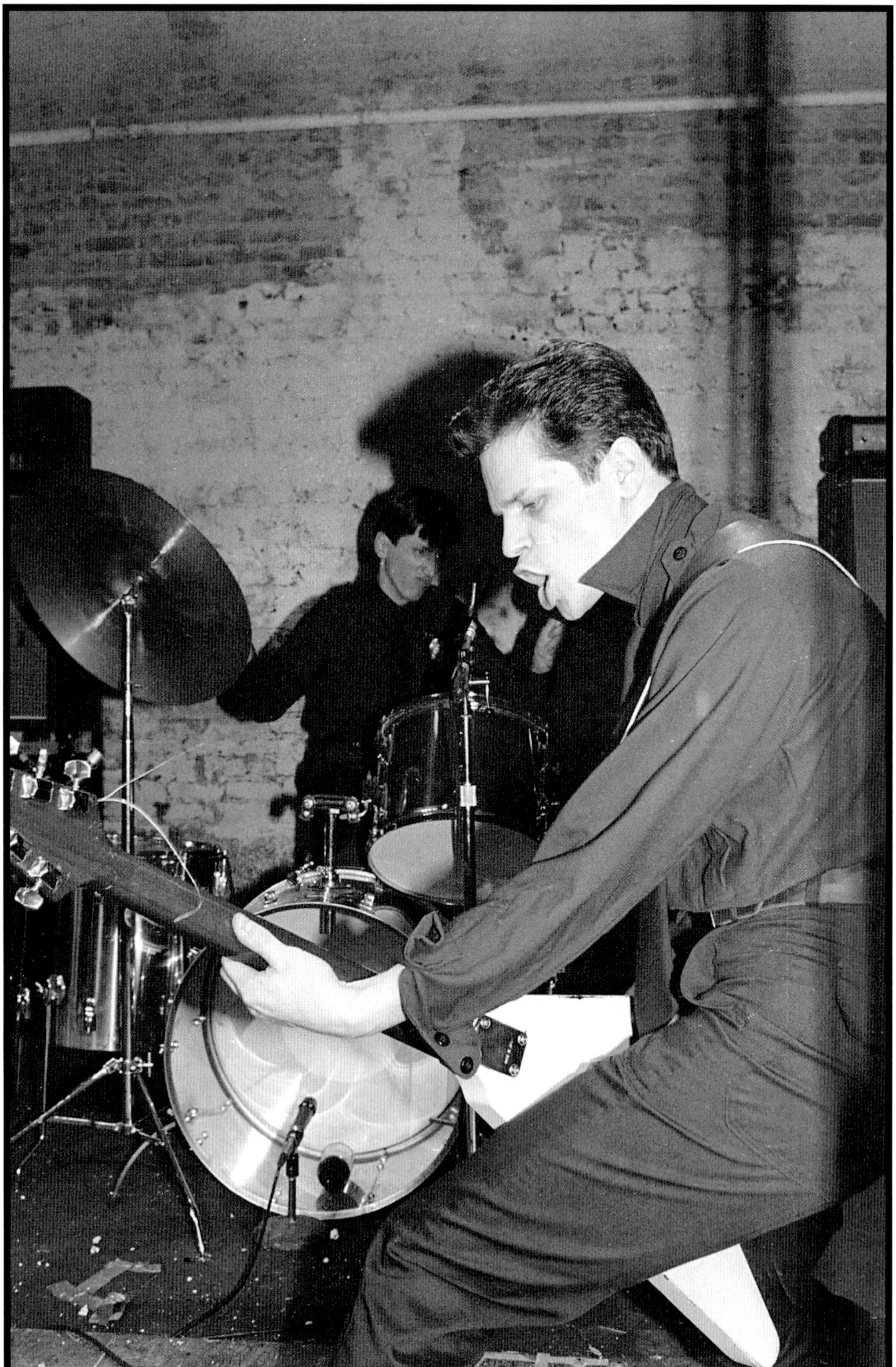

Frankie

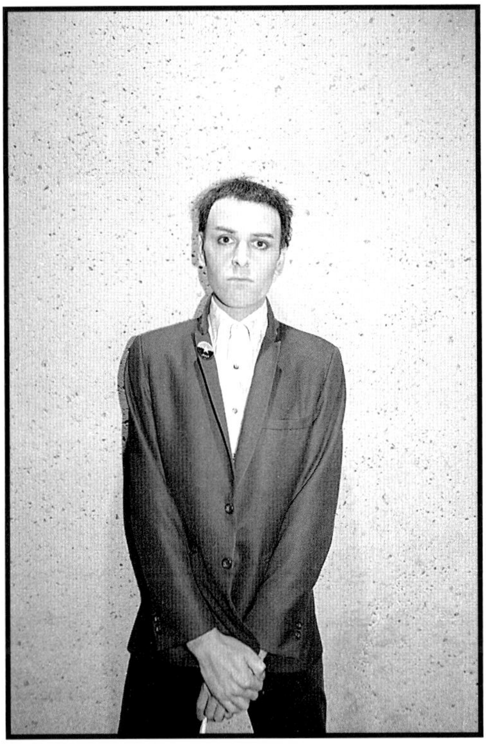

Ron

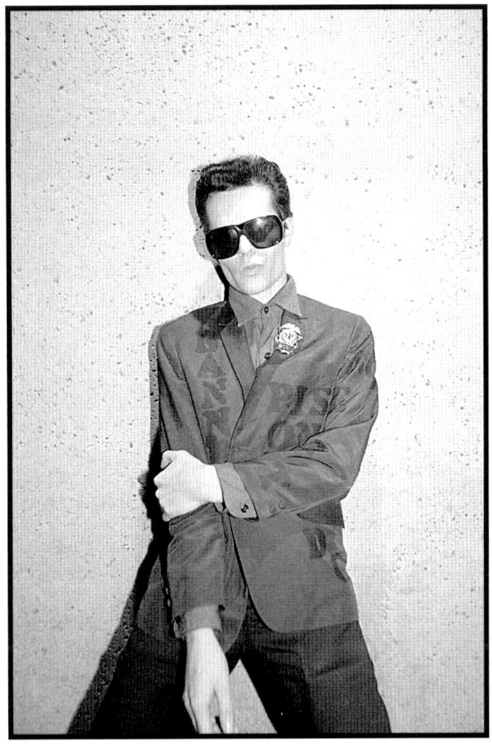

Frankie

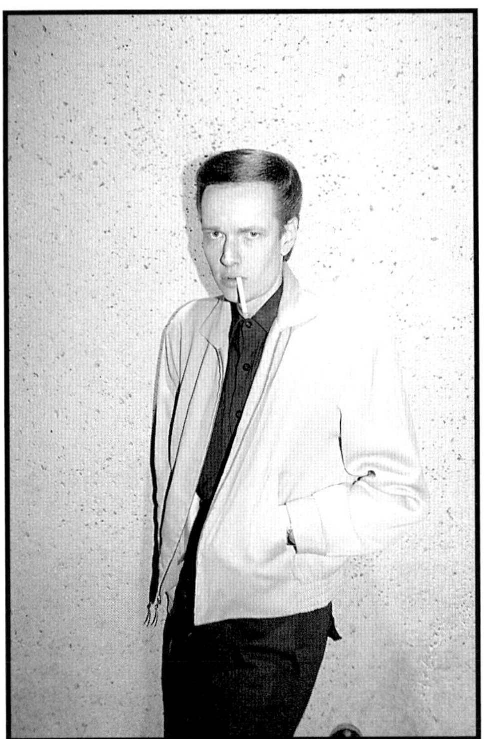

Johnny

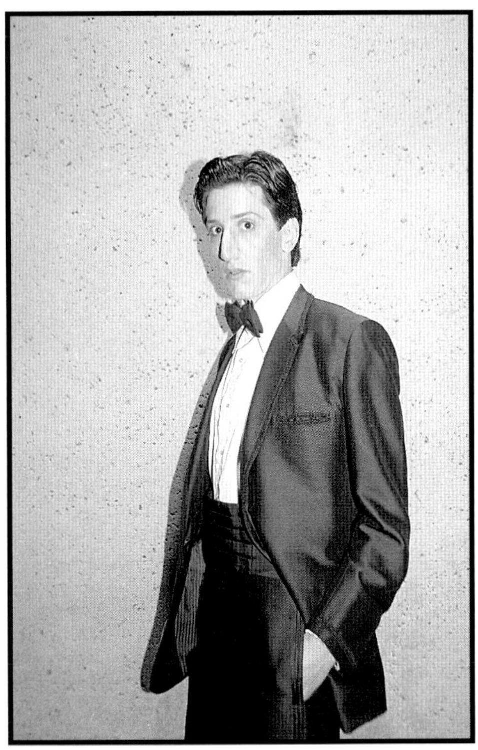

Hank

This was shot one frame per person during a photo shoot.

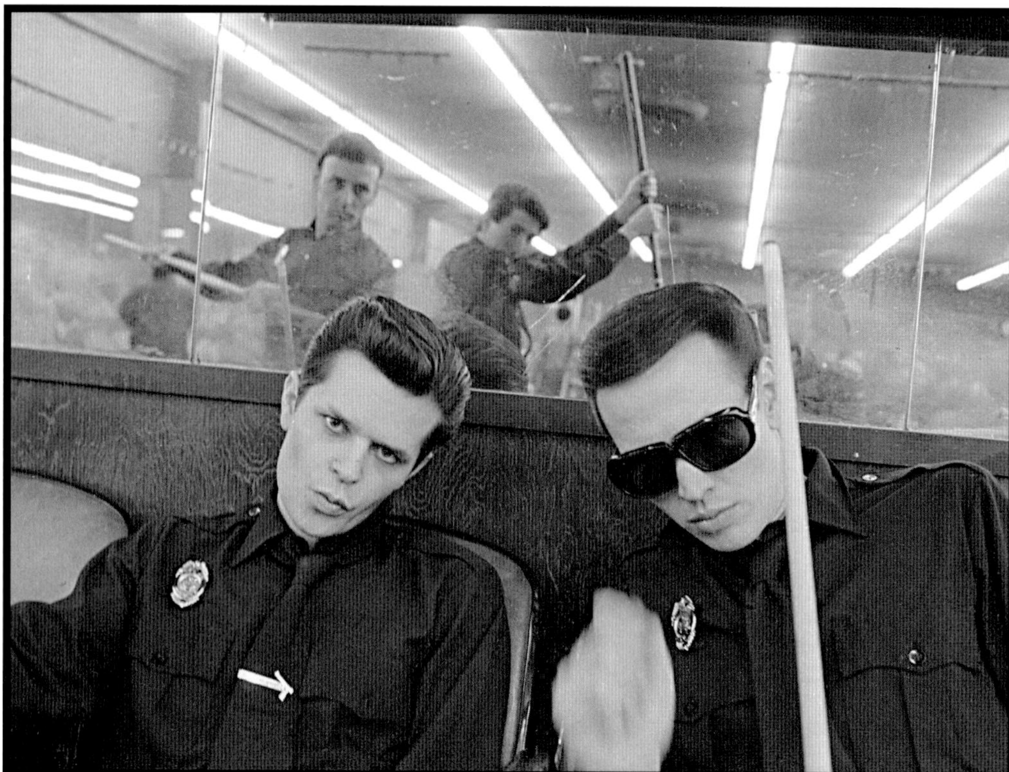

Frankie and Johnny with Ron and Hank in mirror

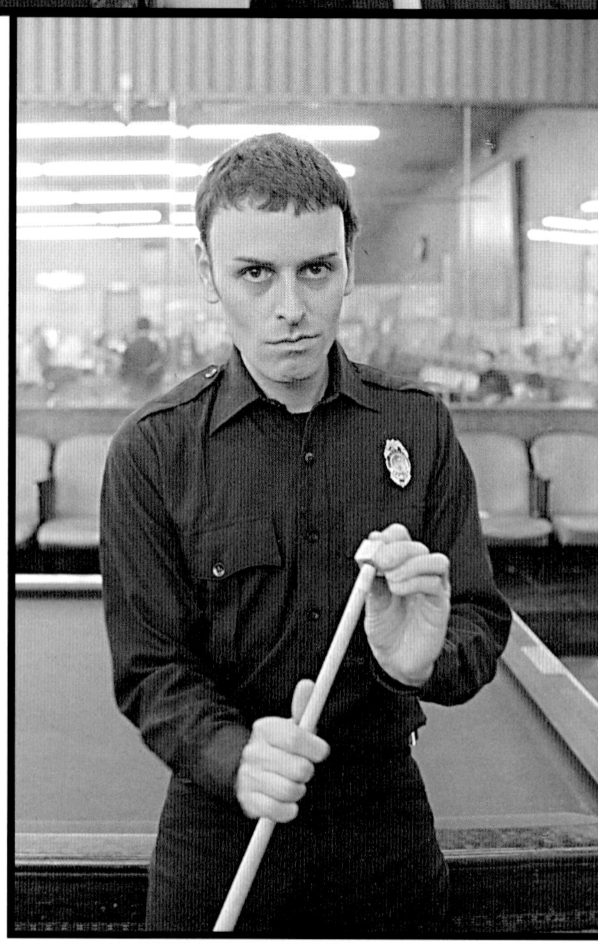

These photos were shot in a pool hall in the rough part of Market Street. It was patronized by the usual mix of pimps, petty criminals, and the like. We were not received with open arms, to say the least. I thought we did well to leave without a fight.

Ron

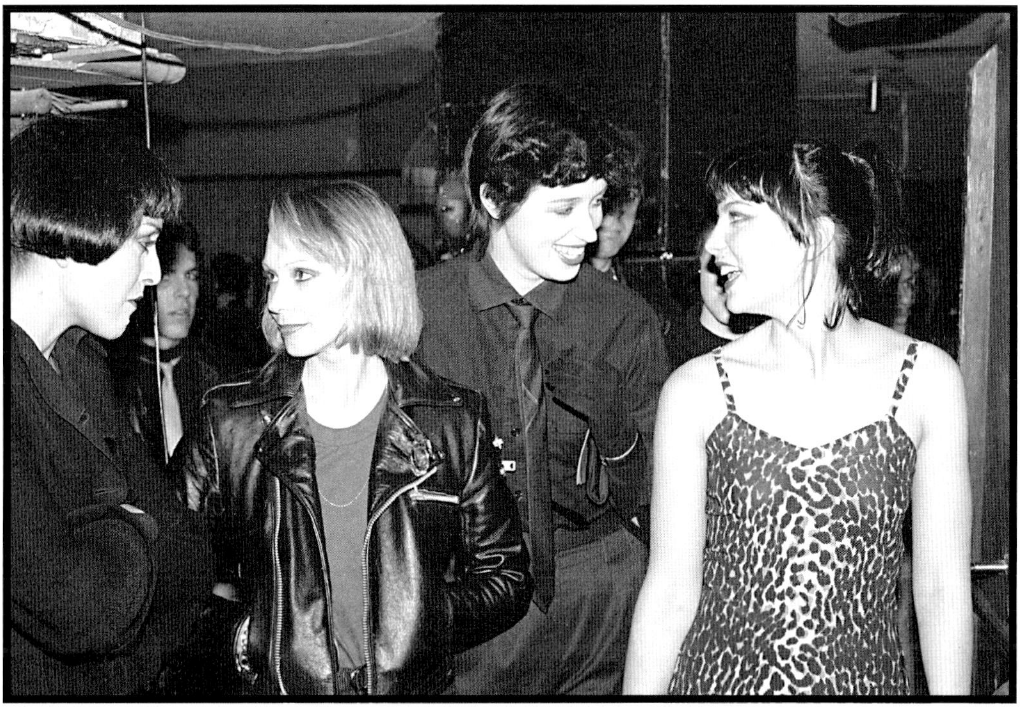

Left to right: Ron's girlfriend Liz, Johnny's wife Jane, Hank's wife Corola, and Frankie's wife Carla.

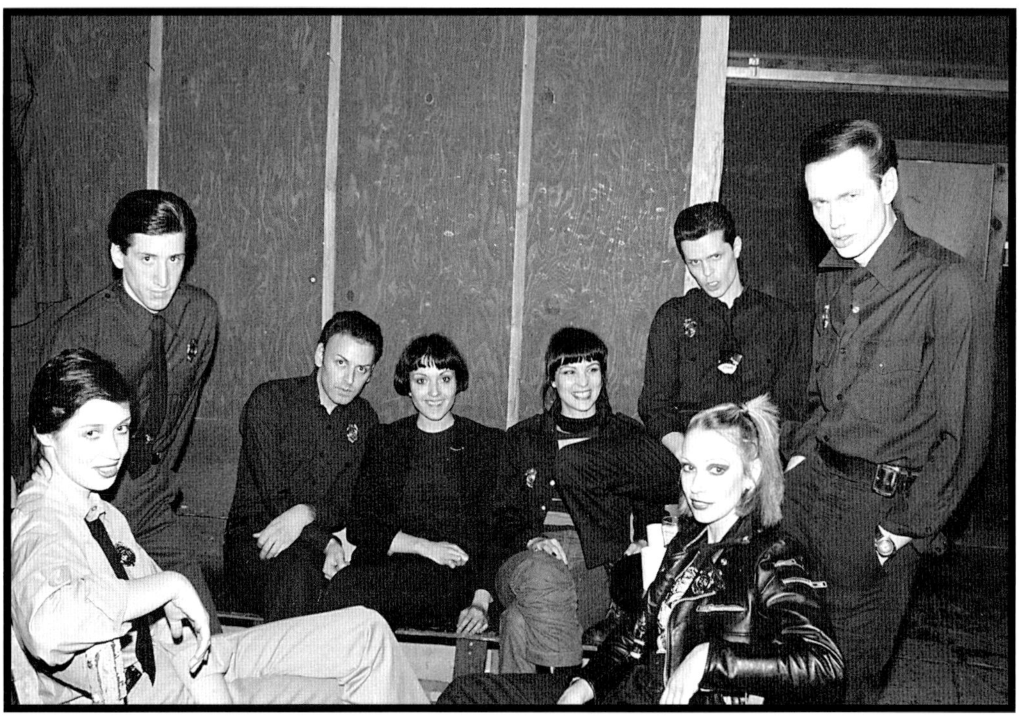

Crime with wives and girlfriends. It's all about the family in rock n' roll.

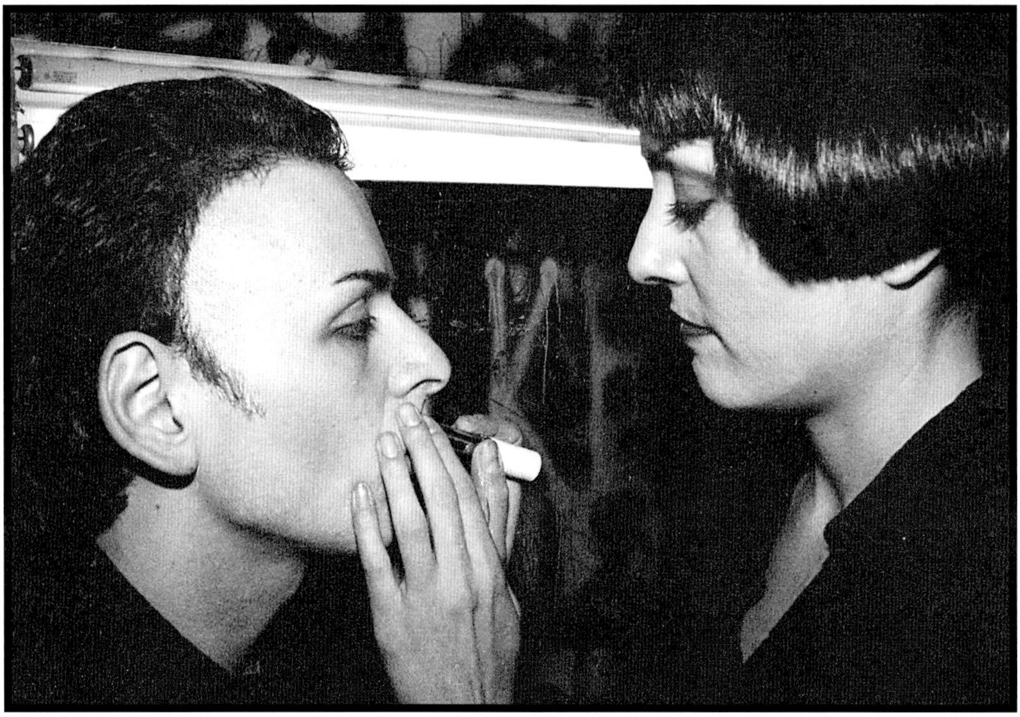

Ron and Liz

Liz sent Ripper a letter telling him how much she was in love with him. Ron went to her apartment and they were together for a couple of years. Later, Ron suspected the other band members had set up the arrangement and even paid her to be with him because he was thinking about quitting the band.

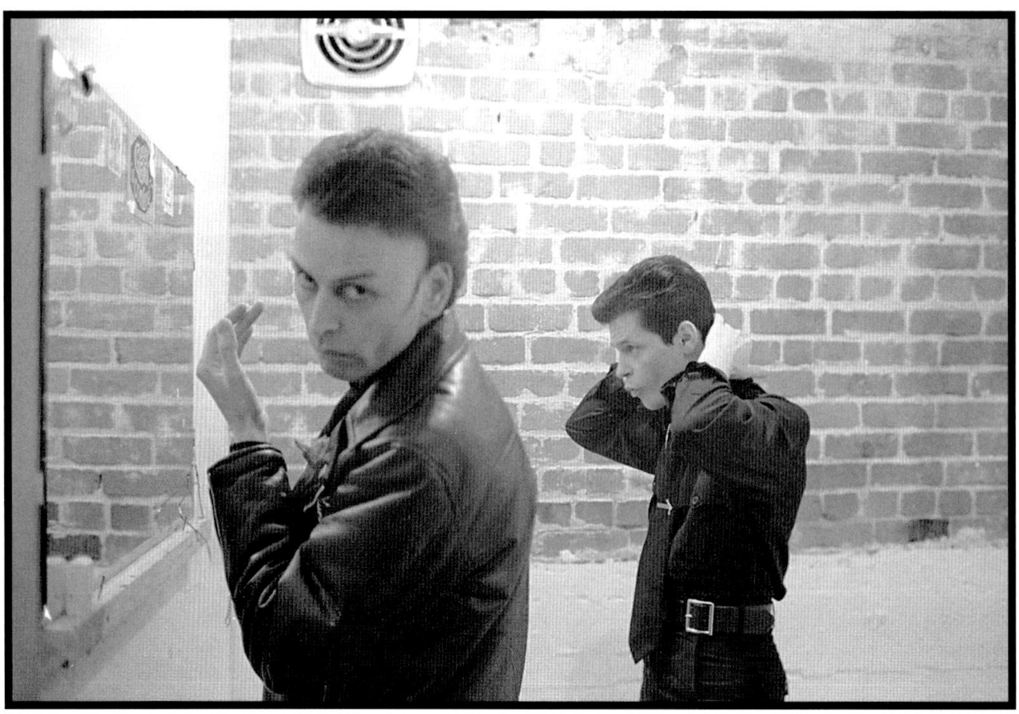

Boys have to keep up appearances

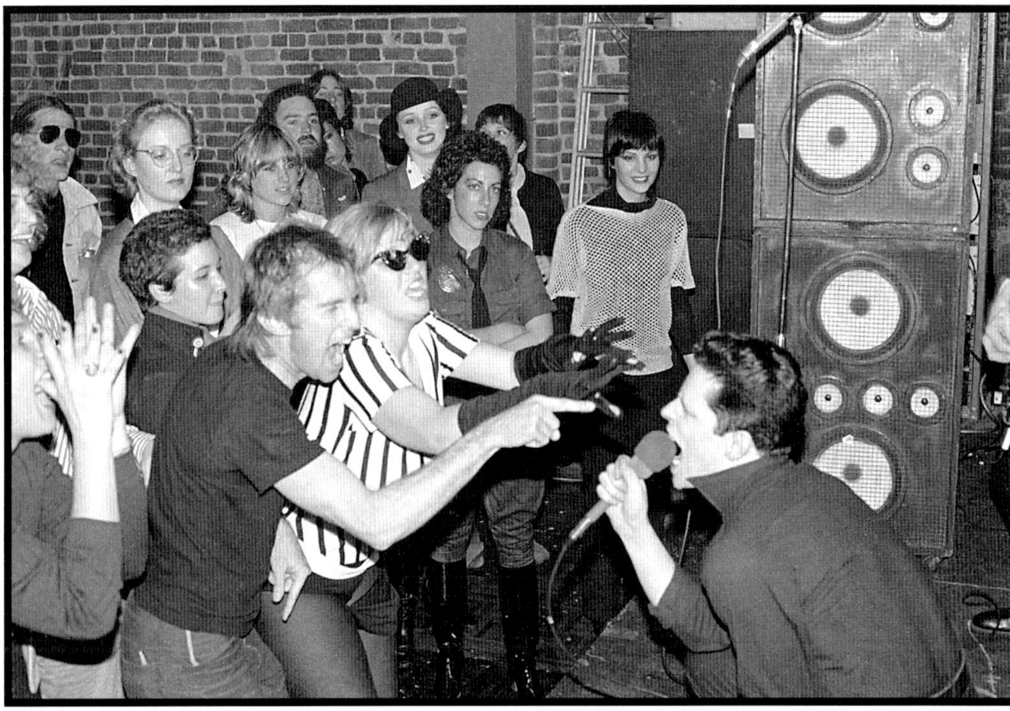

Live at the Mabuhay

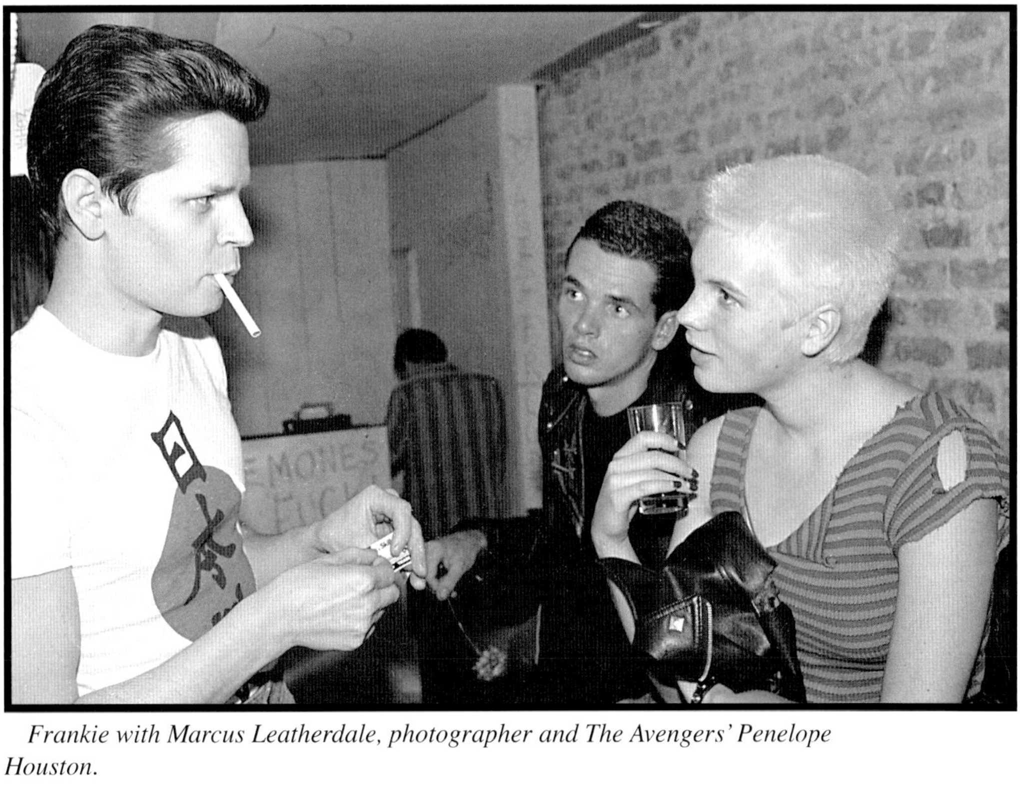

Frankie with Marcus Leatherdale, photographer and The Avengers' Penelope Houston.

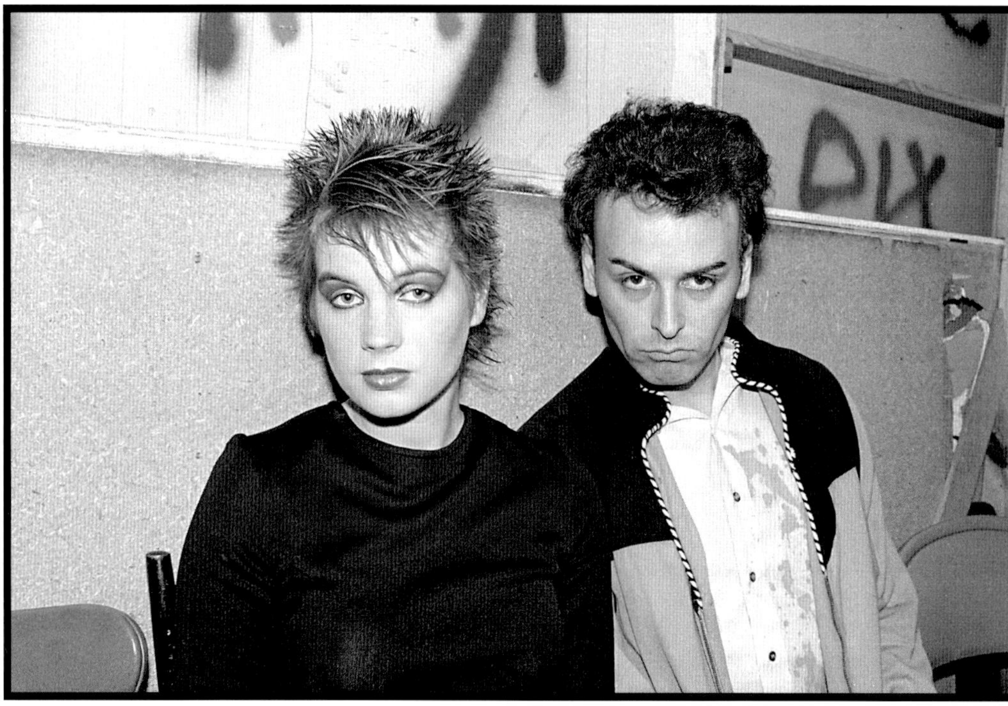

Penelope Houston, The Avengers and Ron.

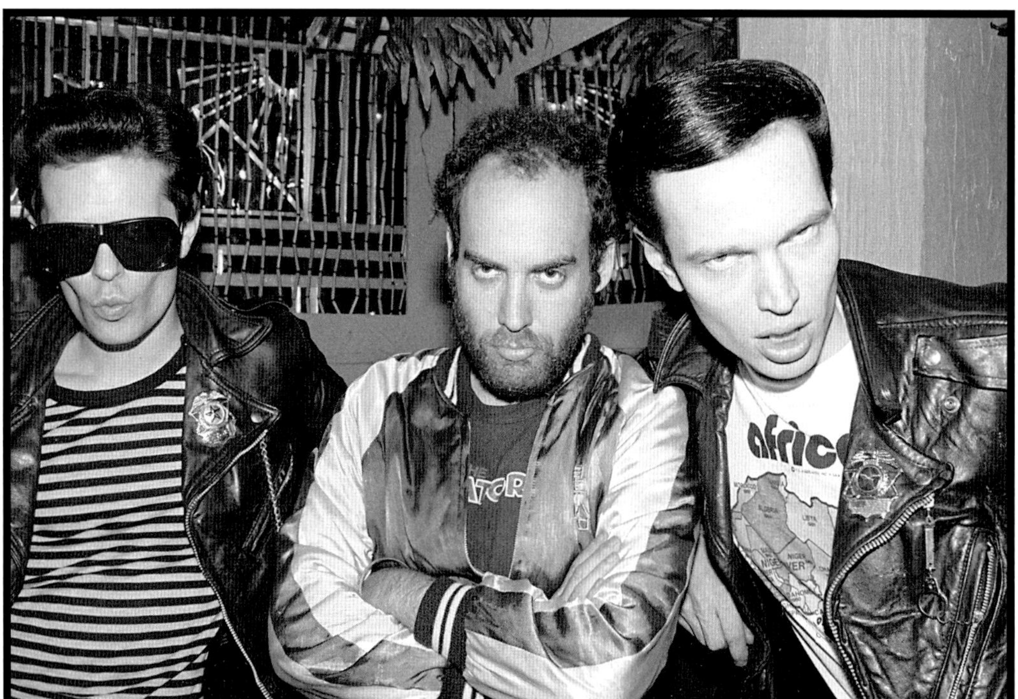

Johnny, Howie Klein and Frankie.

Howie Klein was a freelance writer who was on the scene from the beginning. He pretended to like punk, but in reality Howie was more of a rock guy. He and Kris Knab, owner of Aquarius Records, founded a country music club, Cow Pie, to cash in on the next big thing. It lasted a couple of weeks.

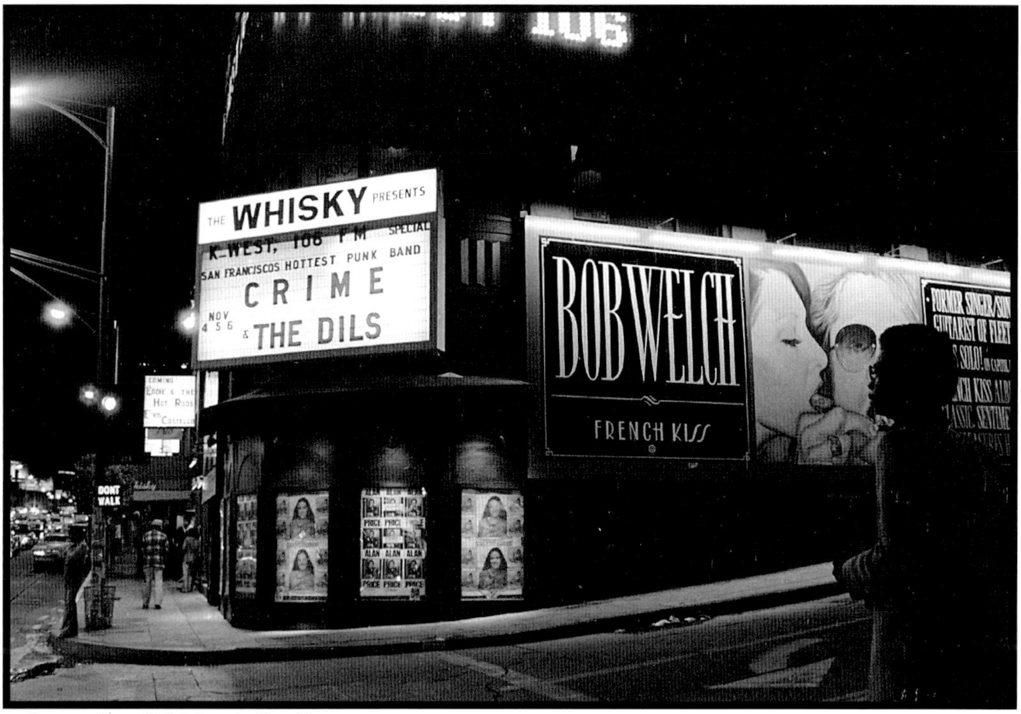

Legendary Whisky-A-Go-Go.

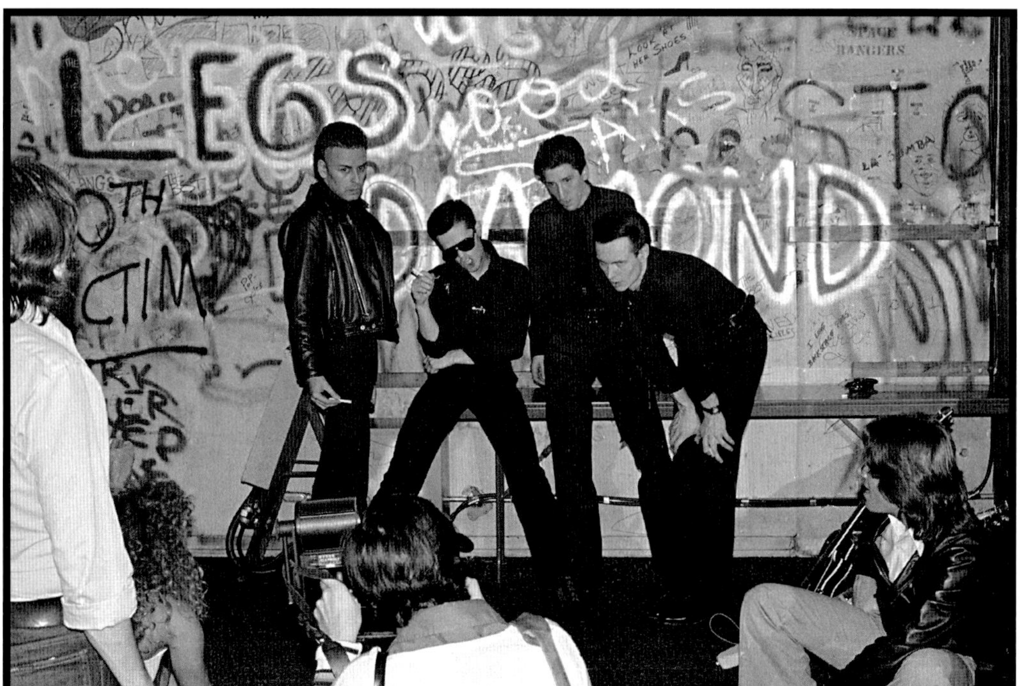

Crime backstage at the Whisky-A-Go-Go in Los Angeles.

In November 1977, Crime played the Whisky-A-Go-Go in Los Angeles. It was their first gig outside the San Francisco Bay Area, and here the band is posing for a few LA photographers. They ran around Hollywood in their police uniforms and created a minor sensation, but they scored no big record deals.

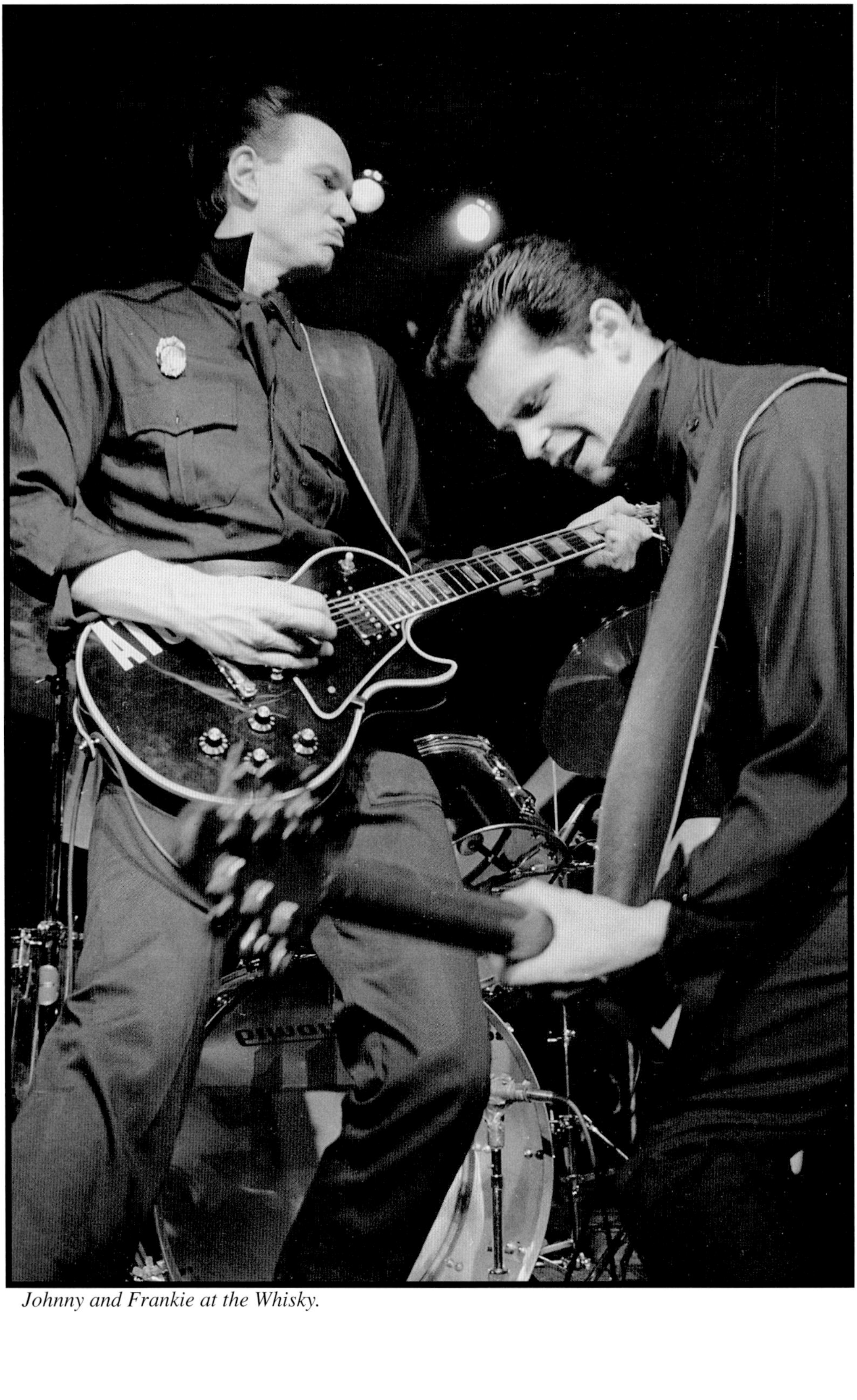

Johnny and Frankie at the Whisky.

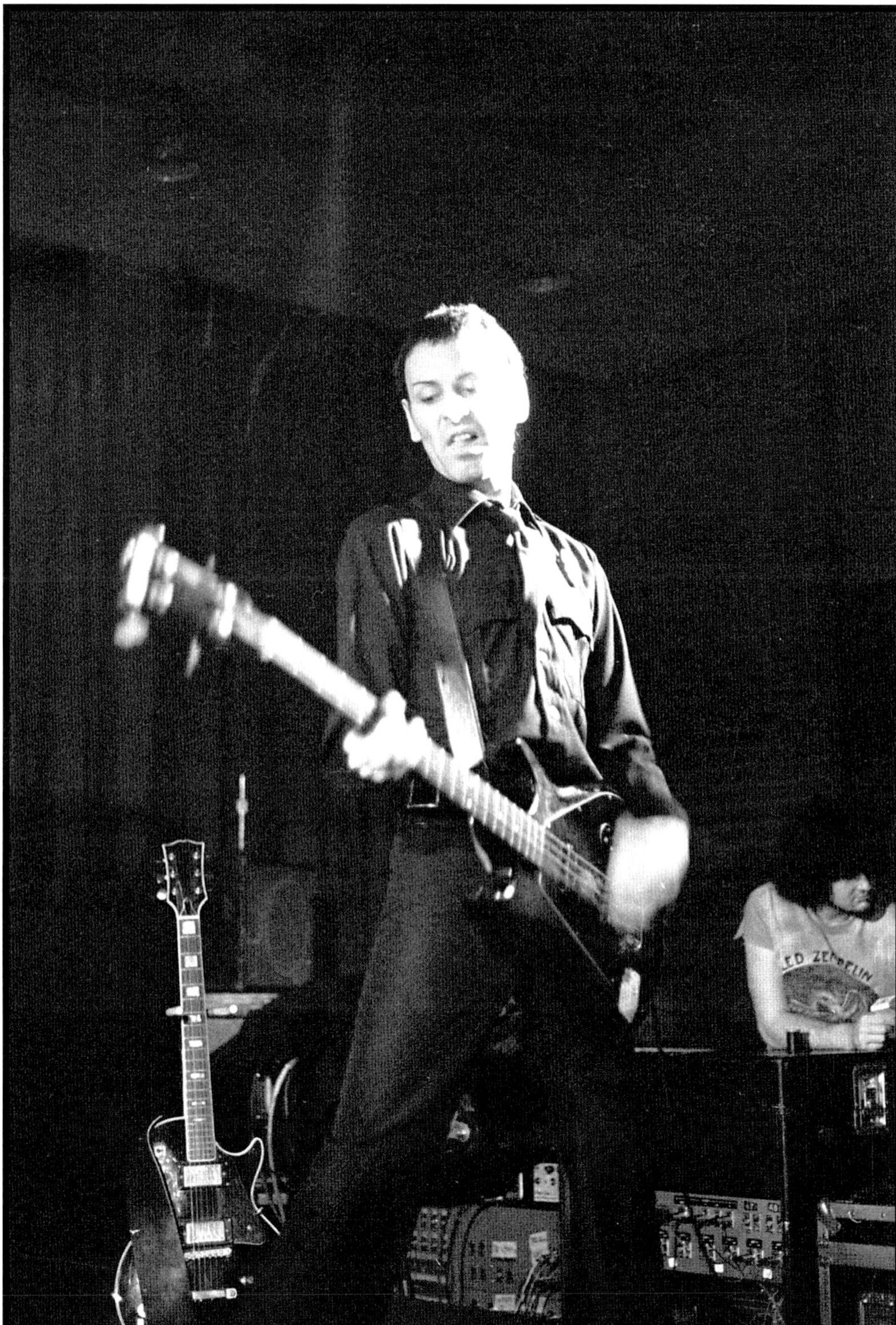

Ron at the Whisky.

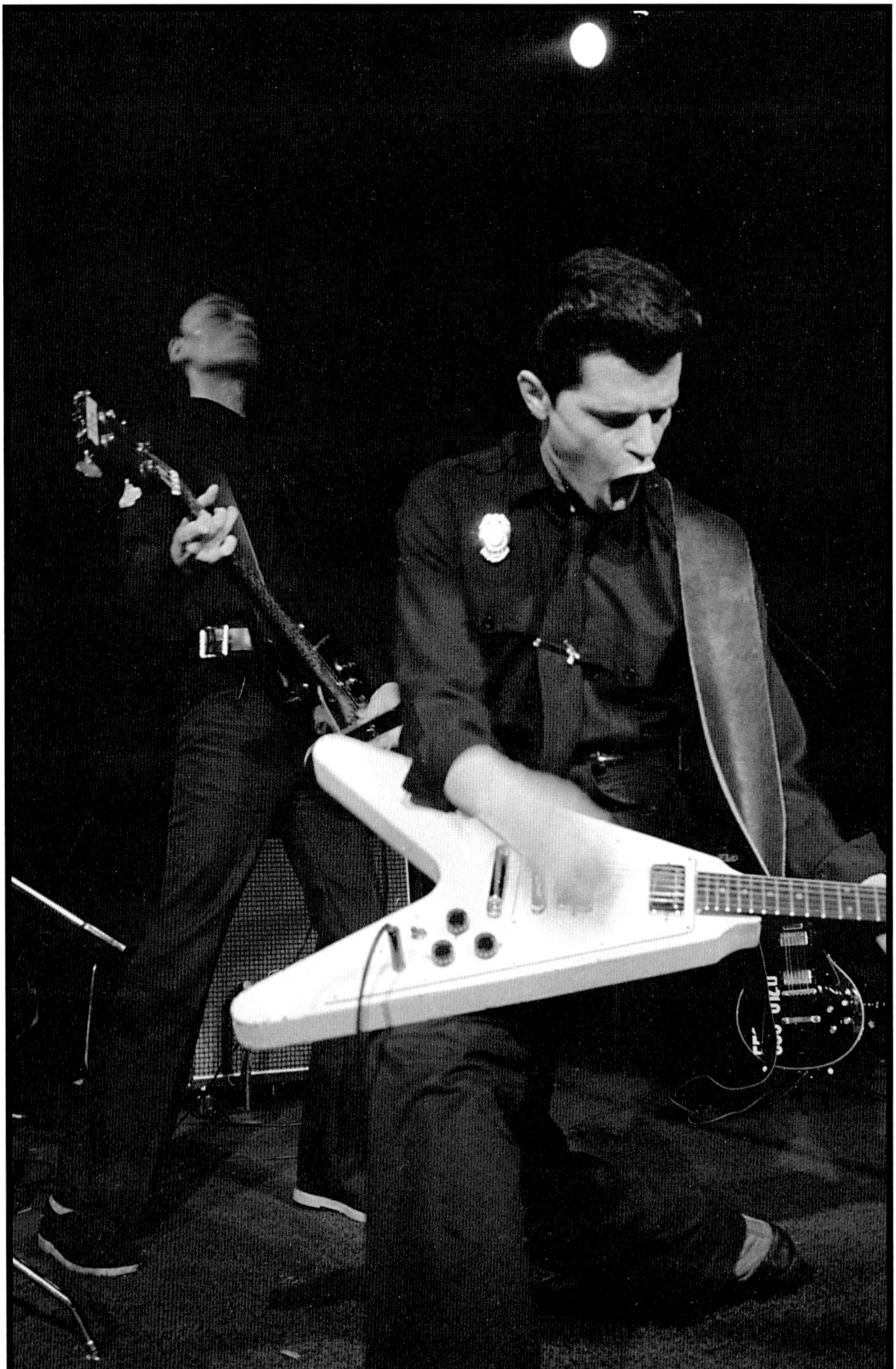

Frankie and Ron at the Whisky.

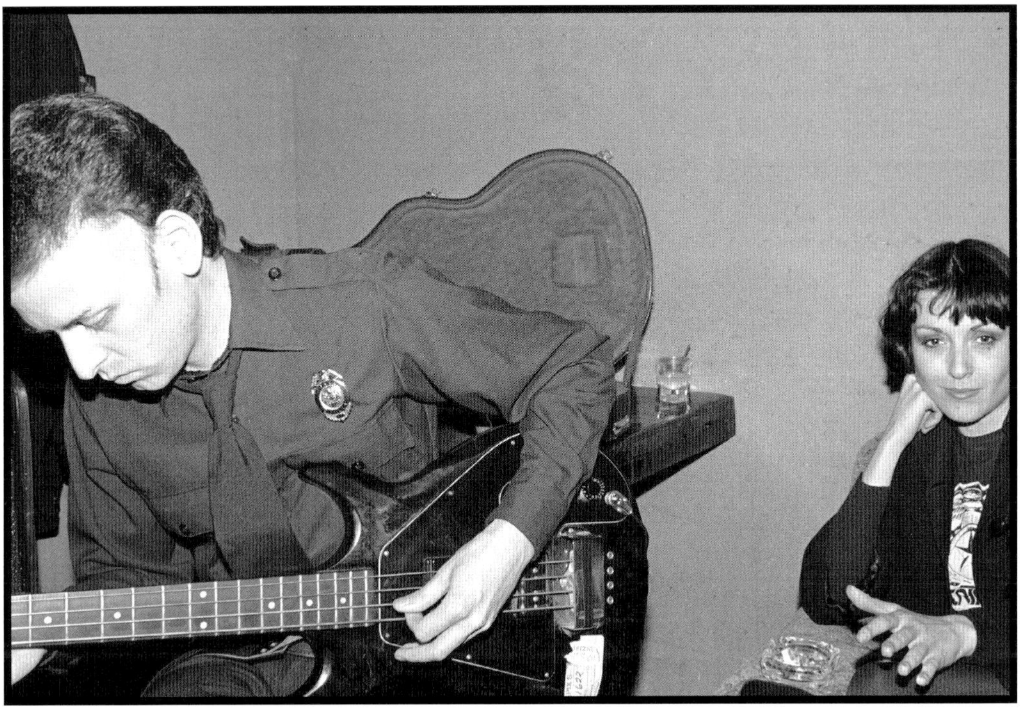

Ron with Liz, waiting.

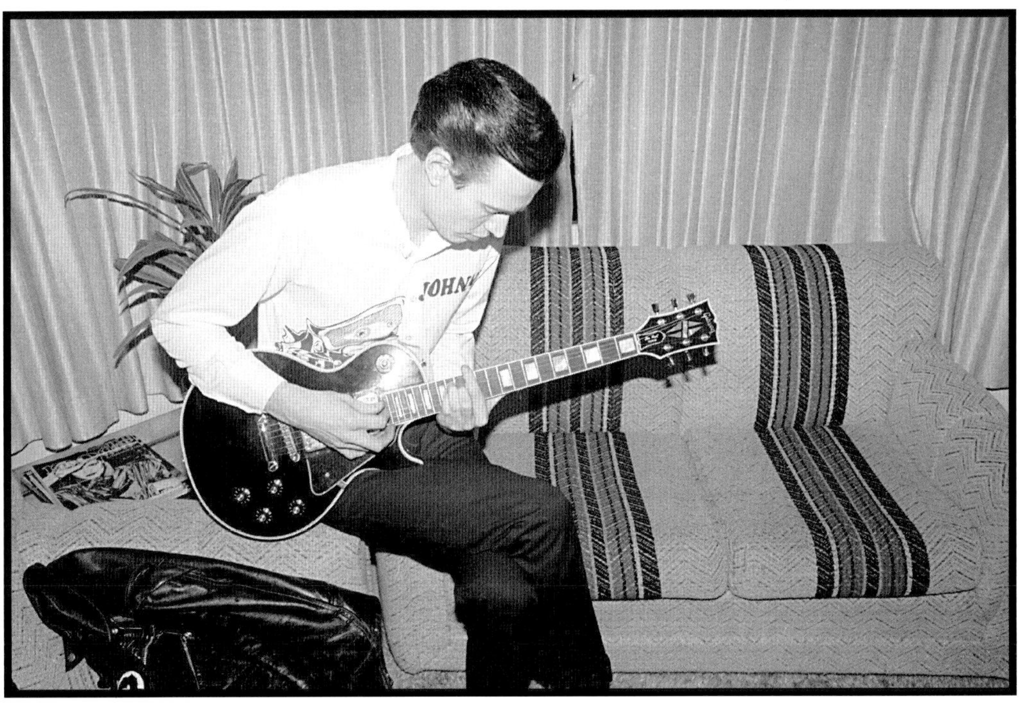

Johnny at home.

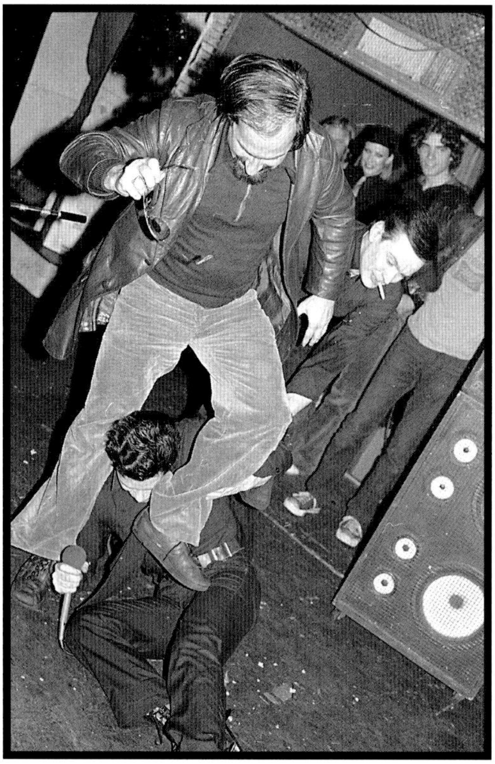

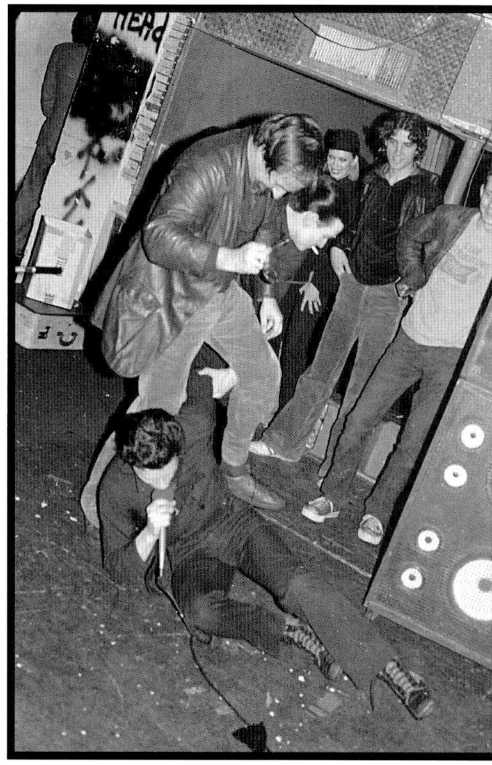

Dirk Dirksen was known for getting into it with band members and members of the audience. Here he and Frankie are getting tangled up. No glasses were broken.

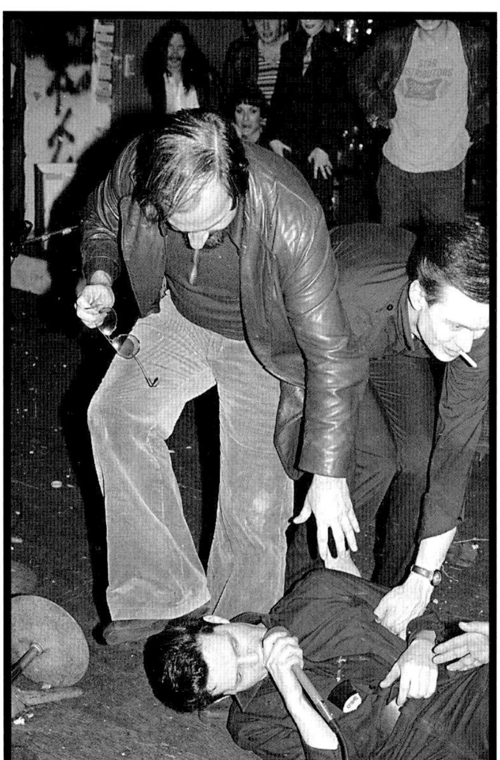

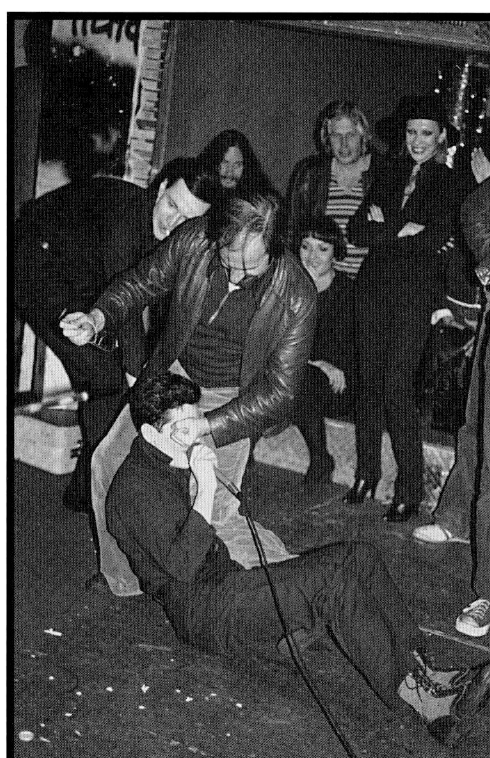

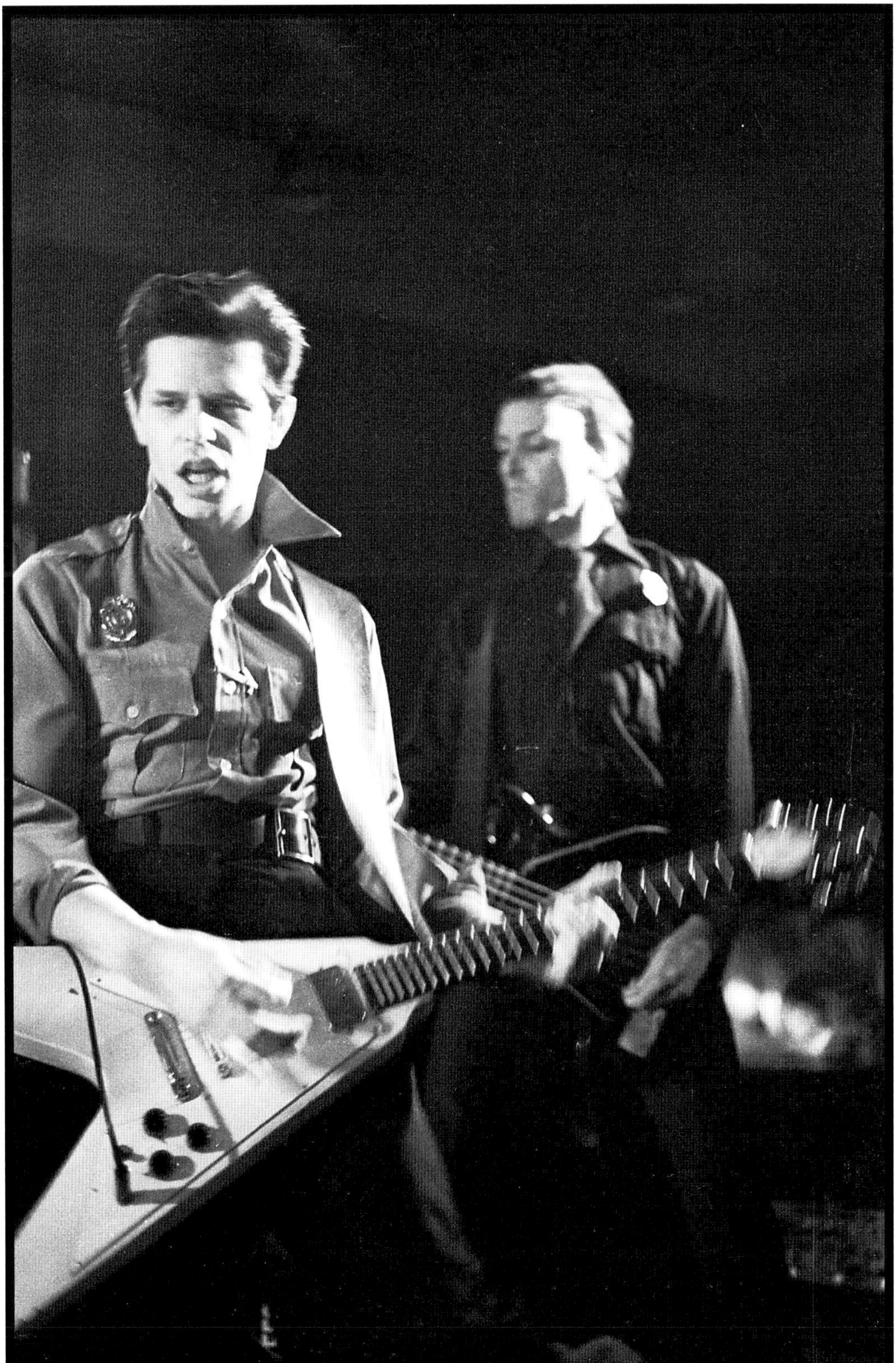

Frankie and Ron

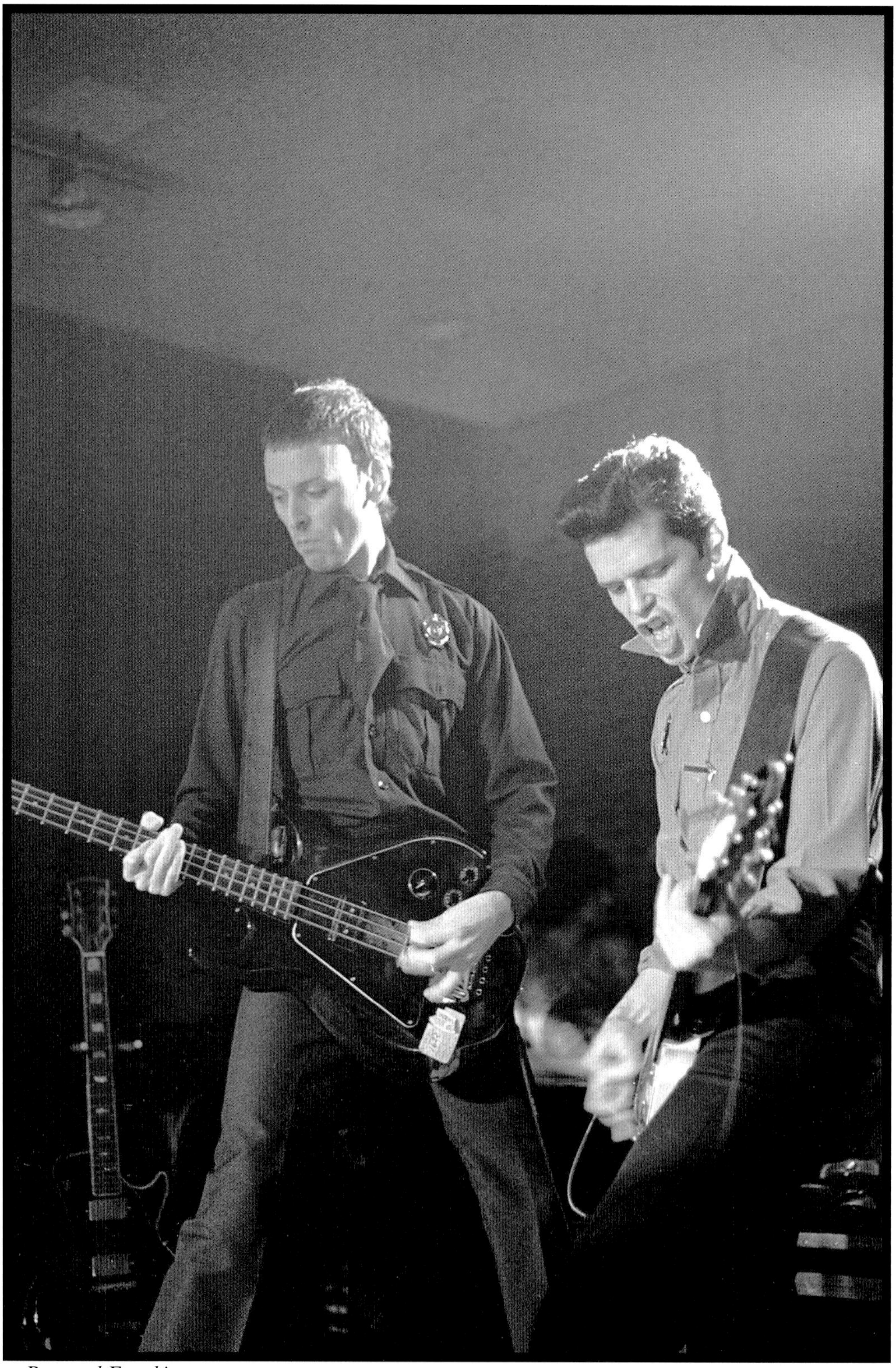

Ron and Frankie

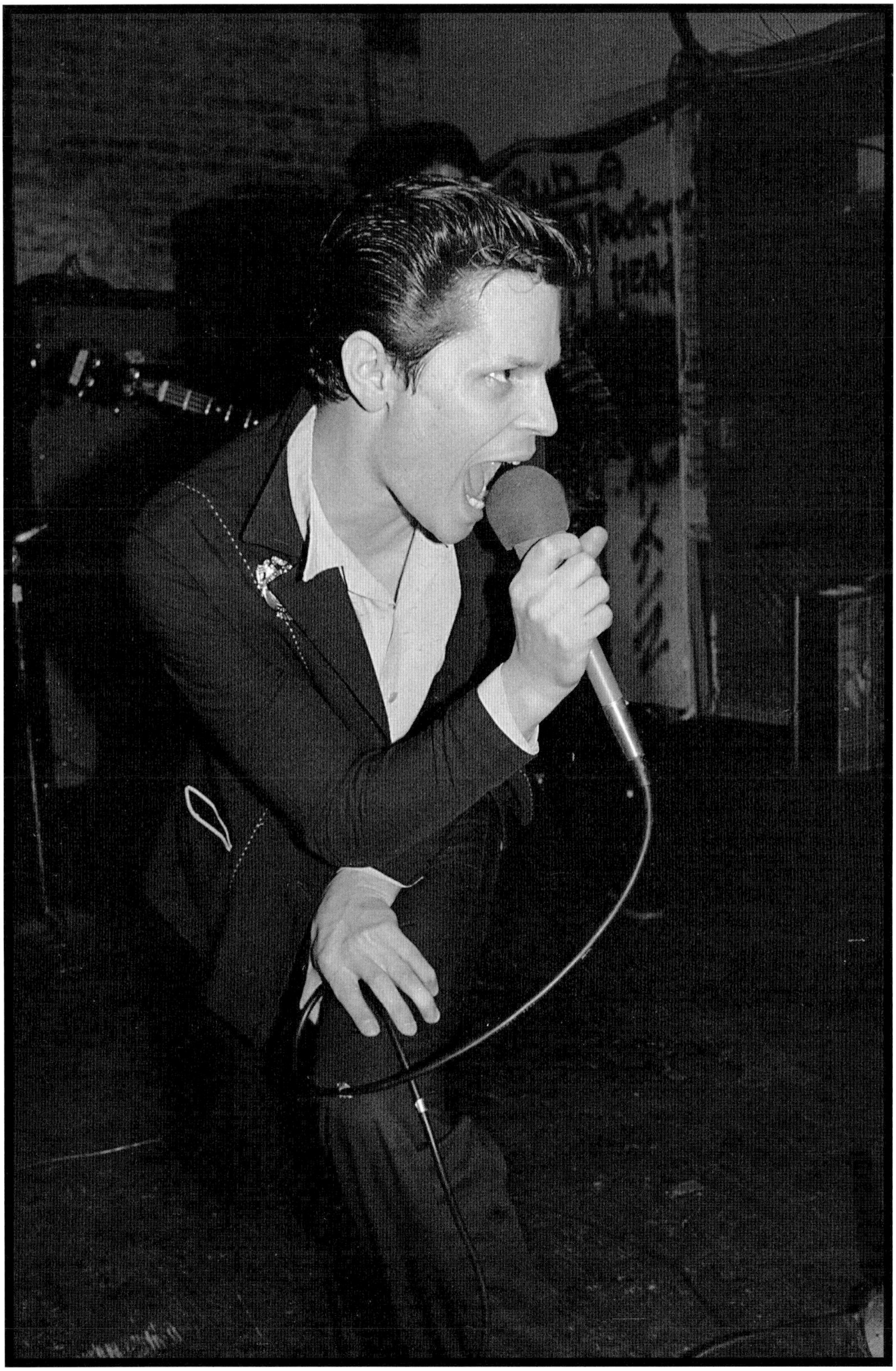

Frankie Fix

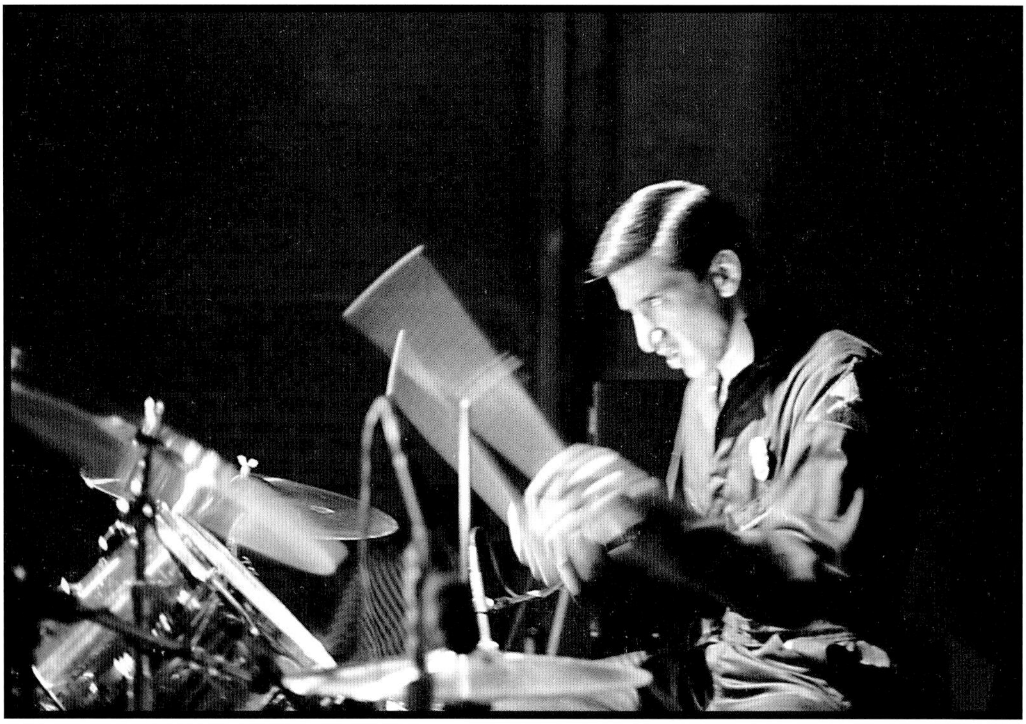

Hank Rank flailing away at the drums.

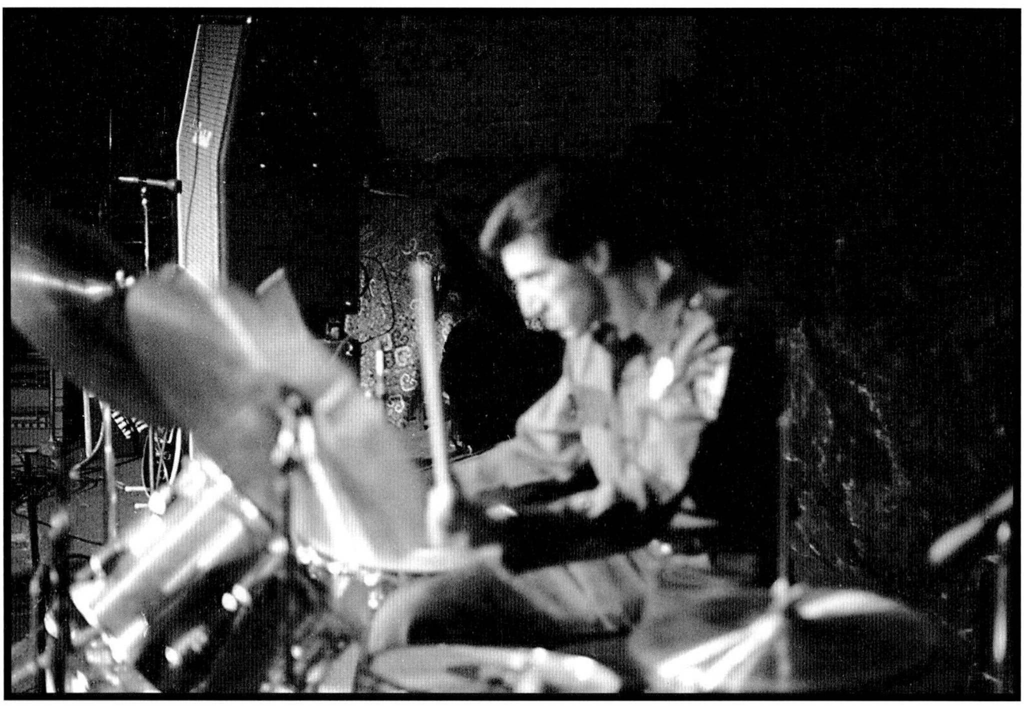

Hank Rank

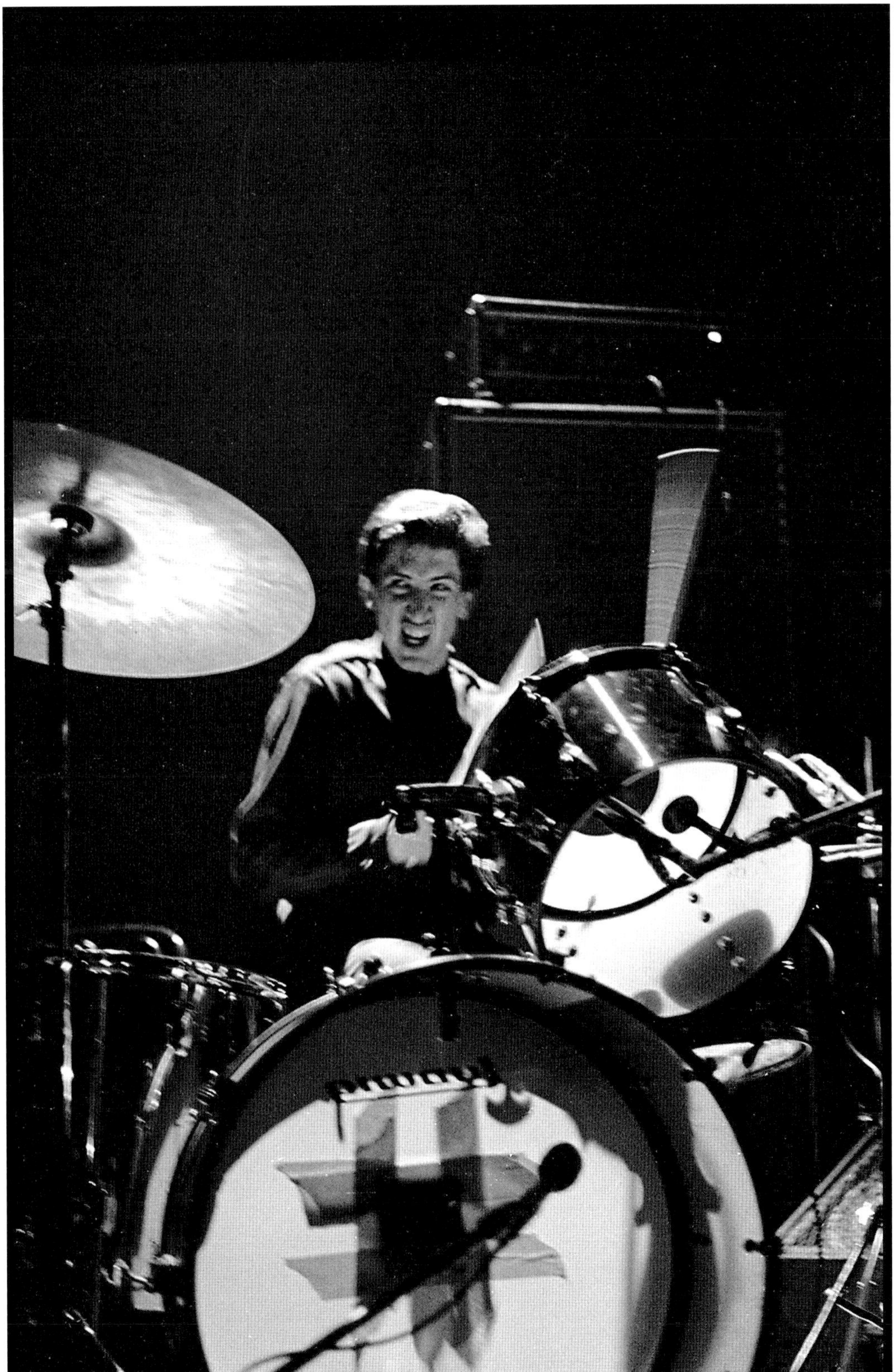

Hank Rank

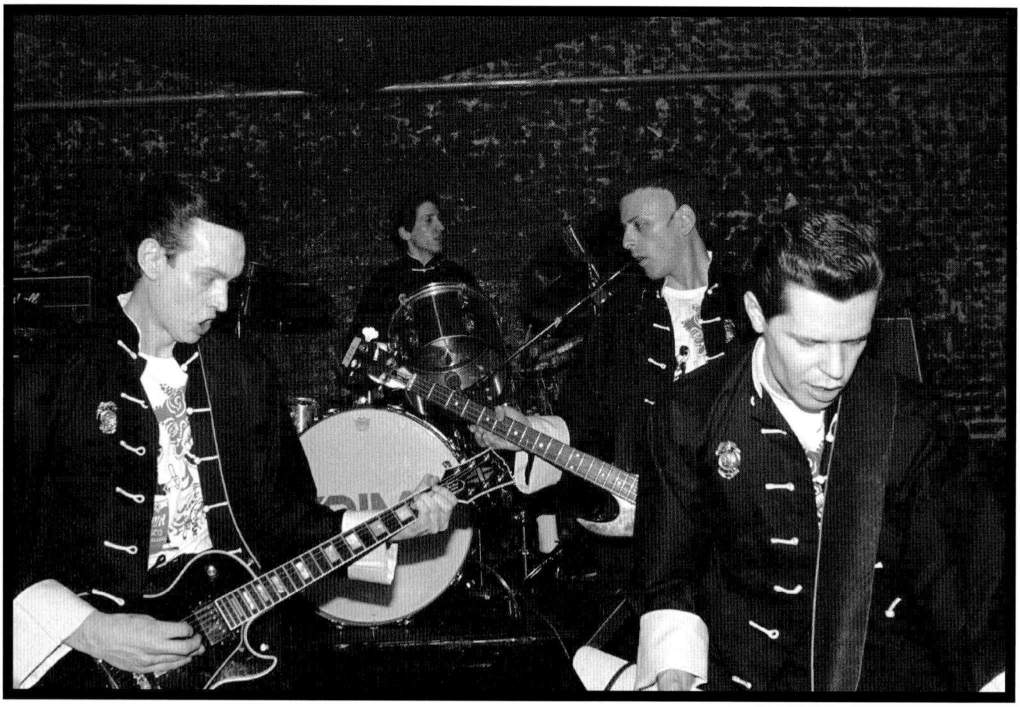

After a trip to Chinatown. Crime liked to perform in different costumes for the night. A lot of these were one-time affairs.

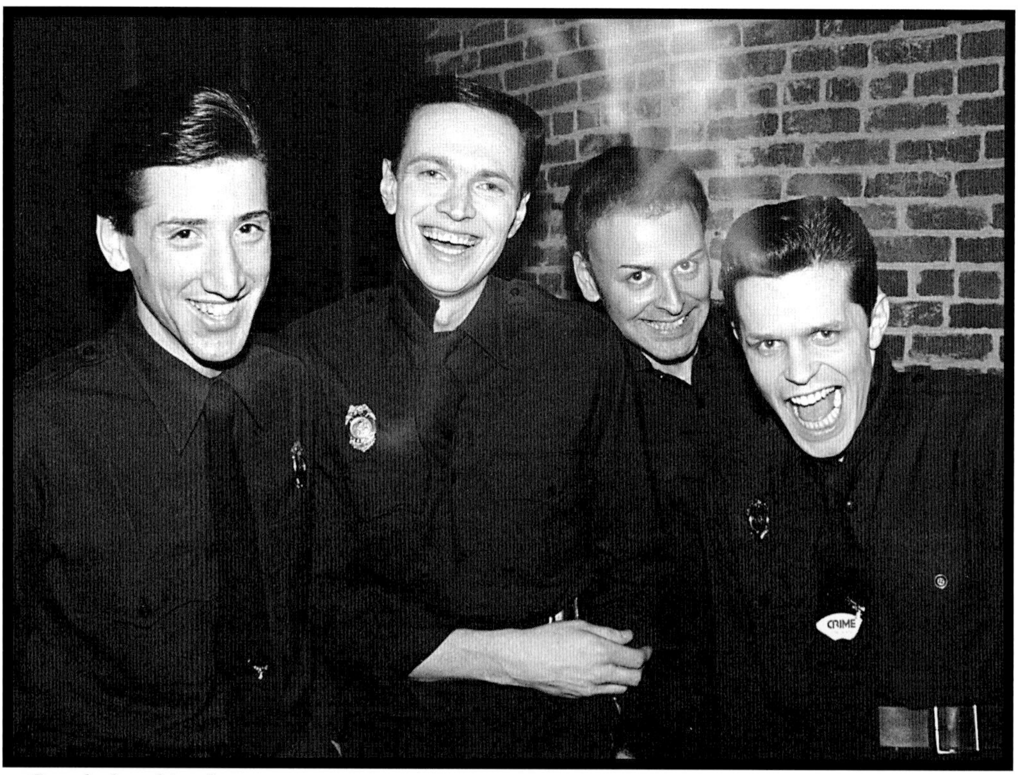

Caught laughing ?

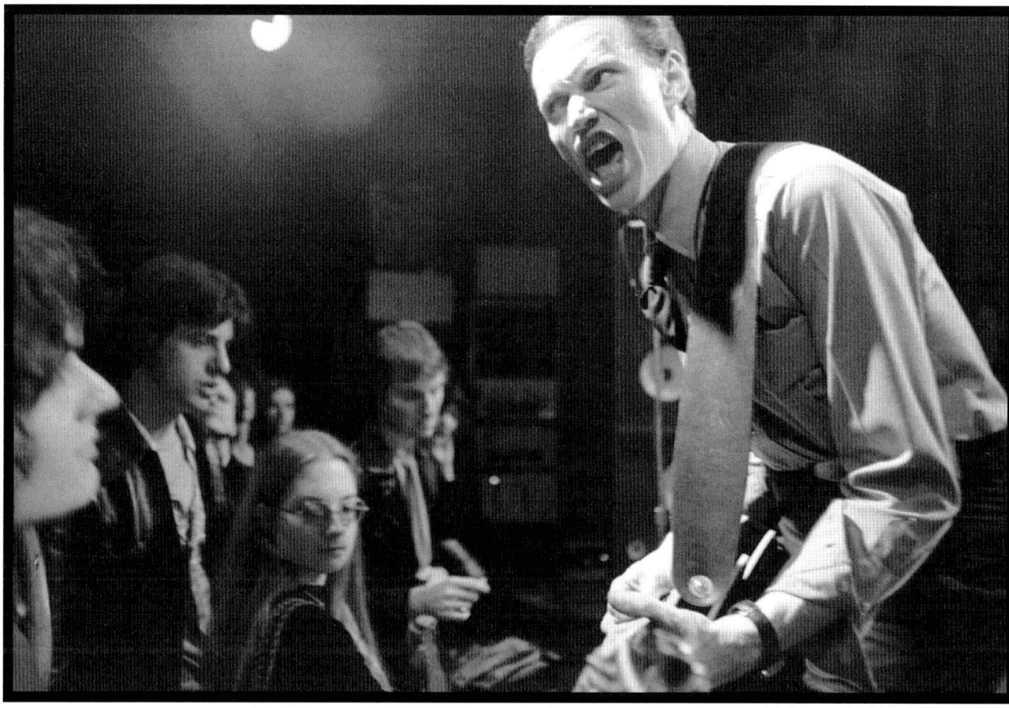

Johnny

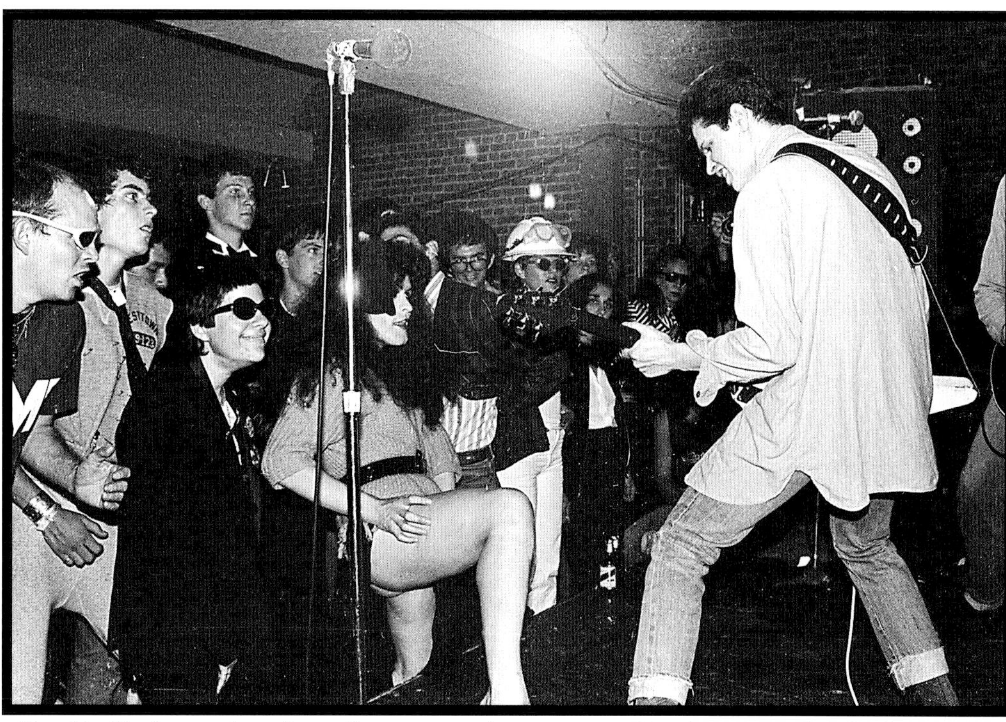

Frankie liked to get into the audience to get them to react. Here he is in rockabilly drag.

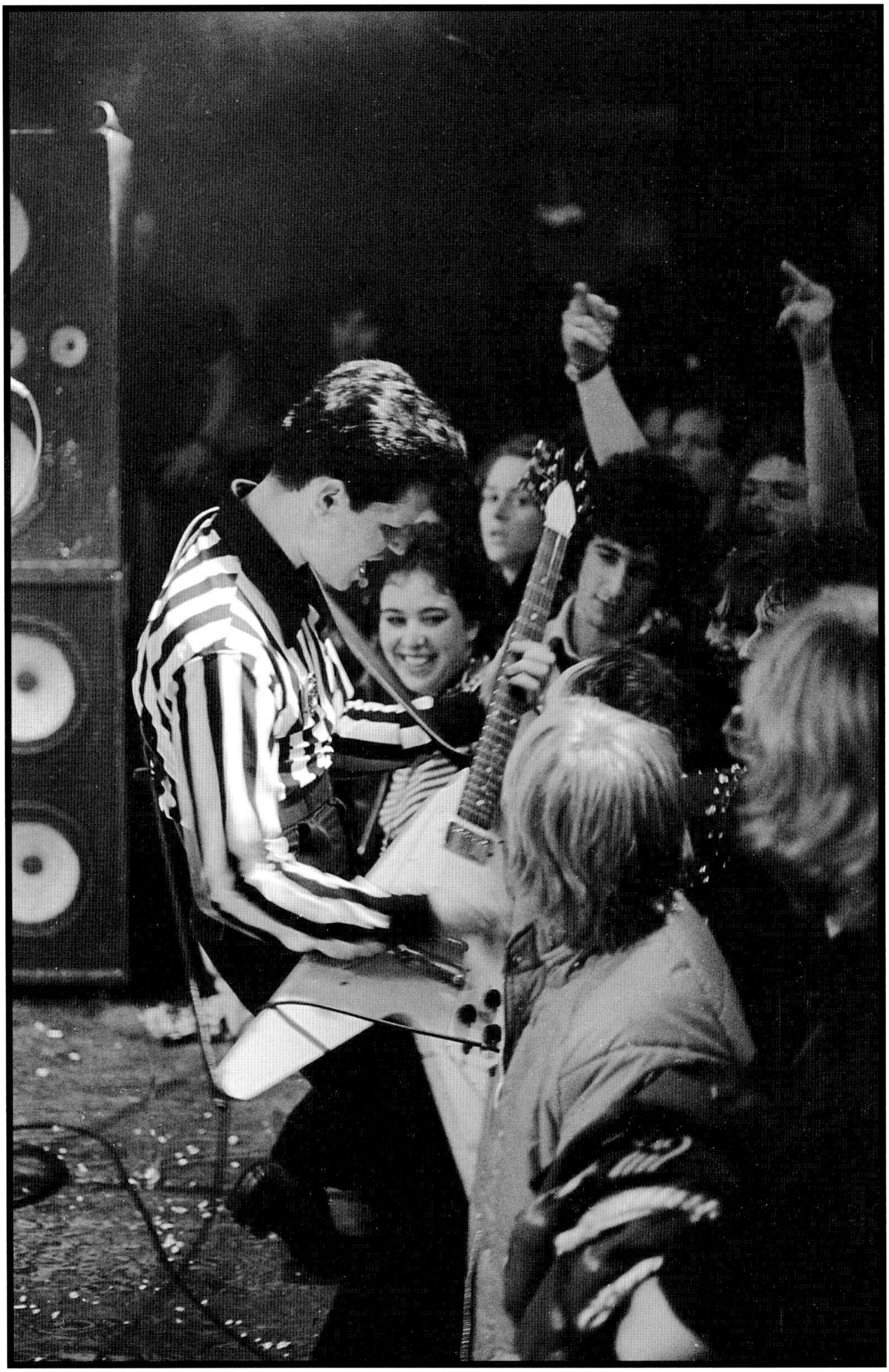

The Mabuhay was a get-in-your-face type of place where the stage was about a foot off of the floor. This broke down the barrier between the performers and the audience.

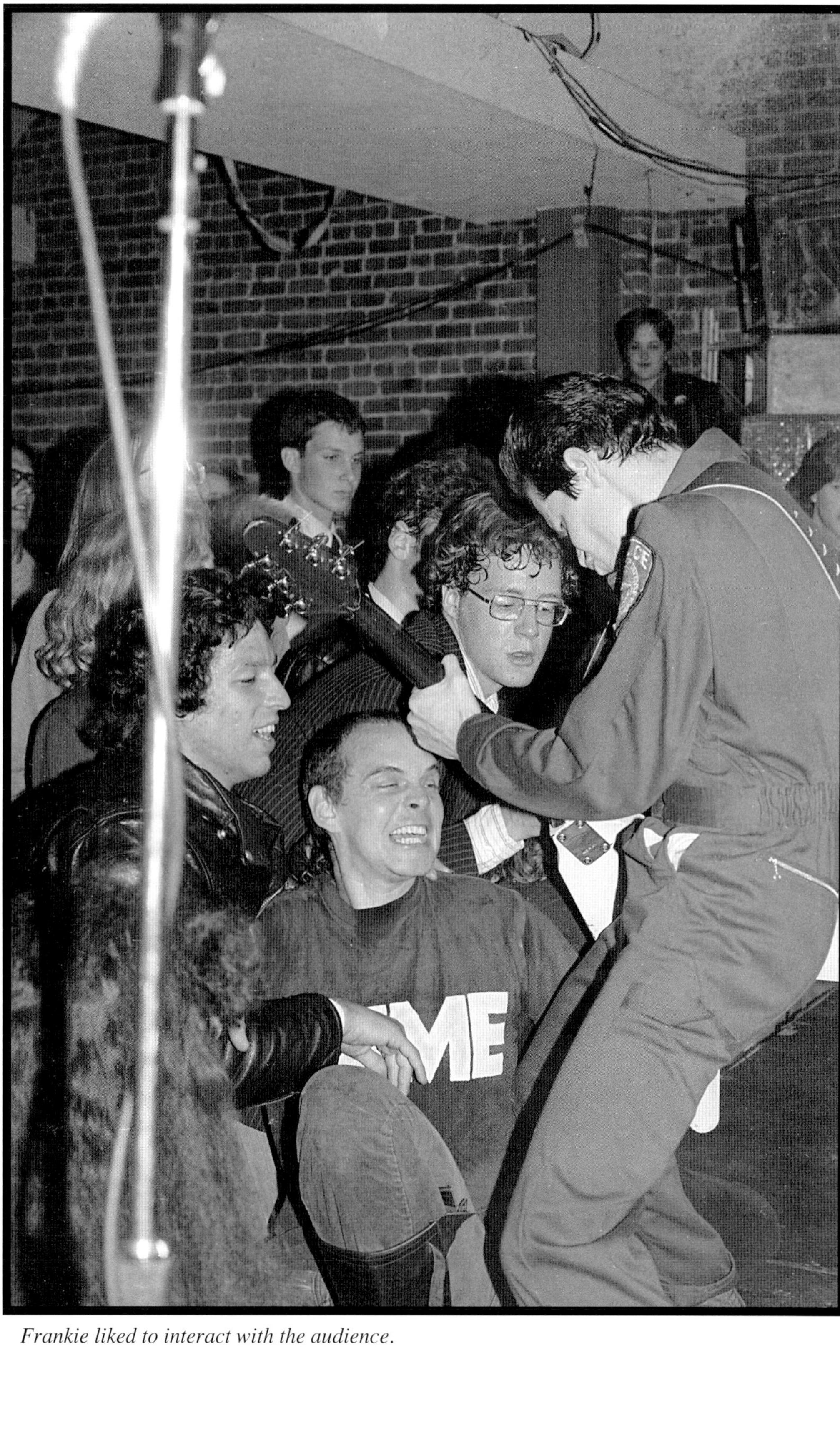

Frankie liked to interact with the audience.

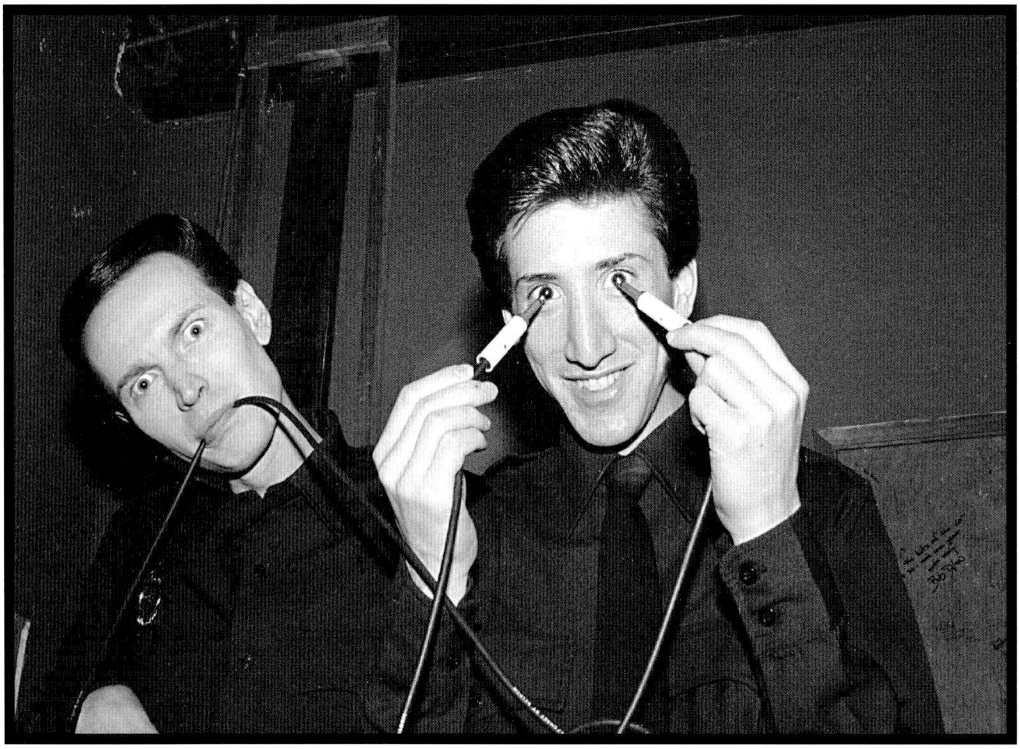

An occassional bit of humor: Johnny and Hank

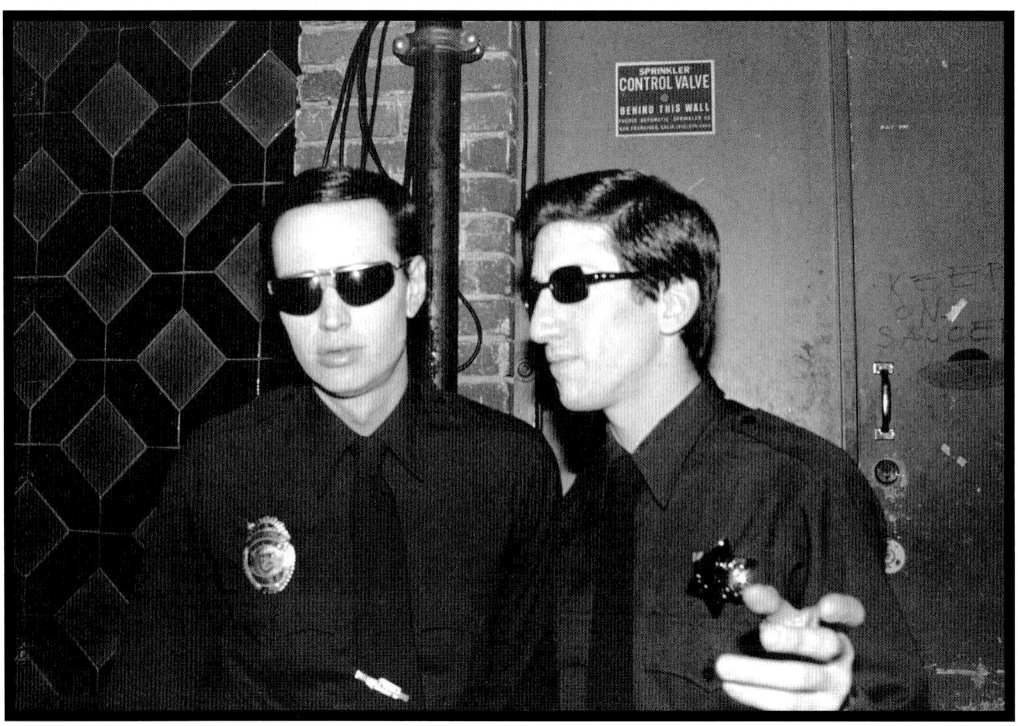

Johnny and Hank

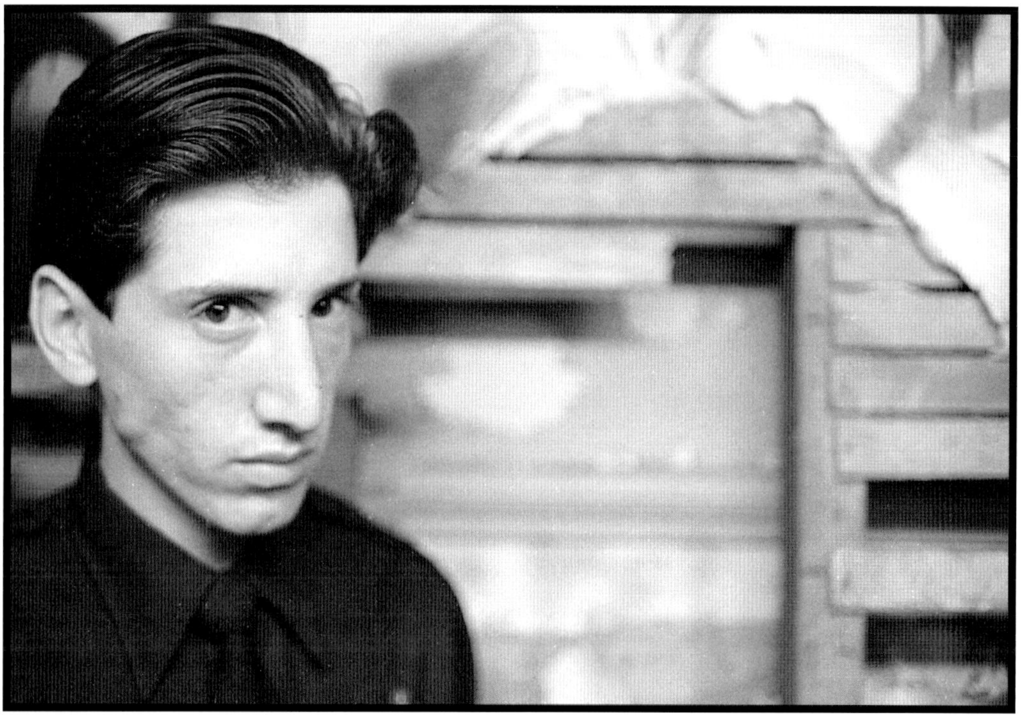

Hank backstage

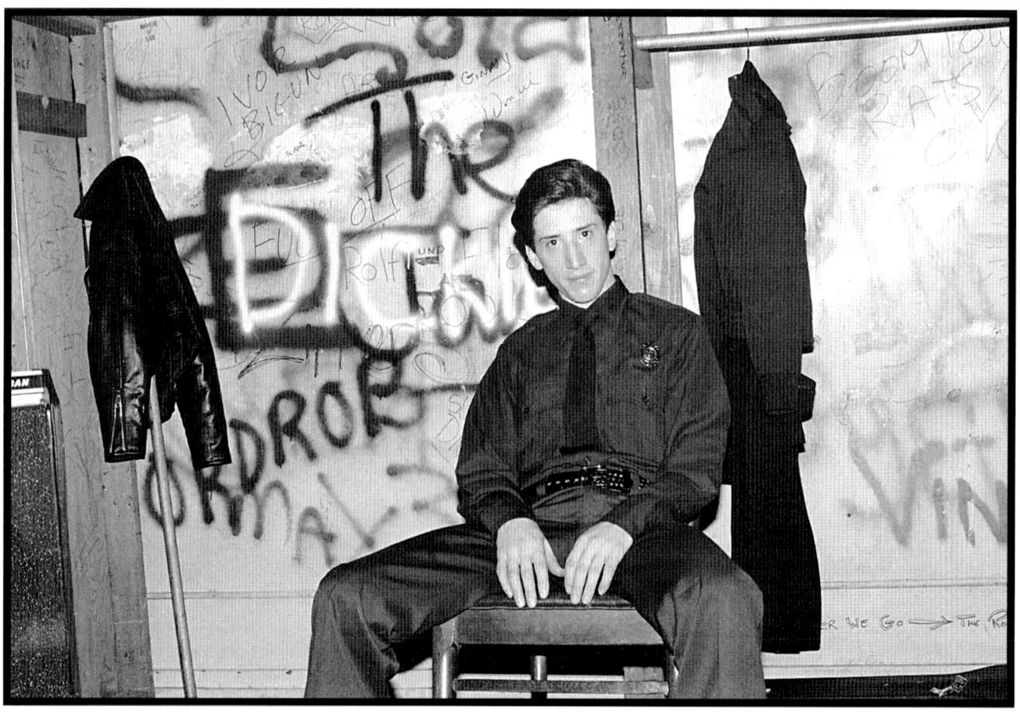

More Hank backstage

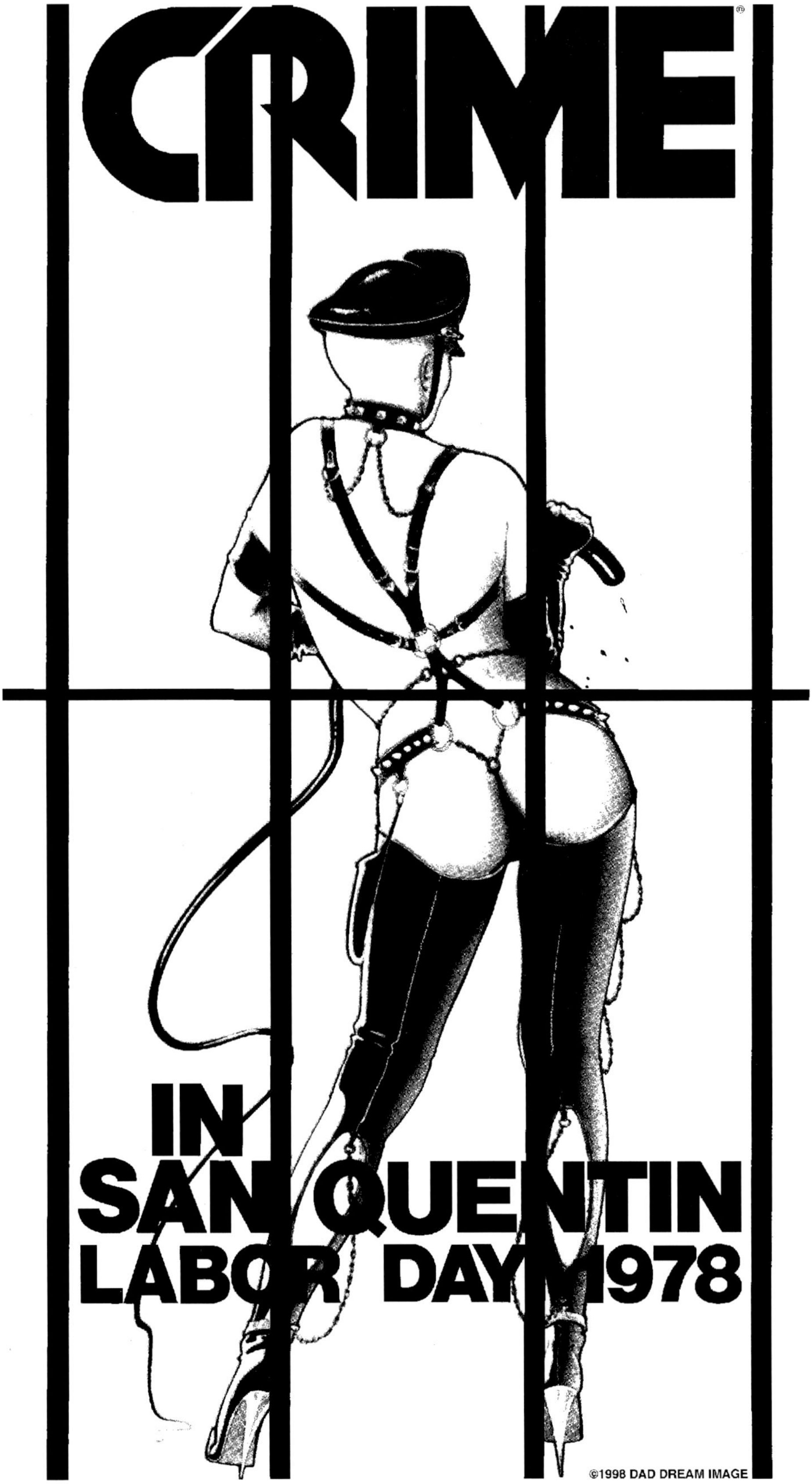
CRIME
IN
SAN QUENTIN
LABOR DAY 1978
©1998 DAD DREAM IMAGE

Brittley's Back

By 1979, I was no longer hanging out with the band. When Brittley came back to play drums with Crime again, after having left to play with The Readymades, the band became fun again. It wasn't as business-like as it had been during the Hank Rank era, yet, ironically, having a real drummer helped Crime get signed to B-Square Records. They added Joey Swails on synthesizer and recorded "Maserati" and "Gangster Funk."

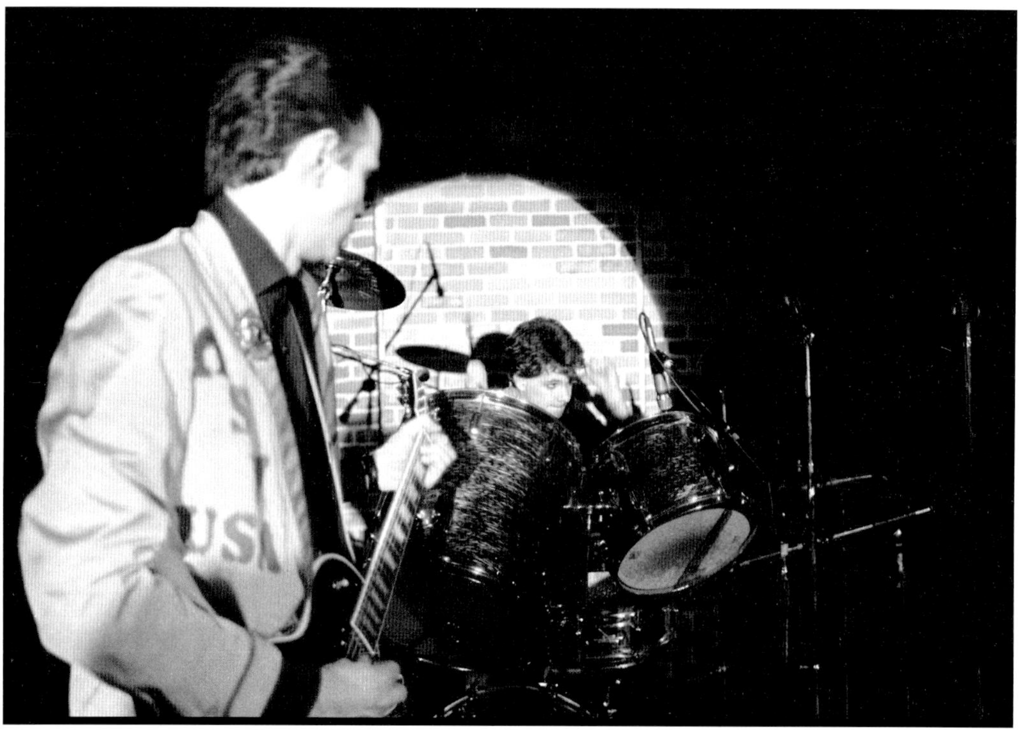

Johnny and Brittley